The Intentional Teacher

The
Intentional Teacher

FORGING A GREAT CAREER
IN THE INDEPENDENT SCHOOL CLASSROOM

Peter Gow

AVOCUS
PUBLISHING

Gilsum, New Hampshire

The Intentional Teacher:
Forging A Great Career In The Independent School Classroom
1ST EDITION

Avocus Publishing
4 White Brook Road
P.O. Box 89
Gilsum, NH 03448
Phone: 800-345-6665
Fax: 603-357-2073

Disclaimer:
Nothing in this book is intended in any way to be libelous in nature. Neither is it the intent of Avocus Publishing to publish any accusatory statement, direct or implied, of improper motives or illegal actions by any individual or educational institution. Any other interpretation of our printing is erroneous and therefore misunderstood. We believe that the public interest in general, and education in particular, will be better served by the publication of the author's experiences and opinions.

Printed in the United States of America

ISBN 978-1-890765-03-3 $26.95 Softcover

For my children
(but no pressure!)

Table of Contents

Acknowledgments

This book is the product of a career's worth of good advice and great examples. Most of these have come from my students; those I have taught, coached, advised, and looked after in dormitories probably number a couple of thousand by now. The rest are the gifts of colleagues, readings, and a lifetime's guidance from my father, David W. Gow, himself a second-generation teacher and the retired head of The Gow School, founded by my grandfather and a preëminent boarding school for dyslexic boys (and my own first teaching gig). Along the way my mother, stepmother, uncle, and a few cousins have also worked in independent schools. It's in the blood, apparently.

More than thirty years ago I learned some pointed and valuable lessons from Bill Rice, Rod Eaton, and the late Evan West at Providence Country Day School, and I hope that in the end I repaid Dary Dunham's faith in me at Fessenden School. Gow, PCD, and Fessy are all great places to have been along the road to where I am.

In my nearly three decades at Beaver Country Day School I have worked with some extraordinary professionals of both the old school and new. Jane Baker, Tom Bigda-Peyton, and the late Ann Grayson and Shelley Tyre endured my presence long enough for me to learn a few things, and Bernie Weinraub's wry humor and no-baloney manner made me a high school teacher, at last. Other Beaver colleagues: I owe you more than I could possibly fit into these pages. Fellow members of the ISED listserv and the Independent School Educators' Ning deserve equal credit, as does David Mallery, whom I am privileged to call a friend.

Since the mid 1990s Beaver Country Day and I have thrived under the wizardly headship of Peter Hutton, whose clear vision and instinctive grasp of how to incorporate great ideas into a new evolution of Progressive education have given me space and inspiration to grow as well as extraordinary opportunities for me to help others become intentional teachers. In the heat of the moment I have no doubt often neglected to express to Peter my eternal and enormous gratitude for entrusting me with this work, and so let me make clear that many of the concepts that frame this book are as much Peter's as my own; perhaps our common boyhood experience at a very traditional high school clarified ideas about teaching and learning for both of us.

My dear friends and frequent sounding-boards Rebecca Yacono, Kate Silver Rabinov, and Anne MacLeod Weeks have worked their way through early drafts of this book and made it many times better with the power of their ideas, to steal an apt phrase. My spouse, Mimi Harrington—yet another independent school teacher grafted onto my family tree—has added her wisdom and editorial expertise.

For specific permissions to use ideas and materials I must thank project-planning genius Kathleen Jordan, observation maven Steve Clem, and above all Grant Wiggins, who has been an inspiration to us all. Brad Rogers reminded me of a few things new teachers must know.

The late Craig Thorn, the excellent Catherine O'Neill Grace, and the ever-generous Nancy Raley were all early cheerleaders for this project, and to astute copy editor John-Michael Dumais, principal Ernest Peter, and editor Dave Eisenstadter at Avocus Publishing I am most deeply grateful: to them I owe the existence of this book as a physical object and not just a cloud of ideas swirling in my aging head.

Preface

THIS BOOK HAS been written for two purposes. The first is to guide prospective teachers toward being the very best, the most effective and the most satisfied they can possibly be. I also hope it will be useful to schools committed to helping their faculties move onward in a career trajectory that combines efficacy and happiness.

I find myself writing almost exclusively from the perspective of independent schools. In the United States, independent schools are a distinct subset of schools called "private," and the category includes not only schools that are truly *sui generis* in their mission and organization but also schools with strongly faith-based programs that are not under broader (parochial, diocesan, or synodic, for example) operational control. A century ago, independent schools arose largely as places for the privileged classes to educate their children; but happily, in recent decades the real privilege of independence has been that in most jurisdictions the schools themselves are able to independently set their own missions, curricula, and standards.

It is a tragedy that American public education of late has been dominated, serially, by the strictures of union contracts and by successive avalanches of public policy requirements in response to the anxieties of the moment. The most recent trauma for schools has been the manic imposition of standardized test requirements aimed at evaluating, variously, the effectiveness of their curricula, the abilities of their students, and the skill of their faculties. Although polls reveal that most citizens are pleased with their local schools and schoolteachers, we are continually bombarded with reports from the field suggesting public school teachers are disheartened, threatened, and at worst, disengaged. It would be hard to blame them if they were, but I believe that the impression given by the media criminally misrepresents hundreds of thousands of men and women who are devoting their lives to doing the best work they can under often trying circumstances and on shifting sands.

Independent schools, for whatever reason, have been able to ward off most legal and economic impositions, and, more importantly, they have maintained and even enhanced their competitive (and in many instances leading) place in the educational marketplace. I would suggest that independent schools' continued success lies precisely in the way they train and teach their faculties, and so I draw upon their practices in laying out a course of action for individuals and schools interested in optimizing teaching quality. While public schools have been forced to respond en masse to circumstances largely beyond their control, independent schools have been able to continue to focus on improvement on a smaller and more human scale, school by school, teacher by teacher.

Few issues in our society are more fraught with extreme and divergent points of view than the matter of teacher competence. Politicians rail at the apparently poor quality of America's public schools by focusing attention on the effectiveness of classroom teachers. As noted above, the public is quick to insert a caveat before any sweeping condemnation of the nation's classroom professionals; families and students are generally pleased with the quality of the teachers in *their* schools and *their* communities. In other words, most Americans seem to feel that the teachers they know best are doing a good job, despite a feeling that teachers at large are part of a deteriorating system.

This apparent contradiction illustrates for me the special role that teachers play not just in our society but in our lives. Those closest to a community of teachers within a school tend to see a group of hard-working, dedicated, and often under-rewarded adults who each day give their time, their expertise, and above all their spirit in the service of children. Some of these are recognized by their communities as "good," others as "bad," a few maybe even as "great." The definitions of what it means to be a good teacher are as varied as individuals willing to attempt definition. It is no wonder then that when we look at a school we see, rather than a finely tuned educational machine or a carefully assembled all-star team, an agglomeration of individual skills and a generally positive will, and it is no surprise that their customers tend to judge these collections of individuals benignly.

The communities that create, support, and are in fact created by independent schools are no different. A handful of schools seem to employ a vast preponderance of "great" teachers, and cocktail party or carpool caucuses are quick to identify them, even if these informal juries sometimes miss a thing or two. Students know best of all, of course; they know which teachers truly care about their well-being, really know their subject, and are adept at helping students learn and understand challenging material. A school with enough of these great teachers tends to be regarded as a great school.

How, we should ask, does one become a great teacher? How does a school collect enough of these folks that it becomes itself great—that it can bask in the reflected glory of the many giants on its faculty?

Frankly, spin and careful public relations work can set up a sense of false greatness all too easily. Schools may be judged by the quality of their students rather that of their teaching. Some schools are fortunate enough to be able to manage their enrollments so as to ensure at least a critical mass of high-profile students. The academic success of these students, as measured in public ways by college lists and performance in academic competitions, will be notable and will thus throw a positive light on the school. In reality, many of these schools might not truly deserve the accolades they garner, as super-bright pupils accepted as middle schoolers might require only the most basic of teacher attention in order to earn admission to Harvard a few years later. These students may in actuality experience only a few teachers of better-than-adequate skill, but they will thrive under almost any conditions. Conversely, schools with extremely fine faculties may be pilloried for aspects of their mission, values, history, and governance.

I am interested in schools that actively work to create a transformational experience for their students. This is much more easily said than done, and to a degree the schools that are very good at this do so by a kind of alchemy that cannot always be fully described or copied. But it is my belief that the basis of excellent teaching lies in the intentionality of the enterprise, and this can be replicated.

Business books devoted to leadership make up a hot genre, and the "smartest" of them maintain that organizational effectiveness is based not on the degree to which businesses can squeeze every nickel out of customers or out of their own processes but rather on the degree to which they can define their purposes and then set about developing practices and finding and training people who will creatively support and passionately commit to these purposes. Businesses can go from "good to great," play leading roles in the "flattening" of the global economy, and achieve "excellence" only if they understand their own strengths and how to capitalize on them. Intentional organizations tend to become successful ones, and the best of the business books do not neglect the notion of work-corps satisfaction in their definition of success.

The underlying purpose of this book is to help teachers focus on their own intentions—to understand and define their personal missions as educators and then to figure out how to make the most of their skills, energies, and passions in the service of their missions. Gone is the era when an independent schoolteaching career could begin with the new graduate being shown into a classroom and then progressing in stately and tweedy fashion over the decades toward a punctilious retirement, full of years if not so many honors, with the teacher doing little more than showing up each September. Effective teachers are constantly engaged in the re-examination of both practice and purpose, and while this has always been true of the good and great, I argue that anything less—mediocrity—is simply no longer viable. It is my belief that anyone with the will to teach can achieve and is in fact obligated to him- or herself, to his or her students, and to the school to work toward a kind of greatness, a fully realized capacity, that can only be realized by intentional effort.

The second audience of this book is of course schools, most especially schools that have committed themselves to hiring and then retaining a faculty of the most admirable sort: a faculty of teachers who are all truly good and great; impassioned educators who believe in their students, in their schools' missions, and in their own ability to participate in providing their students with transformational learning experiences.

Such schools are themselves intentional. They use their missions as touchstones against which to consider even the slightest of policy changes, and more importantly they talk about their missions and their values as if these were living, breathing entities. It would be difficult, in fact, for a school of passionate intentionality not to become the kind of place where teachers learn and grow. It is just as important for such a school to know what sort of teacher will thrive in the throes of carrying out a clear and specific mission amid a community committed to clear and specific values.

Most independent schools have come around to an understanding that professional development is an essential part of improving their practice and their competitiveness, and most teachers understand that there is always more to learn. This book is ultimately for schools and for teachers who are ready to take their commitment to improvement to the next level and who are ready to submit to the discipline that true intentionality requires.

All I can promise is that this discipline will not hurt—in fact, it should feel quite good. Intentionality may bring a realization of the dimensions of the unknown, but it will also provide a clarifying understanding of how to do things in a better way. This is immediately, and not just ultimately, satisfying. Furthermore, it will help one's teaching become more successful; the intentional teacher is likely to see more of those "aha!" moments that make teaching worthwhile and that are evidence of those transformations that are the ultimate aim of all educators everywhere.

I urge the reader onward, then, toward a level of understanding and a commitment to a practice in which the good teacher understands *why* he or she is good, and happy, and on which any school can draw in its own quest to move from good to great.

CHAPTER I

A Teacher's Will

"School is for kids."

— Peter Hutton

This chapter might well be titled, "So you want to be a teacher?" I am not going to try to talk anyone out of teaching, but there will be tough talk about what it takes, or rather what it should require, to make the decision to enter the field of education as one of the tens of thousands of classroom teachers who begin their careers each fall. Teaching is not for everyone, it is true, but neither is it only for the few; the need precludes this kind of self-selectivity. Instead, the contention here is that many sorts of people, with widely divergent talents and aspirations, can become excellent teachers if they possess the personal will to do this and are supported by professional structures that support individual growth at every stage.

Who is a teacher?

Teachers come in all shapes and sizes, and many of those who teach most often and most effectively are not always thought of as teachers by profession. By the most basic definition, a teacher is one who teaches.

This description raises a question of intent. We read often that the youth of our society are being ruined or corrupted by aspects of the culture in which we live. Advertising and public relations experts know that their job is essentially to teach consumers of culture, goods, and services to incorporate new ideas and new products into their lives. The intention is to teach, but in this case the teaching has an instrumental purpose: to inculcate specific choice-making behaviors that will bring economic benefit to their clients.

"Role models" must also be considered. We are told, especially when a star athlete is caught doing something wrong, that society's designated role models, often the rich and famous, teach children how to behave and that they must be blameless in their conduct. Here, at least, some difference of opinion exists; not everyone believes that each celebrity is *de facto* a full-time instructor of the young, but nonetheless we tend to denote such people as having a teaching role.

Most vocations involve an instructional component. Even the most modest service-industry positions involve on-the-job training, the newest worker often learning skills and routines from the next-most-recently hired. Concerns about employee layoffs are almost always connected to the need for more and better education and training, on-the-job and otherwise. Thus are we all teachers, from time to time, by choice or by default.

But teaching school is a different matter. I often ask teaching candidates at our school what it is that has brought them to the idea of teaching, "The money or the prestige?" They all understand the joke, sorry as it is, because most people entering the teaching profession, or moving around within it, are fully aware of the sacrifices that one makes as a teacher. Salaries may be rising, but no one will grow rich as a classroom teacher, and few people, except those who have left the profession and produced popular memoirs or exposés, have become famous through their work in front of a room full of children.

In the current economy, the choice to become a teacher, even for a time, involves a conscious setting aside of the typical or casual reasons that people choose careers. Money, prestige, glamour, perquisites, and fame are not in it, nor is the prospect of quick success, early promotion, and an eventual partnership presaging early, affluent retirement. To head into teaching is to take what looks to law school-bound classmates or investment-banking trainees like a vow of poverty, with a corresponding vow of humility.

A millennium after Christian monks and nuns first took up teaching as a religious and social duty, that the educational profession still looks monastic is a national tragedy. There is no good side to this, as the rigors of being a teacher do not weed out all but those with a "true vocation" to teach, nor would it be a good thing if this were the case. That teachers are somehow possessed of a greater purity of soul, or purity of motive, is a fatuous and patronizing supposition. Worse still, the poor rewards of teaching are seen in some quarters as attracting the poorest students ("those who can't, teach"), thus adding to the overall notion that teachers are lesser beings, either romantically disconnected from their own self-interest, tragically isolated from "reality," or too craven or too pitifully underequipped to compete in the rat race of business and commerce.

A teacher needs but three basic characteristics: a deep affection for children, an undiminished joy in learning, and a dogged commitment to

the success of others. I would add optimism to the list, but I think that the other three essentially add up to just that.

Affection for children

Prospective teachers often say "I love kids" when asked why they want to enter the profession. This is a pretty general statement, so much so that some interviewers find it suspect. I do not concur with this reaction, but I always want to hear more. Many young people do in fact discover a joy in interacting with children; babysitters, summer camp counselors, daycare volunteers, and even happy cousins seem to keep coming along just when the adult world needs a respite from the demands of kids and just when kids need time with a near-agemate as role model (yes!) and guide.

The truth is that not all teachers, even the greatest of them, "love" all children. Some seem to have a single grade, or a single demographic, with whom they work best and with whom some ineffable chemistry creates a bond of mutual respect and affection that makes learning feel natural. Many have "bands" of age levels with whom this chemistry is manifest. We probably all know people who seem to be "born" pre-school teachers; "born" tenth-grade history teachers appear to be bit more thin on the ground, but they exist.

The potential teacher, even if convinced by experience or predilection that he or she "loves kids," should consider as precisely as possible what this might mean. Has this conclusion been based on concrete experience—a really great eighth-grade year, a summer as a junior camp counselor, late-night discussions on the meaning of life with younger friends—or is it based on more abstract considerations? How deep does the putative love run: to listening to sixth-graders sort out social hierarchies, to cleaning up after incontinent five-year-olds, or to confronting high schoolers caught in acts of seriously bad judgment?

The best questions for the aspiring teacher are about hypotheticals, based on personal experience. Successful teachers who have found "their" age group are able to enter into, or at least to respect, the most solemn realities of their students' lives—to understand what it means to be in that age group and to acknowledge without judgment the things that matter most to its members. The chemistry, of course, lies in the teacher's understanding and acceptance of the importance of this reality while at the same time being an accessible, reliable, and inviting bridge to the systematic requirements—the curriculum—that adults are required to impose upon the children. What sorts of childhood reality does the aspirant believe that she or

he will be capable of entering? About what age group might the aspirant be ready to care the most? When did the aspirant feel as though he or she had truly begun to come of age, or when did the world, or the first passionate interest, open up? If the aspirant were left alone on a park bench to observe kids of all ages, which age group's activities would consume his or her attention?

For some who choose to become teachers, particular age groups offer particular attractions and aversions. The responsibility of having to teach children to read discourages many from the taking on the lower elementary grades, while the supposed recalcitrance or mercuriality of high schoolers makes others shiver at the thought of teaching teenagers. The thought of successfully bringing justice to social dramas makes some people yearn to become middle school teachers, as does the idea that uninhibited eagerness still occasionally shines in the eyes of seventh-graders before it is eclipsed by the shadow of adolescent coolness.

I do not mean to give the impression that a good teacher has only one "good" age group. Most have many, and a few blessed souls have careers that encompass the successful education of toddlers through graduate students. But it is important for the potential teacher to see himself or herself working respectfully, energetically, and above all happily with a specific group of children, and then to seek opportunities to test that vision.

Joy in learning

The second requirement, a non-stop joy in the feeling of learning, necessarily includes both a passion for what is to be taught and an equal passion for the experience of giving *and* receiving insight, skills, and judgment as well as content knowledge. The great teacher is a great learner, unselfconscious in the experience and generous in sharing the pleasure that he or she feels, no matter which side of the classroom desk he or she is occupying.

In practice, this joy takes any number of forms. A high school English teacher may read passionately or write poetry in spare moments, or a biology teacher may spend summers tramping rain forests, looking after endangered species, or volunteering in a biotechnology lab. Hordes of elementary school teachers spend their summers as camp counselors, perhaps working with different age groups or with children with material, social, or even physical disadvantages. These people just cannot stop themselves from remaining engaged with the essence of their work, even if they are not being well paid. Most educators have had professional development experiences in which they have been asked to step far outside their comfort levels, oftentimes finding themselves in groups of those who teach other ages and

other disciplines. Reserved high school humanities teachers can find themselves put to shame by elementary school people when called upon to dance or to drum; the best of those elementary teachers share with their young students the ability to enter the moment, uninhibited and exuberant.

This excitement with the process of learning, of being able not just to "do" the learning but to enter fully into it, may not even correspond exactly with the subject matter. Some happy souls are able to transmute their love of mountain climbing into an ability to put algebra or world history across with contagious joy that brings students deeply into the process.

Many who consider teaching as a career express a distaste for the idea of taking courses in education, often based on the dreary reports of others; this is especially true among independent school teachers, who are generally untethered from certification requirements. These reports are too numerous to be ignored; many schools of education seem to have serious work to do. Unfortunately, such stories undercut another aspect of the requirements for effective and satisfying teaching. Prospective teachers must be at least more than a little interested in how to do the work well and in learning more about the nature of the children they are to teach.

In the last 25 years, the knowledge base in pedagogy and curriculum design has expanded significantly, and important ideas have been put forward about the nature of the learning process and about the psychological, social, and moral development of children. If the prospect of many hours in an education school classroom daunts, the prospect of being systematically and thoughtfully exposed to good ideas about how to teach well should not. The days when teaching could be done entirely from the gut are long gone, and anyone thinking about teaching needs to be as ready to learn as they are to teach.

Perhaps the best ways for prospective independent school teachers to gauge their passion for the process of learning is by a combination of self-reflection and self-instruction. Here again, it is worthwhile to consider matters through the lens of the age groups or subject matter that might be taught. What kinds of reading or activities are truly energizing to the aspirant, and to what extent can he or she visualize sharing this or that interest in a classroom, on a playing field, or even in informal connection with children?

Some teachers come to teaching out of the love of a specific subject or discipline; I believe that this alone is not enough to make a great teacher. This may be heresy, but I have seen a number of teachers who are truly experts flounder, at least at first, in the classroom. Their troubles have stemmed from one of several causes, in each case something that the struggling teacher had not fully considered.

Expert teachers who are joyously and obsessively in love with their disciplines may be at first shocked and then dismayed to learn that not all of their students share that love. Especially against the backdrop of a popular culture that devalues academic learning, it may take time to win over a room full of skeptical or even resistant adolescents, and some teachers find it all too easy to judge reluctant learners harshly, even turning against them and becoming cynical about their prospects and sometimes even about the educational process itself. Sometimes these teachers feel betrayed by the students and even by the school that had been so weak-minded as to admit such a sorry lot of learners and that has obviously abandoned all standards in retaining and promoting them. Often these teachers recognize the issue and remove themselves from the profession to find work that truly honors the depth and intensity of their passion. Occasionally they stick with it long enough to discover that something else—students, not subject matter—can inspire them, and they become brilliantly effective classroom teachers and school leaders.

Another expert and passionate sort who is likely to find teaching unsatisfying is the teacher who has come into the job bringing a fairly narrow perspective. Often and sadly, this perspective is that of a practitioner of the narrowest kind of traditional teaching, focused on the "one right answer" and on one-dimensional and oversimplified explanations, reasons, or received interpretations. Such teachers often find themselves locked in a futile, painful battle to protect their precious subject matter, whether mathematics or literature, from the inconsistent, error-prone, and sometimes admittedly shoddy efforts of children to master it. The devotee of Emily Dickinson whose students just cannot make out the symbolism in a beloved poem or the intuitive mathematical thinker faced with youngsters unable to grasp the beauty of the associative property are likely to be disappointed. At worst, teachers of this sort work to strengthen the barricades that protect their subject matter and become contemptuous of their students. At best, they begin to see that their task is to seek out new ways to guide students into unfamiliar or daunting topics, to help them negotiate the challenges of undiscovered routes, and to welcome them when they arrive, no matter how they got there.

I am presenting many cases here in harsh terms; the teaching prospect needs to understand that accepting children where they are and displaying a real generosity of heart and mind are equal in significance to enthusiasm for learning, and that these cannot be separated. To consider one's own potential for encountering problems is not about searching for character flaws, but a real prospect for harm exists when individuals find themselves disappointed and embittered in the realization that teaching is not all that they had imagined it to be. Those who overstay their time in the classroom, increasingly disrespecting the children they teach and the enterprise of teaching itself, are a lasting danger to themselves and to the spirit of others.

I would maintain that a love of the learning process is something that can be both acquired and expanded in adulthood; it is simply a matter of understanding *what* is to be learned. I know teachers who entered the classroom because they were fond of history and discovered only after a while that they also loved learning about child development and various theories of learning. A single new idea, or an old idea seen from a new perspective, has sparked the full-blown renewal of any number of teaching careers, often in people who did not even realize that such a personal and professional renascence was possible. Many of the most radically inventive of today's theorists in the areas of curriculum and pedagogy were long-time and very traditional teachers who awoke one day to a whole new way of looking at something essential to their practice. They did not set out as 20-somethings to devise novel approaches to their work but kept pondering something vaguely unsatisfying until they changed everything about their work except their passion for it. Great teachers have to be able to keep alive the ability to learn, even from themselves, as long as they teach.

Commitment to student success

The third important characteristic of effective teachers is the ability to project one's passion for young people and for the act of learning onto others in the form of a single-minded commitment to the success of one's students. If one idea unifies today's most traditionally minded and most radical education reformers, it is that educators at every level must believe that every child can succeed and that a combination of demanding standards and hard work can elicit from every student a high level of performance. The aspiring teacher must above all things be an optimist about children and be willing to make a significant investment in every student.

No characteristic may be more central to successful teaching than optimism. It is not absurdly Pollyannaish to look upon a classroom full of seven-year-olds or 15-year-olds and see the potential for success within each child; it is absolutely necessary. The teacher who does not believe in the possibility of success, or if necessary redemption, for all students is doomed to misery, a fact known to every educational theorist going back to Socrates. To believe anything else is to write off a portion of humanity, an act antithetical both to good teaching and to an emotionally whole life.

The matter of optimism lies at the heart of one's views on human

nature. Those who adhere to an anti-social view of human beings as naturally selfish and in ugly competition with one another—in the words of
Thomas Hobbes, the "solitary, nasty, brutish, and short" life of man without the moderating influence of society—have indeed had a voice in the
history of American education; the Puritans, for example, saw childhood
as a time to literally beat the devil out of sinful children in the hope that
they would become godly adults. The 19th- and early-20th-century "fac-
tory" model of education, with lockstep curricula, rigorous sorting of students with the lower tiers directed to vocational training, and such physical
manifestations as desks bolted to classroom floors, is as much a reflection
of the Puritan mistrust of the childish spirit as a response to the need for
a uniformly trained workforce. Fortunately optimists dwelt among even
these most mechanistic and discipline-oriented of educators, always looking for the good in and demanding the best from students not as a means
of forcing failure but in order to produce the best from those in whom they
had faith.

Others see human nature as an essentially benevolent power that education should work to liberate, a view that traces its roots most directly to
the ideas of the French-Swiss theorist Jean-Jacques Rousseau. Two-and-a-
half centuries later we see evidence of Rousseau's thinking in almost every
aspect of contemporary education: child-centeredness, flexibility in curriculum, and the emphasis on moral and social growth in school settings.
Along the way Rousseau's ideas even gained some of the flavor of the Christian "Social Gospel" movement, in which ideals of service and self-sacrifice
in emulation of Jesus became important to the child's learning. Largely
secularized today even in independent schools with a religious heritage,
these ideals show up for instance in the tradition of athletic competition as
an exercise in teamwork, hard work for a common purpose, and humility,
and of course they are also manifest in the idea of community service as a
fundamental aspect of learning.

If I seem to belabor the historical aspects of educational philosophy
here, it is to underscore the importance of ideas about the nature of children to the field of education and to the teacher's will. Successful teachers
will have come to terms, explicitly or implicitly, with their own understanding of human nature, at least insofar as it is displayed in the actions and
potential of children. Believing in children is simply the most important
thing a teacher must do. It is this faith in the wonderful, capable, special,
and even redeemable character and potential of each child that inspires the
fine teacher.

This belief must exist in the abstract, but it is far more important that
it reveal itself in the specific. Any random sample of published biographies

or personal memoirs will yield mountains of evidence as to the power of a caring teacher in a young person's life. Great educators understand that they have an obligation to find something to connect with and even something to love about even their most trying students. This is no small thing, and yet it is surprisingly rare. Over and over again, students polled about the qualities of their best teachers stress the need for teachers to know them, not only by name and by whatever superficialities can be observed in a classroom but deeply, as learners engaged in serious work but more importantly as individuals with their own strengths, stories, affinities, and concerns. Teachers who take the time to learn the story of each of their students make a statement to those students that their lives and aspirations matter, that they are in fact individuals worthy of being taken seriously. What person does not crave this acknowledgment from others?

It is great when the optimism and connection that a teacher demonstrates become the basis of a deep and transforming personal relationship, but here it is worth cautioning the aspiring teacher that getting to those relationships is not easy. Films about teaching, from *The Blackboard Jungle* to *Up the Down Staircase* to *The Dead Poets Society* tend to offer overheated celebrations of the intensity of teacher-student relationships, relationships which appear on screen to most working teachers as nice to contemplate but in the end too good to be true. Some such films often extol the charismatic and even rebellious teacher, and I have interviewed a few candidates, steeped in the ideas of Rousseau and his successors, who can hardly wait to establish their iconoclastic selves in the classroom where they can start right away to save teenage souls. This can be done, but in a good school overarching standards are set and maintained, with a whole community to support and even transform the students. While teaching is very much about helping students to help themselves avoid some of the sleazy and dangerous traps the culture has set for them, a savior complex is undesirable in classroom teachers. We want students to develop belief in themselves, not in their teachers. And above all we want them to grow via intentionally designed experiences that provide them with irrefutable proof that they can, with application and hard work, be more than they had believed. The role of the teacher in this process is to be a designer, a giver of important and meaningful feedback, and above all a cheerleader—a *sincere* cheerleader.

The qualities of a good teacher—affection for children, love of learning, and essential belief in children—may be largely innate, but I believe that they can be developed from latency in all but the most cynical teacher candidate. It is my deeply held belief that anyone who really wants to become a teacher can develop the necessary traits and skills to become a very good one. Preparatory "professional development" for teaching in independent schools involves at the minimum a great deal of personal reflection on the topics covered in this chapter and a modicum of self-instruction around essential aspects of actually being in a classroom with students.

The prospective educator has much to learn. Some is little more than gussied-up common sense, while much is about knowing something about the arts of pedagogy and curriculum design. A bit is even about managing oneself and one's ambitions within an organization. Most, perhaps, is about himself and herself: the values and articles of personal faith about learning and about children that drive the will to teach as well as recognition of the capacity to subordinate one's own ambition and needs to those of students. But if the hopeful beginner is at least modestly confident that he or she possesses the essential traits outlined above, it should be relatively easy to muster and concentrate the will to teach—to enter actively into the process of becoming a teacher as a manifestation not merely of vocational interest but also as an affirmative statement of personal purpose.

CHAPTER II

Finding a Teaching Job

*"Choose a job you love,
and you will never have to work a day in your life."*
— CONFUCIUS

The first order of business for the intentional teacher is to find a job. With the media filled with stories about a looming teaching shortage due to the imminent retirement of the baby boom cohort, this might seem like shooting fish in a barrel, but finding the right position in the right school is a little more difficult than that. The prospective teacher can apply a few strategies, however, to find that "right" school and to present an attractive, compelling candidacy.

Here again the reader is cautioned that the pathway being set forth pertains specifically to independent schools in North America and to the community of so-called "international schools" that share curricular and organizational frameworks with American independent schools. Public school districts, even in areas where multiple routes to licensure exist, have their own distinct ways of recruiting teachers, as do schools with structural religious affiliations. Some chartered and pilot schools have dipped their nets into the independent school recruiting pool, but the focus throughout this book is on independent schools.

One somewhat rarefied avenue into independent school teaching involves internships. A number of schools, both boarding and day and serving all grade levels, have formal internship programs that involve a real education in teaching; some programs are affiliated with universities and award a master's degree. More schools have internship programs that involve part-time teaching and coaching at relatively low pay, with some degree of mentoring or professional development that will serve to give the intern a leg up on a future full-time job.

Once the potential teacher has decided to see him- or herself as that, the now-eager candidate should consider a strategy that has two or even three prongs. Finding the right school, a school that is matched in purpose and temperament to the candidate, requires a bit of "eye training" on how to find and study schools as well as plunging energetically into the world of recruiting and hiring, which is a cottage industry in its own right. Simultaneously the candidate should begin assessing and working to articulate his or her own strengths and interests. Later in this chapter we will read about how, once hired, the successful candidate can enter the culture of a new school as a participant from the beginning and not as a gradually acclimating tourist.

It is not a focus of this book to expatiate on the unique rewards of independent school teaching, but I should emphasize here that one of these is the opportunity to be close to the structures that govern one's working life. Independent schools make their own decisions about every aspect of policy and practice, and active and engaged teachers in these schools can have a significant role in defining the work they do and the conditions under which the work is done. Independent school teachers willing to involve themselves in all aspects of the life of their schools will thus be able to exert real control over the shape of their day-to-day lives as well as over the quality of the careers they fashion. The payoff is such that few career teachers would trade their lives even with those whose salaries and prestige had been much greater.

Identifying appropriate schools

Finding independent schools is not always as easy as it might be. Although New England is full of institutions whose names are familiar as the prep schools of presidents, outside of a short list of "usual suspects," those known to a prospective teacher whose own world has not connected directly with that of independent schools may be few indeed. Some independent schools like to maintain a very high profile as regional leaders, while others keep a lower profile. High schools tend to be better known than those that end at elementary or middle schools, and some schools appear to be so esoteric in their missions or traditions that they simply go unnoticed (much to their own chagrin) unless someone is specifically looking for them.

To find independent schools, the best place to start is to ask around, either of educators or of parents. If this is difficult, several comprehensive annual guides to schools are published by companies like Porter Sargent, Peterson's, or Bunting & Lyon. The latter two offer online information, but a good public library should have recent editions of most of these, and bookstores will carry the latest. Peterson's is the most obviously designed for "consumer" use.

Online searches can also yield "independent schools" by region or type, but another good source of school listings would be to search for an "independent school association" by region. The National Association of Independent Schools in Washington, D.C., is the main professional organization to which several thousand such schools belong (and their website—www.nais.org—features employment listings), but every area has its regional associations; Canadian and international counterparts also exist. Most association websites list not only member schools but also employment openings at these schools.

The good news is that a prospective teacher need not know everything about every school right from the start, as ways of finding important information can be found later, but several important school characteristics can serve to help a candidate identify and sort schools that may be of interest. An important quality indicator of which aspiring teachers should be aware is accreditation. Like colleges, reputable independent schools tend to be accredited by a competent regional body or authority. As it does for colleges, what this really means for accredited independent schools is that at specified intervals, usually 10 years, they are required to complete an elaborate self-study that essentially answers these questions: Does this school do what it claims to do? Does it have the resources and programs to support its students and faculty in fulfilling its mission and its educational goals? The self-study is accompanied by a visit from a team of educators from similar schools who then issue a report and a recommendation to the accrediting body. While the process is emphatically not about ranking the quality of a school's programs, it is very much about the professionalism and care with which a school goes about its work. Most schools will mention the name of their accrediting body somewhere in their promotional material.

Without getting into an elaborate taxonomy of independent schools, the simplest and most commonly used ways to divide schools focus on whether they are residential or day, the grade levels they serve, and whether they are coeducational. A host of philosophical and other variations can also be identified, including schools that focus on students with special learning needs. But these three categories are a good start, and each provides opportunities and challenges that should be noted by the candidate teacher.

Boarding schools versus day schools

In a nutshell, schools with boarding programs tend to focus on older (high school) students, although a handful of "junior" boarding schools exist in the Northeast. Even if they have a significant population of day-only students, schools with even small residential programs are often looking for teachers who are willing to live on campus and to serve as dormitory supervisors as well as classroom teachers. Schools offer various ways of compensating teachers for what can seem like, and even be, 24/7 duty, and a candidate looking at boarding schools should be prepared to ask about weekend schedules (including Saturday classes and the nature of responsibilities on weekends when a teacher is on duty), evenings off, dormitory coverage when a residential teacher is "off duty," and requirements for attending meals. In most locales a job that includes housing is a large economic plus, with a corresponding salary diminution, but in a few areas the rental market is still friendly enough that schools are forced to pay a premium to teachers willing to reside in a dormitory. A candidate should be prepared for an interview process that includes at least introducing his or her spouse or partner and children, and sometimes a position may be contingent upon a candidate's having a family that fits the space available.

Boarding schools are famous—or notorious—for hiring so-called "triple threats": teachers who are willing to live in a dormitory and are able to coach, often at a high level, along with managing a full load of classes. For many years a common hiring pattern involved young triple threats, fresh out of prestigious colleges, who would work at boarding schools for a year or two at relatively low pay before heading off to professional schools or careers in business. Some schools may still follow this model, but it is easy to see how it might not serve students or the teaching profession so well. Even so, a position with this profile could be a great entry-level opportunity, a foot in the door that could lead to a satisfying career. Indeed, much of today's aging independent school teacher force probably began this way; most schools are pleased to hold onto competent young teachers who decide to stay, and some will stay for a working lifetime.

Day schools are generally easier to understand in their programs and demands, although the working day is likely to be longer than for public schools. Day schools tend to require teachers to coach or to carry significant non-classroom supervisory duty and, as in boarding schools, teachers will be expected to attend faculty meetings and perhaps to be part of committees doing important work on issues of policy or even governance.

Grade levels

While most boarding schools offer only the high school grades 9 through 12, individual independent schools can offer a bewildering assortment of grade levels. A handful teach only the "early childhood" years, from preschool to the early elementary grades, while a great many schools offer programs for pre-Kindergarten through sixth or eighth grades. A few schools focus on middle grades (five or six through eight or nine) only, while a great many others start at grades five or six and continue through high school. Age-level groupings (pre-K–4, 5–8, or 9–12) are generally referred to within schools as "divisions," often "lower," "middle," and "upper," with plenty of local variation. A handful of schools, many of them boarding, also offer the equivalent of a thirteenth grade, known as a post-graduate or "P.G." year; students enroll in P.G. programs for a variety of reasons, from having an extra year of academic preparation to focusing on development of an athletic talent to simply gaining more maturity before heading off to college.

It is safe to say that the lower the grade level being offered, the greater the chance that teaching candidates will need some specific preparation for teaching that level. Independent schools may not require certification, but they are likely to look for a degree or significant college-level coursework in early childhood education or some aspect of primary education when hiring classroom teachers below the middle school years. This is not to say that someone lacking this experience will not be hired, but for reasons relating to the known complexity of teaching young children well, formal preparation is considered highly desirable.

Middle school positions may not require specialized training, but those hiring for such positions are likely to be looking for some experience or other visible sign that a candidate is really interested in teaching early adolescents. More than students at any other age perhaps, middle schoolers demand and respond to the ability of a teacher to occupy the mental world, and above all to respect the reality of the strange and wonderful emotional space that they occupy. The aspiring professor focused on teaching subject matter will find this age group frustrating, disappointing, and perhaps even maddening, at least until the existence of a different reality dawns. The martinet or the "control freak" will encounter much the same problem, as the developmental characteristics of early adolescents militate against easy acquiescence or submission to externally imposed authority or even notions of justice.

Middle school positions, it must be acknowledged, are likely to make the most intense demands on teachers during the working day. Supervision and offering extra help can absorb much or all of what looks like "unassigned" time, with the compensatory reward of a somewhat shorter school day and the yeasty pleasures of watching students undergo remarkable personal development.

High school-age teaching is seen as requiring the least specific educational preparation other than solid mastery of subject matter content, and most independent schools place a premium on this knowledge for secondary-level teachers. A major, a minor, or a graduate degree in a specific academic field is regarded as a plus factor for candidates, as can be work experience in a field related to the discipline. It is perhaps easiest for a midlife career-changer to step from an office or laboratory into a high school classroom without extensive training, and schools seem to be increasingly willing to smile upon the professionalism, wisdom, and maturity that such candidates offer. However, it remains true that non-teaching work experience is valued very differently from school to school in salary computations, and a career-changing candidate should not be afraid to ask about this early in the hiring process.

High school teachers, especially, are going to be asked to coach or to otherwise add their age and experience to the leadership or supervision of student activities. Typically these would include clubs, publications, student government, and athletics, but sometimes teachers may be asked to do more humdrum work such as supervising study halls. Most independent schools have some sort of program in which teachers are expected, as part of the general job description, to advise students about aspects of their academic lives. Hours can be long, and a number of evening or weekend activities through the year may be "command performances"; candidates can inquire discreetly about such, but be warned that too anxious an interest in hours and expectations will be seen as problematic by some interviewers.

In many fields and at most levels, one of the benefits of teaching in independent schools is a high degree of autonomy in the creation and execution of curriculum, and this is especially true in the humanities at the high school level. To a degree most foreign language, science, and mathematics curricula are driven by schools' understandings of colleges' expectations, and many of these curricula are still built around established texts; this is also the case for history in many schools. This autonomy is a double-edged sword: it liberates the teacher, but it also requires a great deal of work that teachers with state-mandated curricula do not necessarily have to do. It is imperative that a prospective teacher at any level understand the degree to which their curricula will be their own and also to know who in the school has the responsibility to guide and support the new teacher as he or she creates or adapts learning experiences and assessments for students.

Coeducational and single-sex schools

Like colleges, independent schools in the 1970s abandoned their single-sex heritages in droves as enrollments shrank and the world changed, and nowadays single-sex schools are the exception rather than the rule. However, many single-sex schools resisted, and so a healthy number of fine schools remain devoted to the education of either boys or girls. It should not be surprising that such schools and their leaders are among the strongest voices for the virtues of single-sex classrooms, now the subject of pilot programs in a few public school systems.

Whatever the reasons that once made coeducation suspect, independent schools have been doing it well for many years, and a few elder schools established themselves as coeducational long ago for reasons philosophical, religious, or practical. Today's lower- and middle-grades schools tend to be coeducational, as are many of those schools that encompass the full range, pre-K through 12.

Single-sex schools tend to serve the middle and upper grades, many with a long tradition of service in the education of boys or girls alone. In most cases, today's single-sex schools are not rigorously segregated at all levels, and teachers of both sexes can be found teaching in them. Teachers looking to work in single-sex schools, whether on their own side of or across the gender barrier, will need to examine their own commitment to what is admittedly a somewhat misunderstood, and in some quarters outré, approach to education. The teacher in a single-sex setting had better believe in the virtues of single-sex education, if not as superior to coeducation, at least as its equal in value and validity. Single-sex schools take great pride in what they do; that such schools play a critical role in empowering young women and allowing young men to develop the full range of their emotions are some of the claims justly made about all-girl or all-boy schools at their best. Doing this work should be a source of pride for their teachers.

Getting hired

Once the candidate has identified a group of schools of interest, whether three or 30, further research on the schools' websites can reveal a great deal more about their facilities, values, faculties, and student bodies. Although at first the crisp color photographs and upbeat news can make schools all look alike, in time the thoughtful explorer will note subtle distinctions that may indicate real differences in schools' natures. At the same time, the candidate can soak up knowledge that will make decisions easier, and with luck, interviews more fruitful.

Regional association websites, easily found by searching "independent school association + (the name of a region, state, or metropolitan area)," will have job listings, but so will individual school sites; most school sites now have pages called "careers" or "employment" with current openings and contact information. A fact of life is, however, that such listings may not be complete or current; a candidate should not be discouraged, even if no specific openings are shown.

Hand in hand with finding a group of schools of interest, the candidate will need to make his or her interest known. Typically the candidate should prepare a résumé and a cover letter. The résumé should stress both educational attainments—majors, minor, significant coursework—and the kinds of strengths or experiences that underscore or support the notion that this person has some qualities or interests that are suitable in a teacher; leadership, service, organizational skill, and work with children should be highlighted. The cover letter should make reference to a specific position, if one is known to be open, or to a teaching field or area for which the candidate would be appropriate, were an opening to exist or arise. The cover letter should also make mention of those qualities or experiences that might distinguish the candidate as a prospective faculty member; there should also be some specific mention of the reasons that the school is of interest to the candidate. At the same time, the candidate should also be lining up several people, especially responsible adults with some knowledge of the candidate's qualities as a possible teacher of children and employee, willing to serve as references; ideally, at least two of those should be prepared to write on the candidate's behalf. In other words, the usual principles of job-hunting pertain. Follow-up telephone calls are in order, and there is no harm in asking just for an informational interview to learn more about the school.

Independent schools are unusual among employers in the professions in that many of them rely upon teacher placement agencies to provide them with a pool of pre-vetted candidates. For every school that carefully reads each individual letter from hopeful applicants, at least as many simply contact one or more of the established national and regional placement agencies and let them know of a specific opening. (The names of many agencies can be found in the "Resources" section for this chapter at the end of the book.) The good news for candidates here is that schools pay the often hefty agency commissions, but the less good news is that agencies vary in the degree of support they are able to offer their candidates. But many schools regard the agencies as their prime marketplace for candidates, and some look no further than to candidate files supplied by agencies.

Thus, even as he or she is neatly pasting commemorative stamps on individual letters to schools, the candidate should be busily completing the registration forms that are almost always online, with seldom if ever a fee, for one or more of the placement agencies. If at all possible—and for some agencies this is standard practice—the candidate should do everything possible to make himself or herself known as an individual to the agency, preferably by means of a personal interview. Many agencies also ask candidates to prepare a statement of educational philosophy, and it is worth the time and trouble to be honest and thoughtful in writing this, even if the concept seems rather contrived. The statement ought to focus the candidate's interest in and commitment to the success of students.

The most thoughtful schools will push agencies to provide them with materials on the most appropriate candidates, not simply a pile of papers, and candidates should gently demand equally thoughtful service in finding appropriate placements. The more the agency knows and understands a candidate's strengths and interests, the harder the agency will work on that candidate's behalf. Agency files are often where a candidate's written letters of reference will wind up, but a strong personal statement from an agency staffer can be as compelling as a glowing letter.

Along with school listings, employment listings on regional association sites, and agencies, the candidate should be able to identify myriad other sources of information on openings. Some schools rely heavily on local newspaper employment listings, some advertise in local or regional publications aimed at specific communities, and a few schools have discovered internet classifieds. Several national education publications occasionally carry job listings from independent schools, and several organizations specialize in connecting schools with candidates from historically underrepresented groups.

Candidates should also look for job fairs. Many of these are sponsored by regional independent schools associations; a few focus particularly on minority recruiting. Most fairs have a system for interested schools to interview the candidates who most interest them, but candidates should make a point of table-hopping just to get to know schools; sometimes an offhand contact can blossom into something bigger.

All about interviews

With luck and good preparation, the candidate's telephone will ring, an e-mail flag will pop up, or a note will appear on a job fair board: the candidate has an interview. Sometimes the interviews are the frenzied half-hour chats at fairs or agency "cattle calls"; like speed dating, these interviews give a candidate limited time to make a strong impression in hopes of a callback to the school itself. Knowledge of the school is power here, but so are an energetic, positive demeanor, some great answers, and a couple of thoughtful questions.

The intentional teacher, I believe, should try from the onset of the process to make clear his or her ambition to be a great teacher, and to this end a thoughtful line of questioning ought to be simply, *How will working at your school help me grow as a teacher? How committed will the school be to my professional development?*

If the interview is to take place in a school, the candidate should not be shy about inquiring about the dimensions of the event—who, where, when, and how long? It might be just planned as a preliminary chat with a single administrator or department chair, or it may be on a larger scale. As with fair interviews, focused energy is the key.

At some point the candidate is likely to experience a longer interview, and here it is good to be proactive in asking about such things as a school tour and a chance to meet students. These things may be difficult to arrange, but most schools will try to accommodate this request to whatever extent they can. The candidate might expect as well to meet with multiple supervisors for each of a teacher's likely roles.

Some schools will ask the candidate to teach a sample lesson. For a teacher with little or no experience, this will be a source of terror, but he or she should use common sense and ask as much as possible about the context of the lesson and the learning expectations. The lesson can be thought of as a theatrical scene, with a beginning, middle, and end, and it should have a purpose: What should the students have learned by the end of it, and is there an activity that will produce evidence of the learning? A good sample lesson will have some interactive component—a lecture will not really do—but interactivity can open the door to disorder, so choose an activity that is extremely simple to explain and to carry out, with minimal need for extraneous materials. Above all, the candidate should try to select subject matter about which he or she is knowledgeable and enthusiastic; passion and confidence may well carry the day with students, even if the lesson itself is a bit creaky, and in the end keeping students' attention may be the main thing. If the subject matter is specified by the teacher, the same advice applies: energy, clarity, simplicity, interactivity, and some form of assessment.

If all goes well, the last interviews will be followed by an offer, probably after reference checks. The candidate may negotiate firmly and ask for time if necessary, but as a rule school administrators do not respond terribly well to what might look like a posturing game of hardball. In addition, a criminal background check will be performed; it is advisable for the candidate to be ready to explain any problems that may show up. There is no way to know what kind of information will lead to the withdrawal of an offer, but a forthright explanation and evidence of rehabilitation or non-recurrence can help. Obviously, some issues will preclude a person's working in schools. Schools are increasingly turning to even more comprehensive background-checking procedures, including credential checks, and so any exaggerations or fabrications in an application or on a résumé are likely to be spotted—and an offer promptly withdrawn.

As of 2007–08, the National Association of Independent Schools reports that the median starting salary for a teacher is just shy of $33,000, varying within a few thousand dollars by region, grade level taught, and type of school. In the eleven-to-16 years' experience band, more or less the middle of the experience pool, this rises to over $48,000, and salaries for long-time classroom teachers in a few schools can exceed $100,000. While these sums are not princely, most established schools offer some sort of health insurance, pension or 401(k) programs, and other benefits, sweetening the deal considerably. Boarding schools are likely to include housing, not necessarily in dormitories. Summer responsibilities for teachers tend to be minimal, although some schools require reading or some sort of retreat or collaborative work, often supported with small stipends. The work is emotionally demanding and intellectually stimulating, and the chance to make a difference in young lives is simply part of the deal. While accepting an independent school teaching job may seem like a leap of faith with only modest material rewards, it is not a bad way to make one's living.

Orienting oneself

At last the contract will be received, signed, and returned, and the candidate will have become a "new teacher." Although it is to be desired that all schools would proceed to immerse new hires in useful and connective resources, this is not always the case, and so the intentional teacher should be proactive in establishing as many links as possible with the new school. It may be tempting to spend one's "last summer" taking it easy, but even a small amount of preparation will make the first weeks of the school year pass smoothly and with much less stress than otherwise.

The new teacher should request access to the school's e-mail, at the least, and the names and addresses, including summer contact information, of anyone who will be a close colleague, supervisor, or necessary resource, including teachers who teach or have taught the courses that the new hire will be teaching, the department head, the athletic director, the division director, the business office, and the bookstore. If the school has a formal mentoring program, the sooner the new teacher can connect with the mentor, the better. Independent schools can be shockingly offhand in guiding new teachers with regard to courses they will teach, and the new teacher should be gently insistent on acquiring as much information as possible about curricula, materials, texts, and expectations. If the school keeps a curriculum map, the new teacher should have access to it from the start, and someone in a position to be helpful should be willing to meet for an extended period, in person or electronically, to help the new person plan strategy for the year and some lessons for the first days and weeks of school. The new teacher should also ask for access to any other academic resources, such as the library. The start of the year will also be more pleasant if the new teacher has completed whatever paperwork needs to be done in order to be paid, join the benefits program, or otherwise be in a position to focus on work rather than on life management.

As the start of school grows closer and the pace of planning and associated anxieties picks up, the new teacher might try to imagine him- or herself not so much in a position of vulnerability (which will be quite natural, and accompanied by nightmares of unpreparedness that are an unwelcome but familiar part of summer's end even for veteran teachers) but rather as an anthropologist or cultural historian. The new school is, after all, a new culture, a new society, and a new setting to be explored and understood in order for the recently arrived member to survive and thrive.

Analyzing school culture

In teaching cultural analysis to students, we often use a process known by the acronym PIG'S EAR. Simple enough in concept, the mnemonic sets forth categories for analysis that can be useful to the new teacher in his or her anthropological role:

- **Politics.** What is the flow of authority within the school, and how do decisions seem to be made? What is the individual teacher's role in all this? Are there hidden or obscure sources of authority or power?
- **Ideas.** What are the Big Ideas that guide the school? Are these practical and grounded in extreme practical or material considerations, or are they idealistic? From what sources do these ideas flow, and how are they regarded by the faculty as a whole? Along with this is the matter of **Language**, the lexicon of specialized or esoteric terms that every school has to describe what goes on with it; how does one learn this language?
- **Geography.** How is the campus laid out? What places are important in the life of the teacher as an individual, and what places are important, practically or symbolically, to the life of the institution and the students?

- **Social Structure.** Is there an apparent pecking order within the faculty, or among departments? Which members of the community seem to be especially popular or influential? How do people who do not fit into cultural or social majorities fit in, and where do they find support, satisfaction, and validation? To what extent are student relationships driven by or reflective of hierarchies, and on what are such hierarchies based?

- **Economy.** What are the resources, financial and otherwise, required to succeed in the school, and how are they to be acquired from those who hold them? Is the school itself wealthy and open-handed, or are resources in general relatively scarce and to be husbanded, a source of institutional anxiety or personal rivalry? Does the school easily reimburse teachers for out-of-pocket expenses, or do its structures obviate the need for such expenditures?

- **Arts.** What are the sources of and outlets for creativity in the school and its community? How are creativity and initiative acknowledged and valued? How do the school's programs in the art relate to traditional "academic" areas? What are the agreed-on aesthetics with regard to neatness, dress, classroom décor, and personal decorum? Are student achievements in the arts visible and celebrated?

- **"Religion."** On a philosophical level, what do the school and its community believe in? On a personal level, what roles do faith and spiritual ideals play in the daily lives of teachers and students within the school? Are community members' spiritual lives acknowledged as part of their school experience?

This may seem a superficial or even amusing set of questions for the new teacher to ponder, but their answers can be helpful in negotiating the more challenging aspects of a first year. No two schools are alike, and unfortunately a few landmines are always waiting to be triggered under the inexperienced. Circumspection, close observation, and reflection can help avoid many of these.

A most important resource for a new teacher will be whatever formal orientation is offered by the new school. Perhaps the school has a comprehensive teacher's guide or handbook, and at the least the new teacher should carefully read through any student handbook that the school might publish. Human resources are, of course, the most valuable. Soon enough the new teacher will be able to know who the informal sources of support and advice are likely to be. But as soon as or preferably before any formal orientation begins, the new teacher should not be afraid to request or seek out a mentor if the school has not already assigned one, especially after surveying the lay of the land. Whether official or unofficial, a good mentor can guide the new teacher through the first year of school as well as give reality checks when necessary; an unofficial mentor may be a better source of advice on the realities of internal politics, while a formal mentor may be able to draw on more resources to help the teacher. Ideally a mentor should not be a supervisor or evaluator, but someone who can provide both safe space and honest feedback and whose role and guiding belief is to ensure the success of the new teacher as the hitherto abstract stuff of teaching school—students, classroom management, curriculum and assessment, and families—becomes reality.

The new teacher will soon be immersed in the daily life of the school and a whole range of appropriate daily concerns and anxieties related to lesson planning, collegial relations, life management, and student success. This last will loom large in the teacher's consciousness as the first weeks pass and patterns of success and failure, effort and laxity become apparent. Each student will soon take form in the teacher's mind as a puzzle made up of an ever-growing number of pieces. As the teacher's confidence grows, the pieces will begin to fit together, and, as the teacher comes to know each student well, a room full of puzzles will become a room full of people.

I would offer several last caveats, two seemingly trivial, one vital. The small suggestions have to do with health and comfort: buy and wear comfortable shoes, and be aware that a school is a kind of Petri dish for the incubation of small illnesses; the new teacher is likely to succumb to several of these. Thus, good habits of personal hygiene, especially the washing of hands, can make for a happier and healthier school year.

My other piece of advice is likely to contradict what other wise teachers may say. As the new teacher settles in, he or she will doubtless be asked to help out here or there, to join a committee, to advise a club, or to run a reading group. I have heard thoughtful senior educators, eager to protect teachers in this position from stress and strain, remind teachers: Do not be afraid to say no.

I say: Do not be afraid to say yes. A teacher's willingness to jump in and try new things will be seen by the school as a sign both of interest in the profession at large and of the disposition to contribute to multiple aspects of life at the school. The work will be an extra burden, but it is unlikely to amount to exploitation. The experience will be invaluable, adding not just to the résumé but to the teacher's perspective on students and on education in general. And along the way, the extra responsibility might even turn out to be fun.

CHAPTER III

Knowing Students

"Twine yourself round the hearts of your scholars by gentleness."
— Eliza Palmer Peabody

Whether starting a new job, a new career, or just a new school year, anyone in the teaching profession immediately discovers that to teach is to be immersed in the world of students, and that students take absolute primacy over content. While we prefer to imagine that this knowledge is bred in the bone of the intentional teacher, even at the outset of a life in teaching, a room full of faces, even a roster of names, can be overwhelming. In the abstract, "students" can be an amorphous or monolithic concept, a body of blurred faces or "intellectual raw material" to be married with something equally amorphous called "curriculum" to create an amalgam of learners and learning called "education." In reality, it is the teacher's primary task to disaggregate the monolith into clearly differentiated individuals, each of whom will have not only unique needs but in consequence a distinct relationship with the curriculum. Great teaching begins with the teacher's capacity to know students.

The most successful schools, independent or otherwise, share one characteristic: every teacher in these schools is deeply aware of and interested in each student, and no student can fall through the cracks or hide from a faculty of caring men and women. Optimal teaching and learning experiences are catalyzed by personal relationships built on the faculty's collective and individual efforts to know and understand the needs, strengths, affinities, and aspirations of each student. Classroom and non-academic experiences that foster lifelong curiosity, confidence, and satisfaction result from shared purpose and practice, and it is the responsibility of the intentional teacher to combine observation, empathy, and professional skill in generating this synergy. Nothing is more exhilarating for a teacher than those moments when such synergy becomes not just present but palpable; these are the experiences that students recollect and draw upon for lifetimes.

Learning students' stories

It is a truism that every student represents a story. The main element of the story is of course family, in the broadest sense: structure, size, ethnicity, socioeconomic class, experience, and aspirations. Although one can imagine a bell curve on which the situation of most students in a school fits relatively neatly under the largest part, students whose lives are lived under "outlier" conditions may create special challenges or special rewards for teachers. Chapter VIII, "Families," will offer a deeper discussion of the nature of families and how the intentional teacher can navigate the sometimes difficult landscape of families with compassion and wisdom.

For many students, their story is public and familiar in its outlines, but is possible for the teacher to be misled. Independent schools by their nature seek to create complex and vibrant communities from a diversity of students, and in their turn children, by their nature, often work hard to minimize the appearance and the effects of such diversity. Chapter IX will lay out in detail the idea that teaching in a diverse environment and with a truly multicultural purpose requires close observation and understanding of differences, but it also requires that the teacher begin with a set of color- and culture-blind expectations for the success of each student. Thus, the relationships a teacher builds with students must necessarily originate from that point in a teacher's will that is focused on the ideal that each student can and will achieve at a high level. But differences among students will exist, whether they are visible in some sort of racial or cultural diversity or whether they are more subtle, embedded in experience, class, religion, or way of being. In many schools, variations in learning style are significant beyond other kinds of difference.

A day school, for example, may draw students from a catchment area with a radius of thirty or forty miles—students will come to school from many communities and with long daily journeys to school that cross significant cultural as well as geographical boundaries. Nonetheless, at school most students will work very hard to look, dress, and sound in some way typical; most do this by donning the protective coloration of the majority, dressing by the fashions of the moment and exhibiting "approved" behaviors, preferences, and belongings. As we will see, some students perform this daily makeover at high emotional cost, while for others it is a part of life perhaps even to be celebrated. In boarding schools this situation is equally true, with all students "equalized" in some measure by their dislocation, a dislocation that each student will feel in a way that is uniquely his or her own. Teachers are unlikely to know and should absolutely avoid speculation about which students are, for example, receiving high levels of financial aid or are coming from disadvantaged backgrounds; most schools do not share this information with faculties, for good reasons. However, it is incumbent on teachers to develop an understanding of each student's situation as it relates to his or her success, academic and social.

Teachers can get to know students well in three ways: through conversation with colleagues—avoiding rumor and lurid speculation—through making a thorough study of such student records as are available to the teacher, and through close observation. Each of these approaches will give the teacher valuable insight that will enable him or her to tailor learning experiences, advice, feedback, and support to the student's specific needs. Along the way it must be acknowledged that the teacher will experience momentary crises of confidence, disapproval, and even, on rare occasions, revulsion; children's lives can be messy, and their decisions are not always what we might hope. But each student's story, as it takes form from the qualitative and quantitative data compiled by the proactive, energetic teacher who understands the value of that story, will be shaped, as it unfolds, by the optimistic attention and caring intervention of adults.

Talking to students

Talking with students can be difficult, and many effective teachers go through a career without ever feeling that they know how to do it consistently well. The fact is, people hit it off with one another for different reasons, but the more compelling fact is that as a teacher, it is one's job to make the effort. Whether it is saying "hi" to a student in a hallway, holding a conference about work, offering a genial reprimand or reminder, or engaging in a serious conversation, every opportunity that a teacher has to speak with a student is a learning as well as a teaching experience. Informal, natural, and personal banter can transform a mass of "business-related" teacher-student interactions into solid, lasting relationships that incubate greater student engagement and confidence.

It is worth emphasizing here the special and extraordinary value in a teacher taking what may feel like a personal risk to reach out to students who are in some clear and obvious way unlike the teacher in terms of race or some other aspect of identity. Students from groups that have been marginalized by society tend to respond positively to sincere, respectful approaches from a teacher, even if they do not always acknowledge this overtly. The main thing is to take interaction as it comes, setting aside assumptions (a very good idea in any case) and acknowledging difference without pretense; the teacher needs just to be himself or herself. Crossing cultural gulfs is never easy, but once the teacher has done so, the value will be apparent, and subsequent efforts will expand the teacher's comfort zone. A reputation among students and families as a teacher willing to talk straight across lines of difference can palpably enhance a teacher's effectiveness with all students.

The secret to talking to students well goes back to the idea of respecting each one in the place that he or she presently occupies, of withholding judgment and pontification as one listens—listens!—intently to what the student has to say, working to understand their point of view even when one finds its premises or reasoning flawed or repugnant. At the same time, the intentional teacher is not too quick to jump in with exaggerated support or agreement, or to share in such a way that the conversation becomes about him or her instead of the student.

Above all, the teacher must recognize that professional boundaries lie well on this side of personal ones. To listen to a student, to share ideas and even preferences with him or her, is not to become a friend—at least not beyond the limits of professionalism—a confidante, or most egregiously, a therapist. Savvy teenagers can sound very, very grown up, but their brains and emotional lives are still very much under development and different from those of adults. The teacher is an adult in a position of authority, for better or worse a true role model with significant power, and to invite, offer, or even allow confession or intimacy is to step into serious danger of many sorts, from personal embarrassment to professional misconduct to civil and criminal liability. Getting to know students has limits, and a simple test of judgment should establish their location: Is this a relationship, or even a conversation, that the teacher would feel comfortable having on camera, with the student's family and one's supervisors as audience? We will speak to this issue in greater detail in Chapter XIV, "Professional Behavior."

Student records

Most schools encourage teachers to read through students' files. At the least these may give a "bare bones" educational history of the student, or they might contain information vital to an understanding of the child—testing results, for example, or information on family matters. Even information such as the student's home address is worth noting, as such can offer some hints at socioeconomic background or just such basic information as the length of a student's commute. The existence of siblings, blended families, or absent parents can help a teacher understand much about a student, although it is dangerous, as always, to read too much into such data.

If information on testing or learning differences is on file, the intentional teacher should take note of this, and then seek assistance within the school to understand what this information might mean in the context of classroom learning, behavior, and social interactions. There may be information in student medical records on medication, although most frequently information of this sort is protected as confidential under federal HIPAA (Health Insurance Portability and Accountability Act) regulations. Teachers should be also aware that a student's educational records, such as permanent files, are protected as confidential under the Family Educational Rights and Privacy Act (FERPA). While having students score one another's tests has withstood a court challenge under FERPA, public dissemination of student grades, even through careless handling, and certainly report cards or transcripts, may be actionable under federal regulations.

The teacher-observer and concepts of intelligence

The teacher's most effective tool in knowing students is simply observation. As a first-year teacher I attended a workshop in which the presenter spoke of the "teacher-observer," and I have never forgotten the power of that designation. To take note of how a student behaves and learns is to amass invaluable information that can be used to adjust teaching and assessment methods so as to reach the student most effectively.

The key to effective and useful observation is to have in one's mind a set of categories regarding learning and capacity and to have in one's teaching toolbox some strategies for responding to specific learning behaviors. Without getting into a disquisition on cognitive theory and adolescent psychology, each student, as part of his or her individual story, has his or her own learning style. This may involve preferred modes of learning—aural or visual or kinesthetic—or preferred ways of processing information and putting learning into practice.

In the past few decades enormous amounts of work have been done to try to identify specific characteristics in individuals that can be useful in understanding learning and in designing learning experiences that reach all kinds of students. Some of this work has involved digging into the notion of intelligence itself, long imagined by psychologists as a fixed and unitary quality referred to by psychologists as *g*.

In the 1980s, however, Howard Gardner of Harvard's famed Project Zero and Robert Sternberg of Yale (now Tufts) began promulgating persuasive theories suggesting that intelligence is neither unitary nor fixed. In Gardner's multiple intelligences (M-I) model, intelligence is a bundle of specific intelligences—linguistic, musical, logical-mathematical, spatial, bodily-kinesthetic, interpersonal, intrapersonal, naturalistic, and existential—that are variously mixed in individuals and that can be capitalized on in the design of school curricula. A number of schools and curricula have worked to build M-I ideas into educational programs, but awareness of Gardner's categories can also help the individual teacher to discern preferences and strengths in a classroom full of students: Who gravitates toward which kinds of activities, who excels in which kinds of work?

Sternberg's "triarchic" model of analytical, creative, practical intelligences moves the discussion toward a set of ideas that has been seen as very useful in school contexts. For Sternberg, intelligence as an abstraction cannot be separated from the individual's behavior: how successful the individual is at negotiating life's many challenges and problems.

From Sternberg it is a short leap to the idea of intelligence as a constellation of what educators call habits of mind, dispositions and predilections that in their definitions embrace both the idea of intelligence as manifold and complex and the intellectual and emotional tendencies that students display as they learn (in the broadest sense). Most theories of habits of mind (or dispositional intelligence, as the underlying idea is sometimes called) list such characteristics as intellectual curiosity, perseverance, optimism, creativity, flexibility of thought, empathy, and circumspection. Experience suggests that habits of mind can indeed be taught through intentionally designed learning experiences, and a number of schools have embraced the idea that having students develop an identified group of habits of mind is a highly suitable mission for a school. The intentional teacher should both take careful note of the degree to which his or her school subscribes to different ideas on student capacity and take advantage of opportunities for professional development to learn more; Chapter XII, "Continuing Education: Child Development," will offer more on this.

Related is the idea of emotional intelligence, popularized by Daniel Goleman in the 1990s, which proposes another model to explain why certain affective behaviors and attitudes are apt and productive. Like habits of mind, emotional intelligence can be broken down into specific components, and learning experiences can be designed to help students strengthen these components.

For the classroom teacher, awareness of several models for understanding and categorizing the learning and social behavior of children can be a useful tool, giving the teacher-observer a place to begin analysis. In the past decade the work of the All Kinds of Minds Institute has offered teachers an arsenal both of observational and diagnostic categories and of specific techniques drawn widely from best practices to help teachers respond to what is observed. Using what All Kinds of Minds parlance calls *neu-rodevelopmental constructs*, teachers are taught to observe student learning behavior with regard to attention, sequencing and ordering abilities, memory, language use, movement and physical skill, high-level thinking, and social awareness and behavior. Although training in the All Kinds of Minds methodology is lengthy and expensive, it gives teachers a very useful toolbox for understanding how individual students learn and helping students leverage strengths and interests into deeper understanding.

Colleagues of mine have persuasively argued that these neurodevelopmental constructs, like the several notions of intelligence now current, fail to acknowledge social and experiential factors that have enormous impact on classroom learning. Socioeconomic status, family situation, English-language-learner status, cultural heritage, historical (or, sadly, present-day) prejudice or marginalization, and even health-related issues can all serve as powerful variables in the learning experience of students, and so this chapter must end with a return to its first premise: the intentional teacher, to be an effective teacher, must work extremely hard to know students.

It has been said that teachers make many hundreds of instructional decisions each day, decisions that play out in the way they experience the classroom and the school. Almost all of these decisions, following what planning may be possible, are made on the fly, and almost all of them have some specific emotional content for students as well as for the teacher. Most of this content falls within a predictable range as just part of the affective side of being in school, but all involve expenditure of intellectual and emotional energy. To know students well is to be able to focus this energy where it can do the most good.

CHAPTER IV

Classroom Culture: *"Management"*

*"School should be the most interesting and
stimulating part of the student's day."*
— EUGENE R. SMITH

The idea of riding herd on a score of children may unsettle the aspiring teacher, and for some teachers, even some great teachers, classroom management remains a point of discomfort for the length of a career. Whether the children are kindergarteners or high school sophomores, in a faceless, abstract mass they might as well be, for some teachers, a cage full of tigers. A few who enter the profession are quickly undone by the challenge of classroom management; they leave the profession voluntarily, or they are sent packing, their worst nightmares realized.

This is tough talk to start this chapter, but classroom management is hard work that can also be perilous, perhaps more so than any other part of teaching. Nonetheless, some basic principles should keep the intentional teacher in control and on top of any class. Running through each of these principles are the ideas of honesty and trust; the teacher must be ready to see him- or herself realistically and trust him- or herself and to trust students and their intense desire to learn, to grow up, and above all to be taken seriously.

What the teacher must do: five principles

The first principle of building a classroom culture in which "management" becomes secondary to learning, and the best advice I ever received as a teacher, at a time when I was heading off to school each day literally quaking at the thought of facing five classrooms filled with students at four different grade levels, is: Be yourself! As the reader will recall from *The Catcher in the Rye*, young people can spot and dismiss a "phony" instantaneously. The teacher who starts the day by putting on a game face and imitating—who? Tommy Lee Jones?—may feel well armored against mischief and disrespect, but students have seen all the movies, and some will feel the need to test the armor for weak spots. On the other hand, anyone hoping to woo students by being *The Coolest Teacher in the School* may draw in a few acolytes for a while, but students soon recognize a posture, even when it's a slouch. In any case, too tough or too cool will destroy the teaching and learning process. Teachers should dress professionally, be adult, and speak clearly in proper English; save the slang or *au courant* usages for those rare, surprise moments when they can achieve a specific educational effect. The intentional teacher avoids using a "teacher voice" or other mannerisms that he or she would not produce in front of family or friends.

Above all, no teacher should for one second believe that being "the teacher" has elevated him or her to a *moral* plane above that of students. Yes, the teacher is in authority over classes in a shared voyage toward learning, and the teacher's skills and knowledge are vital resources on that voyage. Students may do unwise, even naughty things, and make questionable, even bad decisions; but the teacher's job is to notice and then to guide, to correct, to model, but not to condemn children. The focus must be on the social and moral import of the behavior and not on the relative moral position of the child. To be oneself in a classroom is not to suppress feelings of disappointment, disapproval, frustration, or even anger (or of elation, amusement, and joy, for that matter), but it is to use the modulated expression of those feelings to build authentic relationships within which students can grow and succeed.

The second principle of effective classroom management is that a classroom is a small society, made up of individuals with their own characteristics, aspirations, values, needs, and strategies for meeting these needs. The teacher, too, brings all this for himself or herself. Just as the school has its culture, so does the classroom have all the ingredients of a culture: traditions, expectations, schedules, rituals, and norms. For the intentional teacher, the secret of "classroom management" is not the management, or containment, of 10 or 20 individual wills but rather the creation of a classroom culture that brings those separate wills into some kind of alignment around core values focused on respect and learning.

This probably sounds almost too good to be true, or at least deceptively simple, and it requires serious and sustained effort to become habitual. The good news is that we have already discussed two aspects of teaching that can make an enormous contribution to building this kind of culture. The first is knowing and respecting students and building individual relationships based on a fundamental understanding of who they are and what they want and need.

The third principle underlying positive and productive classroom culture is organization. The teacher with a plan and confidence in that plan and its purposes brings to the classroom the equivalent of a belief system. If students can see their own interests in that plan and feel the care of the teacher, the classroom can become the moral center of a strong and sustaining culture, rich in possibilities for deep learning.

Above all things, students want and need to see and understand that they are acknowledged and appreciated and that the adults who have been placed, as they see it, in command of their lives, are committed to their needs and their success.

The fourth and fifth principles, perhaps too obvious to mention, are joy and humor. Without obvious and sincere displays of pleasure, and without the leavening of humor (and its helpmate, humility), learning can be leaden and sour, a drudgery and a chore. To take learning too seriously is to kill the spark of curiosity and to trap children in a cave without light, and the intentional teacher looks for opportunities to laugh at him- or herself and to laugh with students at the many absurdities that present themselves in the life of an open, active classroom. After all, it's only school!

Constructivist theory and "Active learning"

It is unlikely that the classroom culture of the intentional teacher will always be silent and orderly. The model of curriculum that we have presented in the previous chapter falls into the category of "constructivist," a student-centered notion based on the idea that effective learning occurs when the learner literally "constructs" meaning and understanding from the intentional learning experiences to which he or she is exposed. Furthermore, current research on brain function and memory has identified the conditions that fortify and extend the synaptic networks that are the physiological basis of learning. Strong emotional or physical associations embed ideas more deeply than does mere recitation, and other kinds of stimuli, auditory or visual, can also reinforce learning. Hard-working brains need, quite literally, to be hydrated, and young bodies need to be active and nourished in order to allow those brains to focus on intended tasks. In other words, plenty of activity appropriate to the age of the students should characterize a classroom in which optimum learning is taking place.

Engaged learning in a constructivist model thrives on interaction, and so the intentional teacher develops a repertory of activities that allow for discussion, question-and-answer, and group work. Skills in these areas take time to develop, but the descriptions of a number of tried-and-true techniques can be found in the literature of teaching, either online or in a good educational library.

For early childhood and early elementary classrooms, the best sources of ideas for classroom techniques will be the literature or experienced colleagues; circles, read-alouds, small-group table work, and break-out groups to work on specific skills are all familiar and effective.

For students in the middle elementary grades and above, there are a number of excellent techniques for fostering a collaborative culture. In the **fishbowl**, for example, a group of students observe another group discussing a topic; the observers then respond with their own discussion. In the **jigsaw**, small groups of students discuss or investigate one aspect of a topic, and the class is then regrouped to share perspectives, with each new group containing one member from each of the previous groups; in time the whole class will have learned about each part of the topic. The **gallery walk** picks up on this idea by having students create or find images and quotations relating to a topic and post these around the room; students then circulate and examine the posted material, after which they discuss the "gallery" of ideas they have experienced. **Socratic seminars**, somewhat complex to manage and evaluate, are formally structured discussions focused on a single text or problem. Students are given specific prompts with which to prepare for the seminar. *Hevruta* **learning** is an ancient Talmudic technique in which students in pairs engage in brief discussions of a single short text or topic and then report out to the whole group. Teachers may ask students to explore particular events or even phenomena in **simulations**, which can be as sophisticated as detailed re-enactments of historical events or literary scenes or as basic as skits explaining or demonstrating scientific or mathematical phenomena. **Webquests** involve structured internet-based inquiry on a specific topic, usually based on materials prepared or specified by the teacher. **Field trips** are an old standby, but effective field trips involve specific prompts or questions designed to keep students focused on the purpose of the trip; the best even involve activities designed to foster observational or navigational skills. **Virtual field trips** take advantage of the many web-based resources designed for this purpose. The intentional teacher might also explore **problem-based learning**, a case-study-like methodology in which students engage in structured inquiry and discussion of a topic as it is carefully unfolded in the classroom; the technique fosters close observation of evidence, analytical skill, and inductive and deductive reasoning.

Audio-visual materials have come a long way from the film strip and the whirring 16-millimeter film with deadpan narration, but good teaching using films or videos has *never* featured a silent class passively watching a screen in a darkened room. Films or digital presentations can be made interactive simply by stopping them to encourage discussion or to answer questions, and students should never be viewing a film or video unless they are also being asked to engage actively with the medium by responding to prompts on a "viewer's guide" as they watch; many experts recommend stopping the presentation when students are writing their responses. The teacher is also free to consider whether excerpts from full-length films can be used effectively to explore a perspective or present an example in the context of a larger lesson without having to use up multiple class periods; sometimes similar short scenes from multiple films can have far more impact than watching an entire feature.

Interactive, web-based technologies can also be the basis of powerful and enormously creative classroom and assessment activities. Many teachers use blogs, microblogs, and other Web 2.0 elements to encourage writing and dialogue beyond the boundaries of the classroom, and developments in the coming years may move more and more instruction into the digital and virtual world.

Especially at higher grade levels, a teacher will sometimes need to transmit content knowledge through the old-fashioned lecture, but giving students a topic outline in advance or requiring note-taking can ensure that active learning will take place even in an apparently passive classroom; the best lecturers, of course, make room for discussion or questions, as well.

Collaborative projects are another important element of active teaching and learning, although they must be employed judiciously and planned with extreme care. Such projects can range in scale from something that takes a few minutes' work during a single class period to semester-length. The essence of a great project is that it combines really interesting and challenging tasks with clear learning goals that connect to the overall goals of the course or study.

At the risk of teaching by using a negative example—always a technique to be used sparingly—this principle might best be illustrated by imagining a classic elementary school science project: the construction of a volcano. Students can use all kinds of materials to create beautiful, topographically complex, and pyrotechnically vivid volcanoes, and exhibition day may be a high point in the students' year. Yet, if students are encouraged to focus mainly on the size, beauty, complexity, or entertainment value of the model rather than on understanding the ways in which real volcanoes are formed, the learning will be largely about plaster of Paris, how budgetary constraints can create invidious distinctions between classmates' projects, or the really astounding things that one can do with vinegar and baking soda in places other than the core of a plaster volcano. All this may be worth it to the teacher who wants to provide students with a memorable experience (which may be objective enough), but if more is at stake, the project assignment and evaluation criteria will need to be fine-tuned to emphasize volcano mechanics.

In Appendix II the reader will find a template for planning more elaborate projects that begins with a planning sheet for the teacher and proceeds with planning sheets for students, even including a "what if something goes wrong?" form. The greatest challenge to assigning collaborative work is ensuring equitable levels of input from each group member; using some method of breaking down and assigning tasks in advance of the actual work is one way of staying ahead of this issue. Equitable evaluation and assignment of accountability are also easier when the teacher has a record of which student was responsible for which parts of the project.

It has been said that the greatest enemy to good learning is an emphasis on "the one right answer," and in the active classroom the focus is on process as much as product. Of course some phenomena have unitary causes, single correct responses (two plus two equals four, at least in a decimal number system), and preferred problem-solving methods, but a classroom of diverse learners will inevitably produce complexity of ideas and multiple ways to solve problems. Where possible, the intentional teacher honors the variety of thought even when it is necessary to steer students toward a single answer or a particular approach. Being able to make reference to rich and provocative essential questions throughout a study can be extremely useful in this regard.

Teachable moments

Teaching can bring surprises, some of them unsettling, but some delightful. Often classroom surprises are the result of a random or offhand comment by a student; sometimes the comment is shocking, sometimes provocative, and sometimes it just reveals a gulf of ignorance; a student or group of students may even have been offended. Whatever the case, the teacher is faced with a dilemma: Does he or she react, take the bait, respond, even if doing so will mean a major diversion from the intended learning experience, or does the teacher press on, perhaps without even acknowledging the buzz in the air?

These are called "teachable moments," and the intentional teacher should be aware that they can be great gifts to understanding, even if they take the class far off track. When a word or statement really requires a response, the teacher had better respond. The teacher may gulp or take a deep breath, but the teachability of the situation is so greatly enhanced by a buzz that signifies stirring emotional engagement that *not* to respond is to lose a great opportunity for learning and perhaps even do a grave disservice to the group and undermine classroom culture and relationships.

The teachable moment may begin when students find themselves vexed by an idea or by an activity that goes inexplicably awry. Occasionally the spark is a particularly earnest or sincerely anguished question of the "What if?" or "Why do we have to learn this?" sort. The class and the teacher may gain much by allowing a fervent and extensive discussion of, say, why knowing algebra may be important in later life or what might have happened if Lincoln had not been shot; these discussions can help reveal to students the actually ways in which mathematicians or historians or simply their teachers think, knowledge that becomes part of reflection and metacognition in years to come.

Oftentimes, and sometimes alarmingly, teachable moments begin with a sweeping generalization; often this reflects a student's narrow point of view, sometimes even a prejudice born of inexperience and unawareness. If the generalization is truly offensive, as it may be, the teacher is obligated to halt proceedings and to confront the issue, *even if no one in the classroom might have been offended*. This is important; inappropriate statements or humor may seem just fine to children, who see and hear such things outside of school with dismaying frequency. But a classroom must be a place of higher values and a higher standard of what is acceptable. Everyone in the class may even *seem* to agree that, for example, "Such-and-such is a bad neighborhood," "My dad says all the Nazis should have been killed after World War Two," or that "Women aren't supposed to be president," but the teacher will need to unpack the statement slowly, carefully, and in clear, non-emotional and non-judgmental language and pose some questions back to the group about the statement. What is the evidence? How might people who call that neighborhood home feel about the issue? Do extreme solutions really help solve problems? What do the laws say about the issue?

And if someone in the class has truly been offended or hurt by the comment, the teacher may have to be simultaneously more direct and more discreet. The offended student may not wish to have attention drawn to the fact that she lives in the neighborhood under discussion, or perhaps the teacher is female. To bring the discussion around to a point where it is a dialogue and not a sermonette may feel daunting; the teacher may just want to express anger or raise a righteous defense of the wounded. But only a firm, rational response will do. Students will feel that the teacher is upset, but the teacher must remain emotionally in control, focusing on finishing the conversation around the issue and on bringing the whole class to a deeper and more empathetic or circumspect understanding of the issue. Teachable moments can be very hard work, especially when they involve the teacher's own "hot button" issues or when they excite a teacher's fierce desire to protect other students from hurtful talk.

The thoughtful teacher will also need to develop sufficient situational and self-awareness to know when he or she is being drawn off topic by the guile of students. Students enjoy digressions of all kinds, and many of them are not above planting a seed intended to move a classroom discussion far from the intended topic; occasionally the seed is a provocation.

Well handled, the discussion ensuing from a teachable moment will be among the most significant work a teacher can accomplish. Because it represents a break from the unusual and because of its affective context, the conversation will be memorable for all students, and perhaps a great step forward in understanding for some.

Managing frustration

When the messiness and disorder of students' words or behavior threaten to undo the teacher's good work, stress and frustration will rear their heads; these times should be the rare exceptions, and not the rule. Successful teachers become expert at dropping corrective advice into conversations in a matter-of-fact way and at bringing students to attention or order in conversational voices; confrontation and the singling out of individual students is to be avoided as much as possible. In a battle of wills, it is not guaranteed that the teacher will prevail, and an audience of shocked (or worse, amused) classmates will only make the situation worse. Never should a teacher's physical gestures seem threatening or intimidating, and the teacher who loses control of his or her voice—shifting to the register of true, violent anger—is lost. If the teacher is prone to angry outbursts, this is one area in which the Be Yourself advice may not be helpful. I would go so far as to suggest that a teacher unable to control anger might either seek counseling in this area or consider a different profession. Some words, when spoken, do not go away, and so the enraged or frustrated teacher who uses profanity, labels a child publicly or even in private, or demeans some part of a child's world has crossed a line from which there may be no return; at the very least, that teacher has opened up a can of professional trouble.

With a "difficult" class, a few strategies can shift the energy from negative to positive. The teacher can engage the class in developing a list of classroom norms (avoid the word "rule" unless one wishes to discover who in the class is born to be a courtroom lawyer, as children are expert in finding loopholes) or "standards" and post these prominently; these ought then to be cited whenever corrective words or action are necessary, and citation must be consistent. Establishing norms for classroom behavior is a good idea in any event; behavioral expectations are part and parcel of every culture, and students will appreciate clarity and consistency.

For more problematic situations, or when a single student seems to defy all attempts to bring him or her to order, a teacher should not be afraid to enlist the help of peers or supervisors. This is especially true when a teacher is at the start of a career; frustration over a difficult class can quickly turn into outright fear, and the teacher's future, like his or her self-esteem, may hang in the balance. The teacher must pre-emptively seek out a supervisor or mentor, describe the situation, confess the anxiety, and ask for assistance. Otherwise, word of a teacher's inability to maintain a productive classroom will soon enough filter out to the school community at large, and recovery when a reputation is at stake can be difficult. The good school has leaders and veterans who stand ready and are committed to helping newer teachers through the tough early moments that all teachers endure, and so the teacher must not allow feelings of shame or inadequacy to stop them from seeking help and guidance; the very good school goes out of its way to invite this.

Feedback

We will discuss the giving and receiving of feedback among the adults in a school in Chapter VII, but a last point relating to classroom culture has to do with the rapidity with which teachers give students necessary and useful feedback.

Sometimes the feedback to be given is behavioral. We have written about "classroom management" and the need to address behavioral issues directly and in real time.

The feedback issue also involves the return of student work. This is a problem area for many teachers—including the author, from time to time—but it is one of which the intentional teacher takes command. We assign work to students not just to see how they are doing but also to give them useful feedback that they can use to improve their learning and their performance. When substantial time passes between a piece of work being passed in and its return with a grade or some other form of evaluative feedback, the opportunity for the student to make use of this information is lost, or at least delayed. The timely return of student work must be a priority for every teacher. Some teachers find the prospect of evaluating student work distressing, and this is an area in which the use of rubrics, with teacher-defined standards, can be very helpful. Having a plan, including a schedule for processing student work and a way of swiftly checking off whether work has been received, can be useful, as well. It should be noted that delays in returning student work can contribute to problems with student honesty, as the teacher missing a paper but faced with the "I put it on your desk four weeks ago" defense has little to stand on.

In the end, thinking occurs constantly in the active classroom. An active classroom culture grows around respect, a teacher's commitment, organization, and enormous amounts of sharing of ideas among students and between students and the teacher. In such a classroom it is almost impossible for students not to develop habits of mind that will carry over into every aspect of their lives: intellectual curiosity, perseverance, the willingness to explore differing points of view, confident self-expression, and all the thinking skills and academic tools for lives of intellectual vigor. These habits of mind, and above all the propensity to be attentive and analytical, creative, and flexible—to exhibit "critical thinking"—represent what has been called **intellectual character**, a noble description of a set of noble dispositions. The classroom whose culture inspires and builds intellectual character is truly an estimable place.

CHAPTER V

Planning, Macro to Micro

"To teach is not to simplify every step until there is no real work for the child to do."
— ABBIE G. HALL

If teaching involves making hundreds of decisions each day, it is no wonder that teachers sometimes find themselves exhausted. However, the intentional teacher can help minimize feelings of enervation by working hard to impose as much order as possible on the fluid, complex, and occasionally even chaotic world of his or her work.

Of course, for a teacher, the attempted imposition of order at some point yields diminishing returns. The teacher who is an extreme "control freak" with regard to curriculum and student behavior is doomed to frustration and failure. But the teacher who is thoughtfully and methodically intentional in his or her work—that is, who sets to work from a group of principles and goals rather than from a list of behavioral expectations—will find that order is not so hard to create, and that creating opportunities for learning that honor the inherent messiness (perhaps a more direct term than "complexity") and intellectual diversity of children's lives can be enormously satisfying, even bringing something like a feeling of order.

I am going to suggest here that the intentional teacher do his or her planning "backwards." In fact, **backwards planning** is a term of art in education, and I thoroughly endorse it. But I mean to take the term a couple of steps farther, to suggest that planning proceed from the large scale to the small, reversing what the most obsessively order-seeking teacher might want to do. Rather than starting with individual lessons, the teacher should consider starting with an entire school year as the design scale.

Curriculum, then and now

When many of us were in school, the "curriculum," such as it was, consisted of nothing more or less than the textbook, or a set of texts, and course objectives for teachers and students were embedded in the idea of completing a set of assigned chapters. Tests, papers, quizzes, examinations, and occasional projects along the way gave the teacher the opportunity to assess learning. For the best teachers, these bare bones were only a start, and they built in opportunities for students to improve or correct aspects of their work; the best of them set goals for learning that went well beyond mastery of a limited number of specified facts and skills.

We are now only a generation or so into some broader understandings of the nature of curriculum. As one of my education professors put it back in 1976, the curriculum is the answer to three key questions:

Where are we going?
How are we going to get there?
How will we know when we've arrived?

These questions encapsulate the three main aspects of curriculum design: goal setting, planning and execution of learning experiences, and assessment. Each of these is applicable to curriculum regardless of scale, from the development of year-long courses to daily lesson planning.

Inasmuch as independent schools are generally free from mandated testing other than what is required of college-bound students in the higher grades, it can be something of a challenge to find the anchor point from which curriculum planning should begin; schools are more or less free to establish their own courses and their own standards. Teachers, therefore, need to understand the school, division, and department's goals as they establish courses of study, and they should also have a sense of institutional history—what has been done before, and where the artifacts of that work might lie. For a teacher newly arrived at an independent school, little information on how courses have been taught previously may be available. It is the unfortunate way of many schools that curriculum lives very much with the individual teacher, whose departure or simple unavailability can leave the replacement teacher or the new colleague who is to teach another section of the same course or another classroom of the same grade feeling the need to start from scratch.

The situation can also arise in a school where a particular unit, activity, or course has evolved over many years as the *opus magnum* of an admired teacher or as the centerpiece of or even a rite of passage for students in a particular grade. The original goals may be lost in time, and so the intentional teacher charged with carrying out such a program will need to be analytical and circumspect as it becomes his or her own.

A *curriculum-planning template*

Fortunately, useful planning templates are available to teachers, and a familiarity with the structure of well-designed curriculum can help a teacher create an effective course or unit relatively easily. The development of curriculum can be broken down into steps using models developed by the team at Harvard's Project Zero or by Grant Wiggins, co-author of the influential 1998 book, *Understanding by Design.* In the independent school community, Wiggins has been a powerful advocate for the development of goal-driven, "backwards" curriculum design and for the use of assessment tools that sharpen students' understanding of material. The design strategies presented here draw heavily on Wiggins's work as well as strategies developed at Project Zero and in school contexts informed by an emphasis on multicultural learning and an awareness of students' learning styles. First we will look at the steps in planning a course or unit of study, and then we will walk through a template for planning a single day's teaching.

Although the reader may infer that the teacher is expected to go it alone through this process, nothing could be further from the truth. At each step the teacher should make a point of touching base with any available human resources, whether colleagues in the classroom, department or division leaders, or other instructional resources at the school or in the area. The collaborative design of curriculum, while not universally practiced in independent schools, is increasingly understood to be one of the most powerful and inspiring kinds of professional development.

Here is an explanation of the planning template, which can be found as a form in Appendix I:

STEP ONE: *Identify the Main Idea*

The first order of business in planning a course or unit is to identify the point of the unit at the topical and conceptual levels. In the language of Project Zero, what is the **generative topic** of the course or unit? This could be as simple as "Algebra I," "Introducing Long Division," or "The Causes and Impact of World War II." Wiggins, who emphasizes the goal of understanding, would ask, What are the **overarching understandings**—the central, interesting issues—for this unit? What, in the broadest and simplest terms, does the teacher want students to know, and to know how to do, at the end of the study, and what habits of mind is the intended study to foster?

A very useful idea in curriculum design is the "**essential question.**"

Essential questions are grand, overarching questions, often almost rhetorical, that can serve as touchstones throughout a study. They are intended to provide both inspiration and focus. Sample questions might be: "How can the properties of numbers help us to express complex problems mathematically?" or "How can the large mathematical quantities be manipulated by breaking down operations into simpler mathematical calculations?" or "Why do humans use war to settle problems among societies?"

Finally in this step, the teacher should lay out what it is that students should understand when they have completed the study. This can be expressed as content knowledge, skills that have been mastered, and habits of mind developed—new dispositions in the ways that they will look at similar content or analogous issues in future school and life experience.

It is important to note that objectives that truly engage students need to be, in Wiggins's term, worthy. In other words, students ought to be asked to do work that has true value or importance. This may be instrumental value, because the knowledge and understanding gained will be useful in doing future, more complex work, or intrinsic value, as learning that inspires and compels. Not every topic that must be studied in school is of equal interest to every student, but the teacher ought to be prepared to justify, even to him- or herself, any work that students are being asked to perform in terms of its true worth. Perhaps more simply stated, students should not be asked to do what is known as "busy work," repetitious tasks or problems to be completed with the sole object of keeping the student working. A fine line divides repetition for mastery from mere repetition, but the intentional teacher is aware of this line as he or she designs curriculum.

STEP TWO: *Determine Evidence of Understanding*

The next segment of the work is to imagine what kinds of behaviors or work students would exhibit to show that they had mastered the intended learning. What kinds of work—projects, papers, problem sets, presentations, test or quiz answers—will demonstrate mastery of the material? What will help the teacher learn whether the students are moving toward responses to the essential questions of the study?

The answers to these questions will start the teacher on building a list of lessons to be developed and work to be assigned. Thoughtfully addressing them will generate ideas for student work that will be worthy by definition, having a purpose in the overall context of the study.

Note here that the sorts of work that will indicate understanding are many. While large-scale projects may be useful to amass evidence of big-picture understanding, tests, quizzes, and problem sets can be useful in gathering evidence of mastery of sets or subsets of important learning. Even asking students to reflect personally on learning, along the way or at the end of the study, can be useful in finding out whether students have in fact learned what has been intended.

At this step the teacher has begun to explore the world of **assessment**. In the technical jargon of education, assessment is simply the business of collecting evidence of learning. It is distinct from **evaluation**, which is the judging of demonstrated learning against standards. To administer a test or assign a paper is to assess student learning; to grade that test or to give the student feedback on the quality of the paper is to evaluate the learning.

At the risk of overwhelming the teacher with more technical jargon, it should be noted that assessment can have several purposes. **Diagnostic assessment** in the form of a pre-unit test or assignment can reveal students' understanding at the outset of a unit or course. **Formative assessment** is used to find out how students are doing along the way in an ongoing study; a quiz on the terminology required to understand a complex process or issue would be formative assessment, as would an exercise in which students are asked to demonstrate safe laboratory technique before undertaking a complicated experiment. Worksheets or speed tests on basic skills are usually formative assessments, designed to give feedback to the student on the quality and extent of mastery and feedback to the teacher on the quality of student learning. Formative assessments, of course, may also be evaluated, or graded.

Summative assessment is used to discover the degree to which students have mastered overarching understandings or met main learning objectives. A final paper, test, examination, or project would be summative assessment, as could be the write-up of the complicated laboratory experiment referred to above, giving the student feedback (and usually an evaluation) on overall performance and providing the teacher with data on the aggregate performance of all students.

(A fourth category, **normative assessment**, is used infrequently by individual teachers but is the basis for standardized test scores, which are developed over time using data from multiple test administrations. A teacher might develop data for normative assessment by using the same test or assignment over several years, developing an expectation for the distribution of performance results for a number of students that can also be the used as the basis of a scheme, or system, of evaluating student work.)

Good curriculum design makes room especially for formative assessment of ongoing learning and as well as summative assessment at major break-points in a course of study.

Above all, the intentional teacher should work to utilize a variety of types of assessment. Multi-genre projects that combine different forms of expression—visual art, expository writing, performance, creative writing, and so forth—research papers, demonstrations, and end-of-unit tests are excellent ways of gathering evidence of learning. But the simplest kinds of paper-and-pencil tests (matching, fill-in-the-blanks, multiple-choice) will always have a place as quick and efficient ways of collecting data on specific kinds of learning. Offering students a varied menu of assessments over the term or year provides them with experience in expressing their knowledge in different ways, and it also allows students with particular relative strengths and weakness related to learning style to find their own best modes of expression and to strengthen their work in weaker areas.

STEP THREE: *Plan the Course of Instruction*

The crucial next phase of curriculum design involves, above all, a calendar. Whether the study is projected to last for a week, a month, a term, or a year, breaking it down into instructional periods—and the specific nature of the instructional tasks involved—is best done against the sometimes insistent reality of a day-to-day or week-to-week calendar.

How to know how much time a study should take is a subjective and troublesome issue. Time is the essential currency of education, and it is both finite and, for the individual teacher, likely to be unstable. In general the wise teacher allocates time proportionally, more or less, to the importance of material, but text-driven curriculum is often pre-packaged in chapters (and thus units) of equal length. While it may be comforting to have the year divided into thirty chapters, all designed for delivery on identical trajectories, the teacher who is an expert in a particular field and who understands the learning needs of his or her class will want to adjust this balance, upsetting the neat design of the textbook publisher as well as forcing a deeper look at the calendar.

Blank calendars are a teacher's great friend, allowing the drafting of courses of study from rough draft to final form.

- What will need to be taught, and how will the teaching be done?
- At what points along the way will the teacher need to administer formative assessments to collect information on the quality of student learning and to provide students with feedback on how they are doing?
- What are the necessary steps students will need to perform in order to complete assigned tasks or projects, and where should waypoints be placed for checking in on student progress?

- What work might best be done collaboratively, and where will students need to work alone?
- What preparation will be necessary for summative assessments, and how and when will this preparation be done?
- Is it important that time be allocated at the end of the study for student reflection, and what form should this reflection take?

This is the design stage where the guidance of peers and supervisors can be most helpful, and the teacher should be ready both to share ideas and to accept feedback. If the course is being taught in parallel with other faculty, collaboration in the development of course calendars is critical in ensuring that student learning is similar from one section to another.

Once the envelope of time for the study has been established and roughly filled in, the teacher should consider what teaching and learning experiences and what kinds of materials, such as texts, resources, equipment, assignment sheets, project specifications, will enable students to demonstrate that they have mastered the intended understandings. The teacher will then need to generate an inventory of useful materials and begin preparing or gathering them.

STEP FOUR: *Design for Engagement*

At this point the teacher needs to step back and ask a fundamental question: What will keep students interested in this work? Without pandering to the lowest common denominator of student engagement, the intentional teacher needs to build points of interest and involvement into any curriculum. With "student-centered" being an ideal, the teacher will need to consider both the nature of the material and the nature of students in order to create learning experiences that honor student interests and needs even as they meet significant, and worthy, learning objectives.

Not every child will be hooked by every task or topic, but part of the teacher's role is to guide students to understand why material matters. The teacher must clarify not only learning objectives but also the nature and purpose of the work that is being asked of students; along with this goes the necessity of explaining the criteria by which their work will be evaluated. As the reader may recall from personal experience, confusion about expectations is a great barrier to learning, even more than confusion about content. Precision in syllabi and assignments is critical: the work to be done must be specified in appropriate language and sufficient detail—more for larger, more complex work; a bit less for more familiar or smaller-scale tasks—but so must the ways in which the work fits into the larger learning. This might include not only "weighting" of the assignment's value but also some indication of what the teacher is looking for—what excellent or thorough work might look like. Forearmed with knowledge of what is expected, students will do better work and understand the reasons why they are doing it.

- This is also the point where the teacher might look for what journalists would call "the hook": the concept, fact, or activity that is likely to engage a broad range of students and generate immediate and sustainable interest and satisfaction. Can a concept be projected through a particular "lens" so as to capture the interest of students—perhaps even in a way that might intrigue a resistant individual?
- The hook might even come in the form of a central project, perhaps requiring students to create and present material in multiple modes or genres. Engaging students might also involve opportunities for them to reflect on the learning experience, either individually or collaboratively. Sometimes students who are asked "What did you learn?" or "What worked well for you in this unit, and what was hard?" surprise themselves and their teachers with answers whose depth and complexity reveals a great deal about how and how well they have learned. The very act of articulating answers to such questions can solidify learning—a concept known as **metacognition**, or "knowing about one's own knowing and learning." Metacognition is a potent skill for students to develop, as evidence shows that students who understand how they learn tend to become more successful and independent learners.

STEP FIVE: *Design for Interactivity and Technology*

- **Interactivity** in the 21st century primarily refers to the leveraging of technology as a means of research, communication, and presentation. With the power of social networks and other interactive tools of so-called Web 2.0, the teacher may be able to construct learning activities that use the power or technology to expand the audience for work as well as to increase levels of both creativity and collaboration. Students working for a broader body of readers and viewers are likely to ratchet up the quality of the work they are doing, and easy-to-use tools for collaboration can not only help students apportion project workloads equitably but work together to improve overall quality control. Evidence suggests that students are more likely to be engaged in work that offers opportunities to exercise "right-brain" creative skills in processing and presenting material.

STEP SIX: *Design for Differentiation*

- To **differentiate** learning experiences is to build into those experiences opportunities for students with different learning styles,
  strengths, proclivities, or interests to experience the learning in ways
  that are personally accessible and compelling. While it is highly
  unrealistic to imagine that a teacher might tailor every assignment
  to every student, it is not difficult to build into a course of study the
  opportunity for students to capitalize on diverse strengths.

For example, a unit might contain opportunities for students to demonstrate artistic or musical talent, leadership or collaborative strength, or
physical agility. While creating these possibilities ought not overbalance
the teacher's objectives, which might include writing, oral presentation,
test-taking, note-taking, or calculation, the teacher who can seek evidence
of learning through a few of his or her students' "multiple intelligences" or
established dispositions can help instill confidence and expand capacity in
students with deficits in traditional "academic" skill areas. The perspica-
cious teacher can almost always find in non-traditional work evidence of
understanding as well as talent that might not have surfaced previously.

STEP SEVEN: *Design for Diversity*

This step acknowledges the value of building multiple perspectives into
learning experiences. Even when the composition of the class does not
reflect broad diversity, for students to thrive in a globalized world it is
increasingly important that they recognize and understand the role that
differences in point of view based on culture, national interest, or way of
being can play in understanding.

Ideally, curriculum should have points in which every student can
see his own heritage and situation reflected. If the study can provide these
points through choices in content made by the teacher, then so much the
better. Otherwise, the teacher should look for places within the study to
address or acknowledge the contributions or viewpoints of different cultures or gender perspectives with regard to content or procedures.

It is equally important that the teacher be alert to cultural effects on
approaches to learning; this will be addressed more fully in Chapter IX.
Where feasible, tasks that students perform in a study should be designed
to access or acknowledge differing cultural or gender perspectives and
approaches to the learning process. It comes down to the question of how
different voices are to be heard in the classroom.

STEP EIGHT: *Design the Evaluation Strategy*

With the learning experiences designed and placed on a calendar, expectations clarified as to the work tasks to be done, and multiple perspectives factored into the design, the last step is to develop the methods and instruments by which work will be evaluated and useful feedback passed on to students.

One highly effective method for evaluating work is the rubric. In its most developed form, a rubric is a two-dimensional grid in which the axes are, respectively, the qualities of the work being evaluated and the criteria for evaluation. The beauty of the rubric is that it allows the teacher to specify the learning goals—that is, the aspects of the work that are to be considered as most important in the context of the study—as categories for evaluation, and to weight those categories appropriately.

We will discuss rubrics in greater detail in Chapter VI, "Standards," as they are the indispensable tool for teachers to set clear expectations for student work.

Daily lesson planning

Every teacher will, in time, develop his or her own approach to planning daily lessons, but as a starting point the most important part of planning on this "micro" scale is much the same as it is on the macro—annual or term—scale: have in mind a specific objective for the day. The relatively short 40- to 50-minute class periods in most schools make it advisable to limit daily objectives to one, or perhaps two, although corollary goals or sustaining ongoing progress toward larger or longer-term objectives are clearly appropriate.

The simple template that has been used successfully by some beginning independent school teachers is shown in Figure 1.

After specifying the learning goal for the class, the teacher is next prompted to note the homework that the students will have done for the class as well as any relevant prior learning that will support the achievement of the daily objectives.

Next, the teacher lists the day's planned activities and the materials that are required, including technological needs. Room setup and audio-visual equipment setup (and rehearsal, if time allows) can also be noted here, as well as any materials that might be needed to assign homework that will be due at the subsequent class.

A teacher should always have a small battery of prompt questions available to guide discussion or to move student understanding in a desired

The Intentional Teacher's 'Daily Lesson Planner'

Class _____   Date _____   Pd. _____

Learning goal for the day: _____

_____

Homework/prior learning: _____

_____

Activities for the day:

1. _____

2. _____

3. _____

Texts/Materials/Technology needed:

1. _____

2. _____

3. _____

Prompt questions to guide discussion/activity:

1. _____

2. _____

3. _____

Predicted signs that it is working: _____

_____

Predicted signs that it might not be working: _____

_____

Homework to be assigned for the next class: _____

_____

De-briefing _____

Did work: _____

Didn't work: _____

Changes for next time: _____

_____

FIGURE 1 *A lesson-planning template*

direction. This is not to deny the existence of teachable moments, as previously discussed.

The teacher should also make note of the homework that will be assigned for the next class; younger students will need, and all students prefer, written assignments, given to them either as printed sheets or online as messages or documents. If the teacher or school culture insists on homework assignments being written on a chalkboard, the teacher really must allow class time for students to copy them down.

Perhaps the most useful aspect of this template is its reminder to prepare for failure as well as success. The teacher who can anticipate trouble spots can also plan tactics for dealing with situations when the best of planning goes awry. What are some areas that are likely to be problematic, and how might the teacher be able to recover and redirect?

Finally, after the class the teacher ought to make some notes on the day's experience, and the template provides space to record high and low spots as well as "how to do it better next time" ideas. An increasing number of teachers "journal" and even blog, which can be much more elaborate ways of recording a day's experiences, but the template offers a starting point for this kind of reflective practice.

The new teacher, especially, will find that things do not always go as planned. The daily objectives may be too fully packed, or addressing a persistent misunderstanding in class may consume more time than expected. Over time the teacher will come to know instinctively when it is time to revert to Plan B or when to shift the focus so as to give him- or herself time to regroup and try again.

Planning is a teacher's most productive weapon in bringing order to learning, but the moment of entering a class and exposing one's ideas and plans to a class of students requires yet another level of thoughtful preparation and another set of skills to be learned by the committed intentional teacher.

CHAPTER VI

Classroom Culture:
Teaching with Standards

"The life history of the individual is first and foremost an accommodation to the patterns and standards traditionally handed down in his community."
— RUTH BENEDICT

A t the core of the most productive and vital classroom cultures are standards, not simply behavioral expectations but standards tied to every aspect of the learning process. With the intentional teacher committed to the success of every student, the definition of success must be clear and present at each moment in the life of the classroom, and every student must understand and engage with the standards.

We have already discussed the development of classroom norms, the basic standards for conducting the business of the class. Whether these are in a list on a wall or merely understood and regularly referenced in the course of daily study, these are fundamental statements of the values by which the teacher wants everyone, including himself or herself, to live in that space.

The higher standard is that implied in the definition of intellectual character, referred to in the previous chapter. Energetic, positive brainwork toward answers and solutions epitomizes the life of the mind and energizes the engaged citizen that the intentional teacher hopes that each of his or her students will become. Even the most casual observer can tell a classroom in which this kind of brainwork is taking place, and the observer can easily see the high value the teacher and students place on intellectual character.

If brainwork is valued, then academic standards will be high by default. Independent schools are fond of describing their academic programs as rigorous, a perhaps-unfortunate term that somehow implies deprivation and pain. School is not always a happy memory for people, which seems to explain this desire to inflict rigor on rising generations simply because that has been the experience of those who have come before.

Standards and grading

High standards are sometimes conflated with rigor, and certainly it should take more than casual effort to meet high academic standards. Much has been made in the press of late about "grade inflation," even at some of the most selective and prestigious universities. In a society that is wedded to the awarding of grades as a shorthand method of signifying the quality of academic work (often quantifying highly subjective judgments), grades and grade-point averages are the coin of the realm: easy to understand, easy to use as a sieve to sort students for some kind of judgment.

In fact the use of letter grades or similar systems is a fairly recent invention in the West, a couple of centuries old and by no means standard from society to society. True to their status and history, independent schools across North America use a variety of grading systems, including the use of no grades at all, with schools serving the elementary grades and below having perhaps the widest variation.

The intentional teacher will wrestle with the matter of grading, and this struggle will ultimately seem to be about standards. However, the thoughtful and open-minded teacher is likely to soon discover that the standards at issue are not so much "what earns an A (or an Excellent, or a 90) at --- School" but rather about the school's standards for the quality of teachers' assessment of learning and evaluation of student work. A school may have its "local norms" for grading, even departmental norms, but grades ought to encode more than a judgment; they should also provide meaningful feedback (for formative assessments, especially), or at the very least summative assessment grades should represent judgment corresponding with feedback received on other assessments of learning.

Grades also represent standards, and while this may be only a matter of "It's impossible to get at A in ---- class," the actual high standards of which teachers and schools may be justly proud are those that students, teachers, and the community understand as worthy and consistent. These standards are authentic challenges to the intellect and the spirit within an academic environment dedicated to giving students the tools to meet them.

Nevertheless, the intentional teacher is going to have to understand and live by the school's standards and local norms around evaluation of student work and around grading. The one and only way to learn these norms painlessly is by working with colleagues to understand the nature of excellent work, acceptable work, and poor work in the context of the expectations of the department, division, and school. The question of grading is often very difficult for a teacher new to a school, and he or she will need to understand the system so as to be ready to explain, and if need be justify, the relative meaning of students' grades, whether high, middling, or low.

In articulating standards, it is best to start by imagining the qualities of the very best work. For many teachers and many schools, the concept of excellent work is couched in the language of "above and beyond," sometimes with more precise descriptors relating to near-perfection in designated content areas. Work at the top level is likely to be precise in execution, masterful in the application of requisite skills, exceeding requirements (if not expectations) in the inclusion and application of content matter, and stretching the conceptual envelope in analysis or logical reasoning. I like to think of the very best work as surprising me in some way with an idea, point of view, an approach to a solution, or a turn of phrase that is both original in some way and especially apt.

The most difficult level of work for teachers to define or agree on is often the nature of "satisfactory." In times gone by (my own Baby Boom generation, say), grades were often thought of as a bell curve, with the letter C or work at about the 75% level seen as the center of the curve. Satisfactory work in such a regime was in the C range, characterized by meeting the basic requirements of the assignment but not distinguished as admirably strong or egregiously deficient; the work represented the task completed adequately in all respects, with some errors that might be classified as "typical" or at least predictable for the age-level and the difficulty of the work. The top of the bell curve resided here because 75% of students were expected to perform at this level.

While this is still a pretty useful description of "satisfactory" work, the top of the bell seems to have shifted in recent years, with "average" grades at many schools well into the B range or equivalent. College admission offices report great difficulty in understanding the true meaning of many student transcripts on which grades in the A range predominate even for students ranked near the middle of their high school class. The teacher whose grades in the aggregate deviate significantly from the norms of the school either by being too "generous" or too rigorous may actually do a disservice to students. The "easy" grader will need to re-evaluate his or her standards, while the "strict" grader may need to consider the matter

Name _____

Topic _____

Writing Assignment Evaluation
Evaluation Criteria

Point Values

4 Exceptional performance. Student surprises with especially imaginative, interesting, well-conceived work; deep understanding

3 Good performance; meets all expectations; carefully prepared; satisfactory understanding

2 Somewhat below expectations; some areas not fully addressed; gaps in understanding or preparation

1 Poor performance, well below expectations; inconsistent or poor effort an understanding

> **General Comments:**
>
>
>
>
>
>

Categories

Content   4 3 2 1

Inclusion of significant topics and accurate evidence; knowledge of topic; depth of research and understanding; use of detail to establish factual background.

Analysis   4 3 2 1

Analysis of trends and themes; use of detail to establish point of view; appropriate point of view; acknowledges differing opinions or viewpoints; logical and accurate analysis

Development of Content   4 3 2 1

Establishment of theme; clear logic and presentation of evidence; development of issues; clear point of view; plausibility

Writing Style   4 3 2 1

Proper sentence structure, paragraph formation, spelling, usage, grammar, and vocabulary. Effective transitions.

FIGURE 2: *Generic writing rubric suitable for middle or high school*

Name __Pat Smith__

Topic __Revolutions__

Writing Assignment Evaluation

Evaluation Criteria

Point Values

4 Exceptional performance. Student surprises with especially imaginative, interesting, well-conceived work; deep understanding

3 Good performance; meets all expectations; carefully prepared; satisfactory understanding

2 Somewhat below expectations; some areas not fully addressed; gaps in understanding or preparation

1 Poor performance, well below expectations; inconsistent or poor effort an understanding

---

General Comments:

Good paper, with effective use of evidence to support your thesis and some original and thoughtful analysis of the various kinds of revolutions. Your discussion of Cuba was especially strong, although the organization of your argument was not as strong as its individual elements.

Well written; just a few small grammatical errors.

Categories

Content 4 ③ 2 1
Inclusion of significant topics and accurate evidence; knowledge of topic; depth of research and understanding; use of detail to establish factual background.

Analysis 4 ③ 2 1
Analysis of trends and themes; use of detail to establish point of view; appropriate point of view; acknowledges differing opinions or viewpoints; logical and accurate analysis

Development of Content ④ 3 2 1
Establishment of theme; clear logic and presentation of evidence; development of issues; clear point of view; plausibility

Writing Style 4 ③ 2 1
Proper sentence structure, paragraph formation, spelling, usage, grammar, and vocabulary. Effective transitions.

Overall: **B**

FIGURE 2A: *Generic writing rubric, as completed*

of evaluating student work in the fuller context of his or her ideas about teaching and learning within the culture of the school.

Rubrics as evaluative tools

In Chapter IV we made reference to evaluation rubrics, an exceptionally useful tool for promulgating a teacher's personal standards and for evaluating student work consistently and clearly against these standards. Figures 2 and 3 show examples of such rubrics, one a generic writing rubric used in high school history classes and the other a rubric used to evaluate a fifth-grade mathematics poster project.

In the rubric illustrated in Figure 2, the teacher has described four levels of performance—excellent, satisfactory, fair, and poor—and defined these levels by criteria for achievement in general terms; each has then been assigned a numerical value, 1 through 4. (It should be noted that an implied "zero" value also exists to denote work that is seriously incomplete or terribly deficient.) In the space below the box for narrative comment, the teacher has designated four content areas that the teacher has decided are important "categories of evaluation." Note that these categories can easily be changed or fine-tuned to match the aims of the assignment, allowing the teacher to emphasize specific aspects of the work. Each category can be adjudged or evaluated on the 4-point scale, yielding in the end a score whose highest value would be 16 (excellent work in all categories) and whose lowest would be 4, or perhaps 0. In use, it is possible for the teacher to split the difference, circling two numbers to indicate work that falls short of one level but exceeds the lower one. Figure 2a shows this rubric as it might be returned to the student. Note that the teacher has taken the opportunity to comment on specifics of the work, and that the teacher has also added a letter grade, converted not as a straight percentage but rather as a proportion, based on a formula that makes the "satisfactory" level or performance equivalent to a B- (what once might have been a C).

Figure 3 is a more visually elaborate rubric in grid form, made using the "table" function of a word processor, although it could also be made on a spreadsheet. Four levels of performance are defined down the left side, with four categories for evaluation listed across the top. This rubric is notable because it gives the teacher an ability to evaluate a creative project that might have driven some students to spend many hours on the design and aesthetic aspects of the project in a way that clearly balances those aspects with the actual content area: two categories relate to the mathematical concept being portrayed, one category relates to the quality of the poster's textual content, and only one category addresses craftsmanship and aesthetics.

My Favorite Mathematical Operation or Property Poster — Evaluation Rubric

Name _____

	Concept Understanding	Concept Explanation	Text Quality	Craftsmanship
Excellent	Student demonstrates exceptional understanding of the concept and its value in mathematical problem-solving and thinking.	Exceptionally clear and engaging explanation of his/her preference in a fully mathematical context. Evidence of humor or original thinking.	Text communicates ideas exceptionally well; excellent and original word choice; lettering is exceptionally neat and well-spaced; no grammatical, punctuation, or spelling errors.	Aesthetically very pleasing; artistic design and creative use of visual elements; exceptionally neat work.
Very Good	Student demonstrates very good understanding of the concept and how it can be applied in different mathematical situations.	Thorough and lucid explanation of his/her preference; thoughtfully related to mathematics and mathematical thinking. Some humor present.	Text is clear and communicates ideas effectively; good word choice; lettering is neat and legible; few grammatical, punctuation, or spelling errors.	Nice to look at; thoughtful and effective design; carefully and neatly done,
Satisfactory	Student understands concept and how it is used in basic mathematical contexts.	Adequate and comprehensible explanation of his/her preference; some mathematical context given. Attempts at humor.	Text communicates ideas adequately; lettering is legible; some grammatical, punctuation, or spelling errors.	Satisfactory visual impression; good arrangement of elements; work is neat
Needs Improvement	Student's understanding of the concept and its application is erroneous or incomplete.	Student's explanation of his/her preference is unclear or incomplete; no clear sense of mathematical aspect of student's choice. Humor or originality lacking.	Text does not communicate intended ideas; lettering not all legible; many grammatical, punctuation, or spelling errors.	Visual elements do not communicate intended information effectively; work is incomplete or messy,

Teacher's Comments:

FIGURE 3: *Rubric for a fifth-grade mathematics poster project*

Clearly, the most important aspect of the project is the mathematical information that the poster is intended to communicate clearly and accurately, and students given the rubric at the same time they are being given the assignment would know to focus on the content area and to pay proportionate attention, roughly a quarter of their energy, to making the poster visually beautiful.

Figure 4 shows a sample rubric for evaluating class participation, originally written for a seventh-grade class but suitable for upper elementary through high school classes in almost any discipline.

In all cases the teacher's standards for performance are clear, and, like most rubrics, these would have been presented to the students well in advance of the due date for the work. Students are made well aware of what is important in the work, what is expected of them in terms of performance, and how their work will be evaluated in the end.

Many teachers will spend classroom time on the exercise of gathering input from students on the design of a rubric, perhaps for all major work or perhaps just once in the year or term to clarify standards. The simple question, "What will make a *perfect* paper (or project, or test)?" will yield suggestions for categories and criteria that the teacher can record and incorporate into a useful rubric—and one that students will understand. This exercise can also be useful to the teacher as a means of assessing students' understanding of the task and the expectations before the due date.

Intellectual responsibility

Another important aspect of classroom culture has to do with intellectual responsibility in its crudest form: simple honesty. News media are full of stories and statistics suggesting that cheating and plagiarism are rampant in schools, and enough well-known adults have publicly toppled from their pedestals due to issues of (lack of) professional integrity that we sometimes seem in danger of becoming a nation of sleaze. The intentional teacher is wary of these things but not so concerned with them as to turn the classroom into either a maximum-security intellectual prison or a place where the presumption of guilt in yielding to temptation creates a culture of mistrust or suspicion.

Students talking about these issues regularly cite stress and competition as the motivating factors in intellectual dishonesty, and so a classroom culture in which overt competition is played down as much as possible can contribute to good decision-making. The Coalition of Essential Schools (of which we will hear more in Chapter XIII) speaks of school as being ideally

Name _____

Class Participation Rubric

If you earned a 4, it means that: Your participation exceeds expectations for thoroughness and thoughtfulness. You show deep understanding of relationship between concepts and facts and demonstrate your ability to apply concepts and an active engagement with subject.

If you earned a 3, it means that: Your participation meets expectations. You show good effort and careful preparation. You also have a satisfactory understanding of concepts and demonstrate a good overall interest in subject.

If you earned a 2, it means that: Your participation barely meets expectations. Some areas are addressed noticeably better than others. You show a basic knowledge of facts and concepts and only moderate interest.

If you earned a 1, it means that: Your participation is deficient in several respects. Your preparation is inconsistent, you have inadequate conceptual understanding, and you show little or no effort or interest.

Student shows respect for others by:

Not interrupting others and raising hand to talk	4	3	2	1
Keeping extra talking and distractions to a minimum	4	3	2	1
Thinking before speaking, responding appropriately to others' questions and comments, and being sensitive to others' feelings and ideas	4	3	2	1

Student shows good listening skill by:

Being in the right place at the right time and being alert in class	4	3	2	1
Making questions, oral contributions, and journals relevant to the class/discussion	4	3	2	1

Student shows strong effort to succeed by:

Coming for extra help and asking questions when understanding is difficult	4	3	2	1
Coming prepared for class (has supplies, ready to work)	4	3	2	1
Coming to class on time	4	3	2	1
Making an effort to contribute, even if not totally confident or sure of answer	4	3	2	1

TOTAL: ..../ 9-------->.............

FIGURE 4: *A middle school class participation rubric*

a place of "unanxious expectations," where standards are clear but not so idealized, exalted, or downright threatening as to make the pursuit of excellence into a win-at-all-costs quest. The best student learning is motivated not by the external promise of reward or glory but by the intrinsic desire to learn—intellectual character.

Teachers can help students make good decisions by clearly defining and discussing expectations around intellectual responsibility and describing specifically what is acceptable and what is not. With students doing ever more collaborative work, it is especially important that the teacher directly address what might constitute abuse of the collaborative process. It is also important that teachers be thoughtful and proactive when administering tests and quizzes; the teacher should move around and pay attention to each student at least for a moment or two several times throughout the testing period; to lose oneself in one's own work while students are in a testing situation is to open the possibility of improper behavior. A colleague of mine reminds teachers each year at examination time that "Paying attention to the kids doesn't teach them that you don't trust them; it teaches them that you care. Not paying attention to them doesn't teach them that you trust them; it teaches them that you're not watching."

With regard to larger-scale assignments, the intentional teacher works hard to create his or her own student assignments, preferably so original that it will be harder for students to find or copy similar work than simply to produce their own. The challenge of coming up with an original essay topic on A Separate Peace or a novel approach to a laboratory experiment on plant growth should be intellectually stimulating to the teacher, and no less so to students.

When some sort of abuse or cheating is discovered, of course, the teacher must confront the issue directly and let the disciplinary process of the school take its course. The teacher will feel at least a bit better about the situation, of course, if he or she has done everything possible to define and clarify expectations in advance and to maintain proper security as work is being done. Children will make bad decisions, but how truly "bad" these are depends very much upon how successful adults have been in ensuring that the children understand what is right, and what is not.

The teacher is advised here to avoid the temptation to handle cases of academic dishonesty outside the system—if there is a system—in the name of compassion. The reasons for this are primarily that students need to be held accountable and secondarily that a subsequent case involving the child will be made all the more awkward by a teacher's revelation that "this sort of thing has happened before" with that student. Good schools will recognize situational and developmental aspects of all kinds of student behavior and respond accordingly, even if harshly. Clarity and consistency remain the hallmarks of good "systems," whether in relation to intellectual responsibility or any other aspect of student behavior, and the intentional teacher will need to have faith in both the student and the school whenever problematic situations arise.

In sum, creating a classroom in which active learning, intellectual character, high standards, and intellectual responsibility are the norm is not so difficult. Based on trust and respect for its members and for its work, this classroom can be a place of joy and exuberance as the teacher and students work together toward shared goals and shared hopes.

CHAPTER VII

The Give and Take of Feedback

"The whole purpose of education is to
turn mirrors into windows."
— SYDNEY J. HARRIS

Part of growing up is learning how to absorb the judgments of others, whether criticism or praise. Even in the most child-friendly of schools, students' skins grow a bit thicker in the rough and tumble of childhood give-and-take among peers and even between teacher and student. Students learn to take feedback in stride and to incorporate it into their subsequent behavior, academic and otherwise.

For teachers, doling out feedback is of course a stock-in-trade, but the intentional teacher gives some attention to the nature of feedback in general and to its most effective application. The best teachers also find ways to make sure that they also *receive* the feedback they need to be at their best in the classroom and at their most useful as members of a school community. Teachers, too, sometimes need to grow a thicker skin if they are to absorb and transmute feedback into professional competence.

We have written of the ways in which teachers give feedback on student work and some methods for expressing academic standards. We have also spoken of the powerful effect that knowing students well and a positive classroom culture can have on inspiring great learning. Both of these are complex systems in which student behavior elicits feedback—in the form of grades, of correction, of praise, of the tacit approval of silence—that reinforces effective action. While judging the quality of work and offering suggestions for improved future performance, is—or should be—quite direct, offering meaningful behavioral feedback is far more subtle and requires diligence in observation (which is always a precursor to judgment) as well as consistency on the teacher's part in living and sustaining the morés of the classroom.

The teacher's role

One of the great challenges of teaching, however, is to align one's own values and standards with those of the school. In the classroom the teacher can be the monarch of all he or she surveys, as distasteful as the authoritarian metaphor might be, and over time many teachers come to regard their classrooms as safe and special havens governed by their personal standards and expectations and, at least most of the time, zones of familiar comfort to all who enter. The danger—a problem that is both professional and institutional—is that teachers become so focused on what goes on in their own classrooms, and in their relationships with their own students, that they begin to alienate themselves in small ways from the school at large. The "rules" and norms of the classroom, even if they are reflective of strong school values, do not seem quite so worth enforcing in hallways or on playfields, and so the teacher hesitates to offer the behavioral feedback to a student in the dining room that he or she might toss off instinctively in the classroom. This may seem a small thing to bring up, but a school in which orderly, productive classrooms are linked by disorderly hallways owing to the excessive provinciality (to put it nicely) of teachers is a place where opportunities to learn are lost. The intentional teacher does his or her best to pay the same attention to students and to offer them the same feedback whether they are in class or elsewhere in the school.

Working one on one with students

We have focused on the class and on student work as the main settings for offering feedback, but for many teachers powerful educating is done in individualized situations. The intentional teacher is by nature focused on the success of each student, and inevitably teachers in independent schools find themselves sitting with individual students to discuss learning in general and work in particular. These one-on-one moments are golden opportunities to foster great learning, and the key, as always, is to be precise in one's observations, professional in one's demeanor and language, and clear in offering suggestions, guidance, and feedback. The teacher should remember that these meetings can be emotionally charged for the student. The teacher is seen as a figure of authority as well as a source of critical advice and assistance, and for students of any age to sit down with a teacher is to expose themselves and their work to critique without the protection of the crowd or the distance of the page; it is the teacher's duty to honor the highest expectations and protect the greatest vulnerabilities of the student.

Some teachers, even very good and very experienced ones, are better working with a group than they are working with an individual; other teachers flourish in tutorial settings but are less in command of a room. Nevertheless, every teacher must develop some tactics and strategies for making the most of one-on-one meetings.

The first point is to be clear on the purpose of the meeting. Is the meeting to take another crack at a topic or problem that the student has not adequately grasped in class? Is it about the student's behavior, a command performance ordered by the teacher? Is the meeting about some kind of personal issue—what students call a "personality conflict"—of which the teacher may not even be aware? Is it to review a piece of work on which the student is unhappy with the evaluation or unclear on some comment or suggestion that the teacher has made? In each case, the teacher must be prepared to listen carefully, to work very hard in the conversation to understand the student's needs as well as his or her perspective, and to be patient and perhaps a little more flexible than usual in trying to find the solution.

Gentleness, one on one, is one of the keys to success. The individual meeting is the time for the teacher to be at his or her most "human," and humane, with the student, gently probing understandings and feelings and reaching out to the heart of the matter. Giving the same explanation over and over as a dogmatic or repetitive response will not do; if the student becomes hostile or falls into the repetition of a single concern or assertion, the teacher will not help matters by playing into the same behavioral pattern. At worst, the teacher should gently but firmly terminate the meeting and suggest the two of them try again at a better time.

At times the teacher may find himself or herself using an individual meeting as opportunity to inundate the student with new information or new feedback in areas outside the intended scope of the conference. While it may be tempting to use one-on-one time, especially with students who may be elusive, to try to pack multiple messages into a single meeting, patience is a virtue here: let matters take their own course, and let the relationship develop without forcing it.

The elusive student

In schools where students are not closely regulated in their movement, teachers may have a hard time pinning down students for individual conferences. As easy as this is to understand, within this simple fact are embedded some very serious messages about the nature of education as well as the effectiveness of the teacher.

For one thing, as students grow older and into the late high school years, it is natural and generally correct for teachers to plan on spending decreasing time and energy chasing down students for conferences. While on one level this is age-appropriate teaching, the rather distasteful possibility is that the teacher might be placing more of a burden on the student than is pedagogically sound. When a situation is serious—when the student is clearly in academic or behavioral trouble—there is no room for a teacher's righteous claim that "I told the student to come, and he (or she) never did. Therefore, the fault is with the student." This assertion made about high school seniors is as inappropriate as it would be for first graders, although it is certainly true that the elementary school teacher may have more leverage in getting the student to the meeting. If necessary, the teacher should have no qualms about enlisting parents, advisors, or administrators in the business of getting students to essential meetings; if the meeting is deemed essential, it must take place.

This may be especially true for students who represent minorities within the culture of the school, particularly in terms of race or cultural background. Students who do not feel completely at ease in the student body and who fear that their performance is in some way to be judged by different standards than their peers' work may endeavor to make themselves invisible to teachers, who seem to stand for the most dire possibilities of judgment and failure. Thus, when a teacher reaches out to make individual contact around an academic issue, the student may respond to this at least superficially as just the kind of criticism they had expected: a private confrontation in which the student's failures and inadequacies are to be reprised by a gloating oppressor. The student, quite understandably, chooses flight—elusiveness—over having to face this dreaded moment.

The teacher simply has to understand this, and then to do something very, very difficult: to persevere, and to have that individual meeting at all costs. I am assuming here that the teacher's intent is not to enact the student's worst vision but in fact to offer the student individual feedback and guidance toward improved performance. While critique may be a part of that guidance, the teacher, by focusing on what the student can do, providing concrete steps by which the student can reach success, and conveying all of this in a firm but compassionate manner, will allay the student's fears and replace them with another, infinitely more potent message: that the teacher cares, and cares enough to work hard to bring the student in for the help he or she needs. The teacher dedicated to the success of all his or her students will risk being seen as the oppressor, dragging students into meetings against their will But this is what it means to be a teacher. This is our work and our obligation.

Of course, no student wants to hear all bad news, and so the old advice to have something constructive to offer along with each more negative item remains very useful. Remember that the deepest and most lasting learning occurs in the brain when it is accompanied by positive emotional associations.

Feedback as an aspect of professional growth

The same principles and challenges apply to feedback directed toward the teacher. Whether or not it is solicited, teachers will soon enough find many sources of feedback on their work—some constructive and energizing, others less so. But to become a better teacher, any serious professional knows that feedback is necessary, and most schools have and all schools should have some system by which teachers are formally evaluated in their work by a system of observation and constructive feedback. The intentional teacher seeks what is useful from among the many sources of feedback available.

A rich and vigorous classroom culture will be, by its nature, a place in which the teacher receives constant input on the quality and effectiveness of his or her work. Informally, a teacher can watch and read the faces of students, and teachers who keep notes on student performance or the impact of lessons will also be collecting information on the effectiveness of his or her work. A teacher should look hard for patterns in student work on assessments: Do similar problems with skills or understandings crop up among numbers of students, indicating ways in which the teacher's intended lessons are not getting through? Sometimes a teacher can know, even as it is happening, that an exercise is failing, but it is important to build into all plans some markers that indicate how well a lesson is working.

It can also be useful for a teacher to develop simple tools for collecting direct feedback from students. Many teachers will read these lines with trepidation, but making the explicit collection of constructive, focused feedback from students a part of classroom culture can take the potential sting out of doing it. Pose to the students, at the end of a project, unit, or term, a reflective question that also asks about things the teacher did that made the experience go well and whether the teacher could make alterations so that the experience would be even better for the next class. Little or no dangers lurk here, for the teacher already has a sense of how things are going, and the query is about making things better, not just fishing for compliments or opening the door to criticism.

Some departments or schools ask or even require that teachers regularly give students some sort of anonymous questionnaire for collecting specific feedback on teacher performance. The best of such instruments are balanced in their questions, asking students for examples of things that went well in a class as well as those that did not. They also avoid loaded language but take their content and tone from the expressed values and mission of the school. In a school that is working to incorporate multicultural learning, for example, students might be asked whether the learning offered students an opportunity to explore the subject from multiple perspectives. Giving students the chance to cite specific examples and to offer suggestions can provide extremely useful data. Above all, the best of such instruments ask only for students to supply specific information based on their personal experience as learners in the teacher's classroom, to provide a report on what was hard for them and what was not, what worked for them and what did not. They do not ask students to make evaluative judgments of the teacher as a person or as an educator. Above all, students, like supervisors, need to be clear on the line between offering feedback that can be used in the context of evaluation and actually evaluating; "The teacher's assignment sheets could have been more clear" is feedback, whereas "The teacher doesn't care whether we understand what we're supposed to do" is evaluation without constructive feedback.

In the realm of unhelpful evaluation and non-constructive feedback, there is a notorious category on online teacher "rating" sites. These are of course entirely anonymous and all seemingly devoid of any editorial control except to remove material that would be offensive (although the teacher's feelings are not considered, of course) or libelous. Teachers should explore these sites at their own risk and be prepared for the worst, although the information posted is quite often more positive than not. Neither schools nor teachers have control over these sites; they are just part of the landscape of our times. Although a major national magazine uses a professorial rating site as part of its college ranking system, the pre-college versions offer educators little or nothing of value.

Clarity in the distinction between observation and professional evaluation is extremely important in schools and to teachers, and good schools are scrupulous about basing all evaluation on both professionally conducted observation and expressed criteria for teacher effectiveness. We have written earlier about the need for teachers to observe and to collect data and to make clear their standards before generating an evaluation of students' work or an assessment of their overall approach to learning; the same applies to the evaluation of the teacher's work in a school. In a school in which this distinction is not preserved teachers can be made vulnerable, for the danger is always present that rumor or a second- or third-hand story may become the basis for an informal but pernicious community "evaluation"—a kangaroo court that convicts a teacher who might not even know he or she

Course Feedback Survey

Course _____

Teacher _____

Term _____   Year _____

1. The teacher of this course explained things carefully and clearly:

Agree mostly   Agree somewhat   Disagree somewhat   Disagree mostly

2. Discussions and class activities in this course helped me learn the material:

Agree mostly   Agree somewhat   Disagree somewhat   Disagree mostly

3. The assignments in this course were easy to understand:

Agree mostly   Agree somewhat   Disagree somewhat   Disagree mostly

4. Material in this class was presented in multiple ways and/or from multiple points of view:

Agree mostly   Agree somewhat   Disagree somewhat   Disagree mostly

5. Projects in this course helped me understand the material better:

Agree mostly   Agree somewhat   Disagree somewhat   Disagree mostly

6. Tests and quizzes in this course helped me understand what I needed to work on to do better:

Agree mostly   Agree somewhat   Disagree somewhat   Disagree mostly

7. The teacher was available for extra help when I needed it:

Agree mostly   Agree somewhat   Disagree somewhat   Disagree mostly

8. The thing I liked best about this course was:

Agree mostly   Agree somewhat   Disagree somewhat   Disagree mostly

9. The thing I struggled with most in this course was:

Agree mostly   Agree somewhat   Disagree somewhat   Disagree mostly   N/A

10. Next year the teacher might want to improve this course by:

FIGURE 5: *A sample of a class feedback survey a teacher might give to students*

was on trial. Good schools work hard to make certain that all teachers are observed and that information on their performance is gathered formally and professionally, so the judgments of the "carpool caucus" or other informal evaluators can be overturned by the school's official, thoughtful, and fair system of knowing the nature and quality of a teacher's work.

Effective classroom observation

For teachers as well as students, the gathering of observable evidence is the basis of the best kind of evaluation, with the teacher receiving useful, precise feedback and suggestions on how to improve performance. First-rate evaluation also—and this cannot be emphasized too strongly—notes areas of strong or commendable work and even suggests ways for the teacher to capitalize on strengths for future improvement.

The teacher newly arrived at a school has, I believe, a right to expect feedback based on observation right from the beginning, and a teacher whose school does not have a system in place for delivering this feedback can do himself or herself no greater favor that to request it. The best source might be a mentor who is not also a supervisor involved in evaluation, but a friendly peer or, in the least ideal case, a supervisor will serve. The teacher can even go so far as to film one of his or her own classes, a process inherently limited by the placement of the camera but one which ensures the teacher some privacy and, not incidentally, lets students know that this teacher is interested in doing his or her best (and that their behavior will also be on some sort of record).

The teacher can make the most of having an observer in the classroom by having a two-part plan. The first part is the plan for the lesson itself, with activities and objectives clear in the teacher's mind and known to the observer; the best guidance for the intentional teacher ought to be based on an understanding of the teacher's intent as well as on how and how well that intent was carried out.

The second part of an effective plan for observation must of course be the plan of the observer. A classroom is of course an incredibly complex and dynamic environment, and tracking a group of students engaged in learning while a teacher is engaged in teaching can be extremely difficult. The art of classroom observation has in recent years become the subject of some very thoughtful work, and in the independent school world, former teacher Steve Clem, who now leads the Association of Independent Schools of New England, has codified the best practices in what he calls the work of "Eloquent Mirrors."

Clem offers a number of possible classroom observation strategies, each with a specific focus but any of which could offer a teacher some illuminating data on aspects of their work in a classroom. Among the most revealing of these is "Verbal Flow," in which the observers note the precise flow of conversation in the class, using the graphic system illustrated in Figure 6 (which has been filled with sample data: a class seating chart and a map of conversational patterns). This system reveals classroom dynamics such as who speaks and who does not, data which can be broken down later to look for calling patterns—gender, specific individuals, or race. Another, "Class Traffic," has the observer trace the physical path that a teacher makes through the classroom, noting time every few minutes. This method is useful when students are working on a lab, in an art class, or on a project and the teacher is "table hopping" or working with individual students on extra help. Class Traffic can also be used to develop a picture of non-classroom teaching, such as coaching or directing a performing

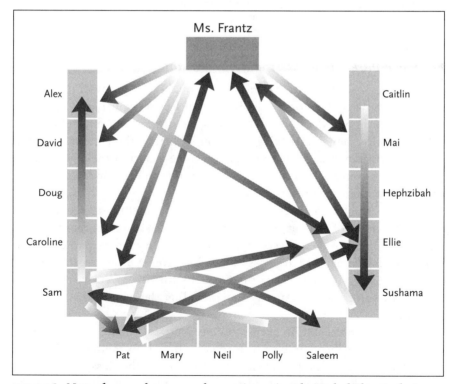

FIGURE 6: *Notes from a classroom observation using the Verbal Flow technique; the lines indicate the flow of conversation in the classroom. Note the amount of "air time" that Sam and Ellie seem to consume.*

arts activity. A third technique, called "Global Scan," involves recording as much information as possible on what is going on in the classroom, including byplay as well as instruction, for two-minute bursts at set intervals during the observation period. This can yield data on student attentiveness and engagement against the real-time flow of the lesson. "Selective Verbatim" involves recording specified data, such as the exact language with which a teacher asks and follows up on questions. The teacher may ask the observer in advance to look for other particular things, from verbal mannerisms to eye contact to interactions with a specific student or group of students.

No matter which technique or combination of techniques is being used, the single task of the observer in the classroom is to observe. Like a camera or an automatic recording device, the observer makes no judgments and offers no critique until the observation itself has been reported in detail to the teacher. The quality and content of the debriefing process, the conversation in which observed data is shared before feedback is delivered, determines how worthwhile and how professionally useful the observation has been.

Feedback based on a classroom observation

An effective post-observation conversation ought to begin with the teacher discussing how well his or her goals for the class were met, and what had facilitated or impeded this. The observer's task here is to listen and perhaps offer no more than a clarifying question. Whether the teacher was well satisfied with the class or disappointed in some aspect of the outcome, the point of this conversation is to tie together the teacher's impressions with the information to be presented by the observer.

Next, the observer presents his or her data, carefully refraining from even the mildest of evaluative language and giving as much detail as possible. This phase of the conversation provides the teacher with a clear and objective picture of what the class looked like from a professionally astute, external perspective. Here it is the teacher's turn to ask clarifying questions until he or she is secure in understanding the picture that has been presented.

When the presentation of the observed data is complete, the conversation can assume the character of feedback. Based on the teacher's goals, the observation, and now the teacher's thoughts on the class, the observer should carefully review what he or she saw that worked and how the observed data supports that interpretation. At this point both the teacher and the observer should understand themselves to be engaged in work with a common purpose: to understand, on as fine a level of detail as possible, what happened in the class in relation to the teacher's initial expectations and plans and in the context of the school's standards and expectations. Even if the teacher and observer do not see completely eye to eye, they are professional colleagues working as constructively and intentionally as possible to make sense of the complexities of a learning experience.

Here feedback has become the basis of evaluation directed at professional improvement based on goals and standards and not on matters of personality or personal preference. The conversation might well shift to technique and become about how a tactic worked or did not. The focus should be on choices and on how the teacher might make even better ones next time. This is the observation-feedback-evaluation sequence at its finest.

For the teacher who is dependent on a self-made classroom film, the process should follow the same pattern, although one might suggest that the teacher sleep on the tape for a night or at least take a deep breath before the first viewing. The teacher ought to suspend judgment (hard to do, but not impossible) and try to apply a specific observation plan to the first viewing—in other words, to be an observer, not an evaluator. The teacher must look closely at the tape and seek unexpected or somehow important moments, observing what is happening rather than merely watching what he or she is doing; that may be done later. Next, the teacher should try to debrief as if one were speaking with a dispassionate version of oneself. The hardest part will be for the teacher to refrain from excessive self-criticism, as the point is to learn how one is doing and not to beat oneself up. Feedback is intended to teach, not to torture.

Feedback as an aspect of professional evaluation

Schools vary widely in the kind of professional evaluation they offer teachers and in the manner in which the process is used. In an ideal world, teachers would receive regular professional evaluation based on clear and stated standards and expectations. Better still, the feedback and evaluative commentary that the teacher would receive in a perfect process would address all aspects of the teacher's job in the school and would acknowledge the teacher's professional and personal goals as well as the school's standards. A few schools have adopted such systems, even using "360-degree" observation in which data is collected from peers, students, and even families to be shared with the teacher in the interest of determining professional status within the school. Even fewer schools have articulated and published their own standards for teacher performance, but those that have done so have created a powerful tool for helping their teachers become better and for creating an atmosphere of common purpose and belief.

The obvious difference between feedback given to promote professional growth and feedback that is part of a system of teacher evaluation is that the stakes in the latter are considerably higher: continued employment and salary levels can be part of the equation, and an evaluation of one's work by supervisors is always stressful. But even in this case, the teacher should be proactive, even if the system in use does not seem to require or invite this, in using any classroom observation as an opportunity to obtain useful, constructive feedback on his or her work.

If the school's teacher-evaluation system does not include pre- and post-observation conferences, the teacher should still request the opportunity to talk to the observer in advance of the observation and then make a point of sitting down with the observer afterward to ask for a description of what was observed—to solicit feedback, in other words—in advance of any evaluation. This may be awkward, and it may not fit into the school's existing notion of how the process works, but the teacher who makes clear his or her desire to maximize the potential of the evaluation process as a growth experience is also demonstrating a notable level of professional enthusiasm.

If the school's teacher evaluation process involves gathering observational evidence on aspects of the teacher's work outside the classroom, the teacher should understand what goes into this data, and the school should be clear on how it is gathered. Most teachers are pleased to have their advising, coaching, dormitory supervision, and other work at the school included in their evaluation, but the same consistency and clarity of process should apply for that work as for classroom teaching, and standards for effective work in these areas should be clear to the teacher.

It is possible that the teacher will be disappointed or even unhappy with the final results of an evaluation, and this will be all the more true in schools where observation and professional conversations only occur during an evaluation process. If teachers are unaccustomed to receiving feedback in the regular course of their work, and if the school's culture is not one in which feedback is valued as an element of professional practice, then the rare moments, annual or even less frequent, in which teachers sit with supervisors to hear about their work may be quite uncomfortable. In this atmosphere, even having small deficiencies noted may feel like an attack, and both teacher and supervisor can find themselves on the defensive, with a conversation that should be about professional growth going nowhere.

While allowing that the existence of this kind of impasse might be an area of school culture that needs to be addressed, the intentional teacher can help avoid it in advance by creating a personal culture in which feedback is an essential aspect of his or her own professional growth and in which he or she regularly solicits and acts upon feedback from many quarters.

At the start of this chapter we referred to the great currents of information that flow through schools and the degree to which much of this information must have, in the end, some evaluative content. It is self-evident that students must be given feedback that helps them understand themselves and their work in order to grow into effective and happy adults, and the greater the precision and humanity of that feedback, the greater its worth will be. But it is perhaps less obvious in some quarters that one of a school's chief responsibilities is to help teachers grow so that their increased capacity can benefit students, the school, and of course themselves. Just as the many kinds of feedback that students receive provide a roadmap to their growth, so should teachers expect to be handed that same kind of information.

CHAPTER VIII

Families

"Let us put our minds together and see what life
we can make for our children."

— Ta-Tanka I-Yotank (*Sitting Bull*)

Whether nature or nurture is more important in human development, the family is the wellspring from which every individual's being emanates. In the context of schools, the parents and guardians are almost always, in the basic sense, the customer; the buyers of independent schooling are not, strictly speaking, the consumers. Families are a school's bread and butter, they are the greatest influence on students, and they are the teacher's greatest source of information, support, and, occasionally, perplexity. But yet, parents and guardians are not the direct recipients of the school's service.

An educational truism holds that schools and families must act in partnership, but to the individual teacher, families, in the aggregate, often represent another world, apart from the school and operating on assumptions and principles unlike and even at times seemingly antithetical to the purposes and values of the school and the teacher. For relatively young teachers in particular, families—parents and guardians—can be a source of anxiety, and for some benighted individuals in the teaching profession, anxiety has given way to contempt. In the worst case, teachers blame family decisions for undermining their work and maintain that "the popular culture" (the world that students inhabit beyond the school grounds, often in their own homes) offers children a vitiated and morally bankrupt value system in which the noblest goals of learning are scarcely to be found. Especially where a school's mission and beliefs are not made clear to prospective families, the disconnect between family values and school values can become a source of dissonance that knocks the whole community out of harmony.

The deterioration of teachers' attitudes toward families in many quarters is tragic and misguided. The partnership between teachers and families is the subject of "the essential conversation," to use the title of a book on this relationship Harvard professor Sara Lawrence-Lightfoot, and it is the foundation of a student's education. While a school and a family may differ in their ideas of what a student needs at a given moment, both are equally passionate about the student's need to succeed, and both should hold the student equally dear. The teacher's role is to carry out the school's commitment to the student and to work in partnership with the family.

The family in the student's life

Teachers might benefit from a sort of field guide to families, which come in many varieties and whose individual characteristics have profound yet sometimes subtle effects on the children they produce. I am often struck by the degree to which teachers, whose own families surely mirror those of their students in many ways in regard to tastes and behaviors, seem to believe that becoming a teacher elevates them to a position in which the vagaries of the average family are somehow problematic.

A veteran colleague once told me that "Parents are the way they are because they love their children." Strip away cultural expectations about admission to prestigious schools, strip away the effect of families paying large tuitions and the expectation of accountability this creates, and strip away the anxieties around class and heritage, and all families are reduced to a set of elemental relationships whose complexity and meaning a teacher can never truly hope to fathom and whose effects on how students learn are unpredictable at best. Eliminate the factors that apply uniquely to independent school families, and little changes other than the stresses and worries that the school and the teacher must do their best to mitigate or redirect.

The number of different family compositions in North America has expanded in the past century, with intact, mother-father nuclear families becoming just one of many. Single-parent households now make up nearly 10 percent of homes, while blended families with step-parents and half-siblings are also common. Not every parent is a birth parent, and some households are headed by grandparents and guardians, who are rightfully sensitive to the assumption that every adult looking after a child is a parent. Add to this families of mixed racial or cultural makeup, partnered or unpartnered gay or lesbian parents, and the simple fact that our continent's diversity of national heritage has been multiplied by great waves of immigration in recent years, and the odds that an independent school might have a "typical" kind of family are vastly reduced. The teacher can reasonably expect, except perhaps in a few schools with very specific missions, that any classroom full of students will consist of representatives of many family types, with an even more extraordinary and largely invisible diversity of experience.

Thus, the intentional teacher is wary of making assumptions about the households from which students come. Along with family structure and heritage, great variety of religious faith and commitment to faith is likely to be present; political affiliations will be just as diverse. Furthermore, while most families and virtually all students are expert at presenting as vaguely "middle class" at school, socioeconomic diversity at most independent schools is broad and in fact growing. While the Bentley in the carpool line or a few choice elements of dormitory room décor might denote wealth, students from economically deprived backgrounds will be at pains to mask what may feel to them like a deficiency relative to their more affluent peers, and their parents and guardians may be entirely absent or working very hard themselves to blend in with the more upscale crowd.

Differences, dysfunction, and secrets

The teacher, even as he or she comes to know a student well, may never know or understand the full extent to which "difference" affects the student's experience of school. In part this is because factors such as heritage and family structure will have driven expectations, explicit and unstated, around learning. A younger child may be burdened within the family with having to succeed in order to redeem the failure of an older one, or the only son of a family from a traditionally male-dominated society may be expected to achieve on a higher level than a daughter; a mother from this same culture may be quietly working against the grain to ensure that the daughter achieves and has the same opportunities as the son, opening for the girl doors that never opened for her. Each family has its own forms of discipline and punishment, from gentle to corporal, and Baby Boomer parents who want both to parent their children *and* to be their friends and confidantes can create their own kinds of household dysfunction. Some children who appear spoiled by materialism may be quickly and wrongly judged as emotionally deprived, and on the whole little correlation, positive or negative, exists between wealth and values. The children of unreconstructed hippies may be working hard to fit in as Young Republicans, and the same oppositional tendency will manifest itself in the alternative presentation of the children of sober conservatives. Professors' children may be anti-intellectual, or they may be among a class's highest achievers. Students with diagnosed learning issues may be working harder at home than a teacher will ever know, and the brightest child, to whom work seems to come most easily, may engage in Herculean struggles with homework and parents each evening. The teacher will experience little of this directly, but for students and their parents, guardians, and siblings these are facts of life, and they color everything.

In a world allegedly made small by modern transportation, the world as represented in a class, on a team, or in a dormitory may in fact be enormous. Children from immigrant or international families may never have grandparents available either to babysit or to answer questions for the oral history project, if they are even alive. Separation and divorce can drive parents far apart geographically and even farther apart emotionally. Many boarding school admission officers actively recruit on three or four continents. Children, in other words, may feel themselves to be missing something in their lives while they are at school; even the child from the inner city neighborhood just up the subway line from the school may feel as though he or she has landed on the moon each day when he or she steps onto the campus.

Children and their families will also have secrets, never to be told in the school and perhaps never revealed outside the home. Illness, which should no longer be a source of stigma but often is, may be one: a parent or sibling in remission, a parent on life-sustaining medication. Suicide, or attempted suicide, is another topic about which families may be reluctant to speak. Even homosexuality—a parent, a sibling, another relative—might be a secret in some families, regardless of the school's welcoming values. Criminal accusations or economic distress will seldom be brought to school if the word can be kept mum. Parents or guardians may have secrets that they keep from children; a few years ago it was not uncommon for adoptive status to be kept from children until their middle school years, adding turmoil to the lives of children in an already difficult stage of life. Alcoholism or other substance dependencies can create extraordinarily complex family dynamics to which the school may remain in the dark forever.

This litany of the issues that families face is included here not to frighten the teacher, but with the opposite intent: to help the teacher understand that he or she will simply never be able to fully know a family. For this reason teachers must learn to withhold judgment and to focus on what matters: the experience of the child in the school. Families, and critically the love that binds them together, take many forms, and what may look to the outsider as a classically "messed up" household will still have its bonds, its coping mechanisms, and its dreams; it will stick together in its own way.

In a subsequent chapter we will address a teacher's responsibility in the case of a student whose family dynamic (or other situation) puts him or her at risk, but it must be acknowledged that at times a teacher will be made uncomfortable by the way a child seems to fit into a family. Unless the child is at physical or emotional risk, however, the teacher should or can do little; the most the teacher can do is pay a visit to the school counselor, either to apprise him or her of the issue or to seek information or reassurance. The student may wish to speak of the matter, but the teacher will need to be very careful to listen and perhaps commiserate in a reflective way ("I am sorry you feel that way; it sounds as though it makes you unhappy.") but neither to judge nor to suggest drastic action—nor to fish for lurid detail. The usual course is to encourage the child to self-advocate, even coaching or rehearsing a conversation if this seems appropriate, although this may not be advisable if the child's home or culture forbid the discussion of difficult issues or express extreme disapproval of certain kinds of behavior. If the child never brings the matter up again, it should be left alone; sufficient embarrassment may already be involved.

The family in the teacher's life

Fortunately, the vast majority of interactions between teachers and students' families are positive and transparent in their content and purposes. In most cases the teacher and the parent or guardian of a student forge an alliance designed to support the student as well as each other in creating conditions and expectations for the student's success. Even in boarding schools, where many parents are not on the scene, e-mail and fax machines make it easy for parents to be a presence in the academic life of their children.

Perhaps 50 years ago and more, the implied contract between independent schools and families was, "You will give us your child to teach and nurture, trust in our professionalism, and in return you will step away from the education of your child. We will meet again to celebrate on graduation day." While such laissez-faire parenting gave the school enormous influence and great power in the lives of children, it also opened the door to arrogance and perhaps even abuse, as the life of the student in the school had been declared essentially off limits to the family.

Although teachers who lived through the historical period of transition might disagree, the age of accountability dawned shortly after the age of Aquarius (and just about the time when tuitions began to rise into the four-figure range), and the independent school contract became one of mutuality and common purpose. Today's parents and guardians expect teachers and administrators to work with them and to keep them apprised of the student's progress and problems. In return, schools expect families to understand and support the mission and values of the institution, made clear in the admission process, and to share with the school information relevant to the successful education of their children.

A teacher's role in this equation is to understand and foster this mutuality. Communication is the most important part of this work, and establishing the proper tone in responding to parent concerns or in initiating contact can make all the difference between stressful relations with parents and easy ones.

Although the culture in many schools is more flexible, I am of the old school, in which I try to recall that parents are valued customers and not my friends. Unless asked otherwise, and usually not even then, I call parents by their honorifics—"Ms." or "Dr." or whatever—and hope that they will do the same with me, although I do not go to the extreme of introducing myself as "Mr. Gow." I am afraid this practice dates me nowadays, but I think that making a point of doing this, at least at the beginning of a working acquaintance, establishes a tone of formality and respect. This might be even more important for a teacher who is closer in age to the student than the parent—a professional courtesy, if you will, that keeps roles and relationships clear.

Sharing concerns with parents and guardians

In formal parent conferences or in casual meetings, it is important that the teacher keep in mind the families' interests. Essentially, all parents and guardians want to be assured that their child is basically a positive community member, is bright enough to succeed, and is trying hard to do so. If the topic of conversation involves concerns about one of these three areas, it will be important for the teacher to set a positive tone that evidences empathy and an acknowledgment of the difficulty the issue is presenting the family. Even if the teacher is utterly exasperated with the child's behavior or lack of effort, the teacher, without whitewashing the issue, must keep matters focused on how this situation is impeding the student's success and perhaps the success of other students rather than on the teacher's anger.

In any formal or scheduled discussion, the teacher must have at hand any specific evidence that might be required not to "win the case" á la Perry Mason but rather to bring the parent or guardian to a full understanding of the issue and its ramifications. The teacher and the family may not see eye to eye on everything, but a positive tone and a free flow of information will maintain a sense of shared purpose.

If the issue is a student's ability, the teacher should never initiate a discussion without first lining up both corroborative evidence from other teachers and being ready to make some concrete suggestions as to a course of action; probably this kind of discussion should be a conference involving academic administrators and not be left to a single teacher.

This should go without saying, but in any interaction with parents and guardians, the teacher had better be as sure as possible of his or her own ground. Teachers make mistakes, and teachers sometimes procrastinate, but a teacher had best not knowingly rise to high dudgeon based on the discovery that a student's work is incomplete a month after that work was supposedly handed in, defend a spreadsheet grade calculation with questionable or hazy parameters, or expect vindication in a disciplinary situation that he or she has mishandled (and knows it). In all of these situations, the teacher has erred and, as wrong as the student may be and as angry as the teacher may be at himself or herself, the teacher must rein in his or her moral superiority. Situations in which the teacher has blundered somehow seem the most likely to escalate into an administrator's office, and although the school may publicly support the teacher if need be, the teacher will have privately squandered moral capital that will be difficult to recover. From the parent's perspective, the accountability and transparency that they expect from a person to whom they have entrusted part of their child's education has been absent, and they will be justifiably confused and angry, for themselves and on behalf of their child.

The single most important tenet of good parent communication is that no one likes surprises that involve bad news. If a problem appears, address it early and return to it as often as necessary if it reoccurs; do not wait until the end of a term to inform a family that their child has failed three tests and is in danger of failing a course and do not wait until the child has punched or been punched by a classmate for the third time to call the parent or guardian. Some bad news just happens, but if the teacher can see justification for the parents' likely question, "Why weren't we informed earlier?", they should indeed have been informed earlier. As hard as it is to initiate a conversation about a child's malfeasance, that conversation will be many times more difficult when it comes too late. Timeliness is everything; if the teacher knows that a communication is necessary, no delay should occur. The only caveat is that a wise teacher might want to perform a quick check with a knowledgeable colleague or administrator regarding the best way to approach a particular parent or guardian: where and when to call, perhaps, or what to expect by way of initial response.

Electronic communication

The intentional teacher must also master a few simple rules of etiquette in the use of e-mail and the telephone in communicating with families.

With e-mail, the basics are timely response (a full working day should be the maximum delay), proper grammar and formal English usage (this is not a text message or an IM chat, but rather a professional communication between the representative of a school and a client), and a neutral tone. E-mail messages should be clear and brief, and any expression of the teacher's emotional state other than pleasure (and the intentional teacher is vigorously encouraged to share good news with families) should be minimized: not "I am very frustrated with Hephzibah's behavior," but rather "Hephzibah's behavior is interfering with her learning." The message is about the child, not the teacher. A new and serious issue should not be detailed in e-mail; the main point of a message in such a situation should be, "Let's talk, please call." Again, e-mail is a place in which I start a message, "Dear Mrs. Smith" and sign my name, always, Peter Gow, but each teacher will make his or her own peace with these issues.

The telephone can be a bit more challenging. While the one-day response rule holds, the teacher may want or need to limit the hours in which she or he is willing or able to call families. The reality is that in many schools teachers are more or less expected to be "on call" from breakfast until bedtime, and perhaps a majority of independent schools now publish teachers' home telephone numbers for families. This does not mean that teachers have to be home every evening or that they cannot screen calls or just let the phone ring, but it does mean that anxious students or families have some expectation of being able to solve a problem or initiate a conversation when the teacher might be grading papers, watching television, or reading to his or her own children. Before answering the phone in the evening or returning a call, the teacher might want to perform a quick self-assessment; exhaustion, irritation, or a couple of glasses of wine can cloud judgment, and the conversation might be best at another time. Parents and guardians, too, may not be at their best on any particular evening, and a conversation that starts to grow uncomfortable should be cut short, with a suggestion of a classroom meeting the following day. Maintaining a calm, courteous, and professional manner is the key to keeping an awkward situation from turning into a bad one.

The intentional teacher should also be aware of some of the smaller challenges of telephone communication. Never, ever should a detailed message be left on a home answering machine—"Please call me" is sufficient; the parent or guardian may not be the first person to listen to the message. The same might hold true for e-mail messages to accounts that have "family" names—4smiths, rather than MSmith, for example. Lengthy voice-mail messages in general are to be avoided, as we all know from having to listen to them. When calling a student's home, the teacher should ask for the parent or guardian by name. If the call is about a problem and the student answers, the reply may be "they're not home," but the teacher should leave his or her name and a contact number and follow up with an e-mail noting the attempt and perhaps a call to a business number the next day. Whenever a teacher calls a family at an unlikely time—during the working day, perhaps—it is helpful for the teacher to start the conversation with a reassurance: "Your child is just fine, there's no emergency; I'm just calling to touch base about…"

A few small points

Potentially awkward situations can arise when the parent or guardian is also a colleague. The fact of the matter is that the student is still a student, and the family is entitled to all the care and diligence that would go into the education of any other child. The teacher of a colleague's child should refrain from offering detailed daily updates to the colleague; it may be that the colleague does not actually want these reports, preferring to hear from the teacher and the school at home or via e-mail, like any other parent. The teacher should also avoid talking freely about other students when discussing the child with the colleague-parent, nor should he or she be drawn into discussions about peers with the colleague-parent; this can be especially difficult when the colleague is an administrator or supervisor. If the intentional teacher *is* the colleague-parent, then he or she should adhere to these same rules and of course not seek privileges for his or her child.

Many schools, especially day schools for younger students, have extremely family-friendly cultures, and mothers and fathers are in and out of the school building as often, it may seem, as their children. While schools should gently make clear where boundaries lie that keep parents and guardians in appropriate roles, many of them will become familiar faces in the lives of teachers and even students, acting as volunteer drivers, grade representatives, library aides, lunch helpers, and other such positions of support. In these schools it is easy to develop strong and authentic relationships with families and to witness in action the best kinds of family–school synergy. But it is also possible to discover in such schools hidden and entirely unintentional power structures and struggles for influence, and the intentional teacher is wary of allying himself or herself or sharing confidences, even inadvertently, with a particular camp or family. In general, it should be emphasized, parents play a benevolent and generous role in schools and in the lives of their children, and teachers should not go looking for downsides to their presence in the school.

In schools supported by not only the tuitions paid by families but also by their contributions of time, energy, and sometimes vast amounts of money, it can also be easy for a few families to gain what appears to be inordinate influence; other families may actively seek such influence. This is a reality of independent school life, but the prudent teacher will avoid as much as possible situations in which a family's influence appears to be in play; every student should be treated in the same way, and requests or suggestions that somehow smack of expected privilege or that seem improper should be gently deflected and the matter discussed with a supervisor. In the same way, teachers should be very cautious about accepting unexpected gifts from families; some schools publish gift policies, while others have a tradition of fairly lavish gift-giving to teachers on holidays or at the year's end, but if a gift seems out of place, a teacher should demur, expressing gratitude but stating his or her discomfort. The same is true when a "professional courtesy" discount from a parent-run business or service passes beyond what feels right. The intentional teacher does not wish to feel beholden to any parent about whose children they are expected to make professional judgments.

Finally, the teacher should be warned that within a few schools some teachers may form an underground culture of mistrust or dislike of families and their influence on children and in the school. Some faculty members may feel that the interests of teachers or of the school and its values are regularly "sold out" to powerful parents, or that large donors can improperly attain undeserved privileges or special treatment for their children. When the intentional teacher encounters this attitude, he or she should back away, keep silent on the issue, and observe and judge matters for him- or herself. Cynicism about parents is just one of the several types of undercurrent that can swiftly and brutally corrode the professional culture of a school and circumscribe the aspirations and ultimately the careers of teachers who are drawn into their turbid waters.

Families, then, are not "the opposition" in schools but an important and extremely valuable asset for the institution and for the individual teachers. Approached in a generous spirit of mutual respect and shared purpose, families are vital allies in the work of the intentional teacher to help students learn and grow. Even when the "back story" of a child's life is obscure and the household situation opaque, the assumption should be that a child's family is the source of his or her strength and purpose and will be regarded and honored as such by the wise teacher.

CHAPTER IX

Diversity: "Getting It"

"For everyone of us that succeeds,
it's because there's somebody there to show you the way out.
...For me it was teachers and school."
— OPRAH WINFREY

The statistical odds in North America are that a teacher is white. The odds that a teacher is male increase with the age of the students or if an all-boys' school is involved, although women still comprise a majority of teachers. Chances are pretty strong that a teacher's educational experience has been among people who share his or her cultural background. This is neither a commentary nor a judgment; it is the nature of our society.

Independent schools, however, have a heritage of idealism. From the venerable schools with a faith-based heritage, whether Episcopal, Roman Catholic, Jewish, or Friends, to progressive schools founded in the tradition of John Dewey nearly a century ago to the community-based institutions that arose in the 1960s, it has been the purpose of many independent schools not to replicate the status quo but to be, in their way, miniature utopias. For the past forty years much of the focus of this idealistic spirit has been on diversity, multiculturalism, and social justice.

Many schools have had great success in diversifying both their student bodies and their faculties, but early on it became apparent to everyone that "diversity" means far more than the faces in the school photograph and that multiculturalism is scarcely limited to special units on famous minority leaders. In point of fact, a racially and ethnically diverse community plus even a healthy dose of culturally sensitive subject matter are only the beginnings of a truly multicultural community. Required to make such a community function as a brave new world are policies, structures, practices, and skills, with effective leadership radiating from the top (including the school's trustees or governors) down.

Diversity and multiculturalism

Multicultural educational communities thrive when a few relatively fundamental conditions exist. The most important of these is that members are able to relate to one another and to communicate about matters personal, professional, and institutional in authentic ways—as real individuals, unconstrained by bias or assumptions associated with role or cultural identity. Authentic relationships in schools must include those between teachers and students, teachers and teachers, and teachers and families.

The second condition is that the school's structures must not include barriers either to authentic communication or to access and opportunity relating either to programs or to recognition. Schools must engage in regular and systematic review of programs and policies to ensure that such barriers do not exist.

Yet another condition involves opportunities for each student to see his or her own experience or own background acknowledged in the curriculum. The very best of culturally comprehensive curricula represent and explore a wide range of content and contributions from around the world and across time, avoiding compartmentalization, as in speaking of race only in conjunction with the Martin Luther King Jr. holiday, say, or of allowing the work of female scientists and mathematicians to be recognized only in textbook call-out boxes.

The final condition involves the ability of adults in the community to understand deeply and respond to the nature and significance of those boundaries of race, culture, and ways of being that exist within the community. Each student is a story, and the more completely teachers can understand that story and its significance, the more effective these teachers will be in reaching that student. In many ways this condition involves the steepest learning curve for teachers.

For the intentional teacher, efficacy as a multicultural educator in a diverse school setting requires acquiring some important skills and knowledge as well as testing a number of personal assumptions. Even in a school with only a modest level of demographic diversity and where institutional pressures relative to cross-cultural understanding are relatively slight, a teacher fully prepared for the educational world in the 21st century must enact certain basic values as though he or she inhabited a fully realized multicultural environment; must be prepared, in fact, to imagine a kind of virtual diversity around him- or herself that requires a rigorously thorough-going response.

Essential concepts in diversity education

A few basic terms and concepts must be mastered before a higher level of understanding can be reached. Foremost among these is **white privilege** (also referred to as **skin privilege**), the accumulation of unearned advantages that accrue in our society to members of the majority, and historically dominant, white race. A seminal concept in race theory, the power of white privilege comes from the analyses and tests of assumptions from which it excuses members of the dominant group. (Essential reading for any educator is Peggy McIntosh's 1988 essay "White Privilege: Unpacking the Invisible Knapsack," a compelling explication of the concept; see Resources.)

More complex but equally important is **cultural capital**, a term describing an individual's aggregated relative "advantage" or disadvantage by virtue of such factors as age, sex, race, religion, ethnicity, socioeconomic status, sexual orientation, and ability status. Many introductory exercises in diversity and anti-bias training ask participants to take stock of their own cultural capital as a way of assessing both the unearned privilege and prejudice-driven disadvantage and the relative power status the individual brings to typical situations; recognition of relative cultural capital is a step toward the acknowledgment of factors that impede authentic, honest interaction.

A term of art in the independent school world is **people of color**, an umbrella phrase used to denote all people who do not identify as white. While not everyone loves it, the term has been enshrined in practice through the National Association of Independent Schools People of Color Conference (PoCC), an important annual gathering of educators of color and some white allies. A college and university usage that is popular in some schools is **ALANA** (African, Latino/a, Asian, Native American) or **AHANA** (African, Hispanic, Asian, Native American).

While the order of the initials may vary, the term **GLBTQ** (gay-lesbian-bisexual-transsexual-questioning) is commonly used to refer to issues relating to sexual orientation and falls very much under the diversity category.

The few terms and concepts offered here are hardly enough to add up to cultural competence. Rather, they are indicators of the degree to which self-knowledge and reflection on one's own situation and status play a role in the development of effective multicultural education. To this list should be added **racial identity theory**. The short version of this concept is that individuals follow a predictable developmental pattern as they grow up and become more aware of their status as a member of a particular group; children's ability to develop more sophisticated constructions of the meaning of race and culture in their lives and in the lives of others increases with age. Just as teachers need to understand the stages of children's psychosocial and moral development, they must apply knowledge of racial identity development to the creation of teaching strategies and programs aimed at social and emotional learning as well as at building cross-cultural connections within the community.

A final indispensable concept is that of being an **ally**. Especially in a setting committed to equality of opportunity, it is imperative that members of majority, dominant groups be able to act effectively in support of subordinated groups. To become an ally—a friend and advocate ready to speak and act against bias and in support of equity and fairness—requires both skill and courage; the skills can be acquired, and those who do acquire them find that having those skills can be a source of both heart and backbone when confronting injustice. Minority teachers and minority students usually find out quite quickly who the true allies are in a school, and it is a status that the intentional teacher should actively work to attain and deserve.

Furthermore, expanding community capacity in the areas of diversity and multiculturalism requires a committed cadre of leaders who are willing to take on aspects of this work. Schools that lead in this area find that the more they learn, the higher their own standards for success become, leading to an ever-greater need for expanding capacity. The utopian goal of becoming a community in which bias and inequity have no place exacts a high price in commitment and expertise.

The "all-terrain" teacher

Many young teachers entering the profession have experienced considerable training in diversity, anti-bias work, anti-homophobia strategies, and multicultural awareness as part of their own high school and college experience. The things that draw someone to teaching may also have drawn them to cross-cultural experiences as part of their education. In any case, the basic principles of effective work in this area are aimed at a common goal. At best each teacher should aspire to becoming what independent school diversity expert Nadine Nelson refers to as "all-terrain," able to adjust to any cultural milieu and work comfortably among all kinds of difference. All-terrain teachers and their counterparts, all-terrain children, are comfortable and humble in their own skins, able to acknowledge and respect difference, and above all, aware of their own biases and able to move beyond assumption and stereotype toward authentic, affirmative human connection. Again, the goal may seem utopian, but in small communities built around deeply held values and missions, why should this not be possible?

The self-awareness required to be an all-terrain teacher begins with the ability to recognize and reflect on the experiences and values that have shaped one's own development in a multicultural context. A common introductory exercise in many anti-bias trainings involves the participants verbalizing and reflecting on their own formative experiences around diversity. For some individuals, either raised in a social monoculture or trained to be "colorblind" (or culture-blind; both concepts have been somewhat discredited in the diversity world as unhelpfully denying the very thing that must above all things be acknowledged in order for its surrounding complexities to be understood), the greatest challenge may be to openly name difference without embarrassment. Even for people brought up in environments rife with prejudice of the most vicious sort, such exercises can be liberating in providing welcome and even necessary chances to surface their own internal conflicts and confusion in the quest for a more highly evolved and productive approach to human difference. The more clear and honest teachers can be with themselves around issues of diversity and difference, the more forthrightly and successfully they will be able to move to deeper levels of cross-boundary understandings and to develop real, honest relationships across those boundaries.

The intentional teacher will seek out those experiences that will expand both self-knowledge and reflection. "Lean into discomfort," goes one of the stated norm at many independent school professional development events: acknowledge and face those aspects of new experience that take one outside one's comfort zone. In almost any town or city the teacher can find many ways to be a cross-cultural investigator of food, entertainment, religion, and community involvement, but the teacher should want to be more than a drive-by local tourist: the goal should be true engagement with all the manifold aspects of diversity.

Gender, sexual identity, and class

Independent schools have long been the focus of considerable research and commentary on issues of learning that relate to gender. Gender properly refers to aspects of being that are imposed on or have developed in the experience of people based on sex. Sex, on the other hand, refers essentially to anatomy; hence, *same-sex* schools but *gender* roles. The body of knowledge about learning and developmental differences associated with gender continues to grow, with some apparent truths but little basic agreement. Just a few decades ago it was of great concern that boys seemed to outshine girls in schools, and schools were accused of "failing at fairness." Educators have been urged to consider the more collaborative, relationship-based ways in which girls learn and to make such adjustments to practice as waiting before calling on students to answer questions; girls, it seems, tend to compose their answers while boys like to shoot from the hip, giving girls a significant disadvantage in access to classroom airtime when the first hand up is always the one called upon. Now, as girls have started to outstrip boys in some high-profile areas of educational attainment (mathematical achievement, for example, and college matriculation figures show a growing majority of female students), other theorists have stepped forward to wonder if there is not a "war on boys," stemming at least in part from developmental differences that make young boys more physically active and that consequently seem to be a factor in the higher level of disciplinary sanctions handed out to boys relative to girls. The culture war here may just be getting started, but the intentional teacher will take the trouble to think and read deeply about aspects of gender and learning.

Although a thoughtful teacher never assumes anything based only on visual cues, he or she must be alert for so-called invisible diversity, which includes sexual orientation, different learning styles and cognitive abilities, non-traditional family structures, and households with limited English-language proficiency; also included here is class difference. In all cases the intentional teacher must proceed thoughtfully and carefully when meeting new students or families, because what may be apparent on the surface from clues such as skin color, dress, manner, and accessories may be the opposite of the actual case. A teacher participating in conversations about the households of students should also be at pains to consider whether all adults in their students' lives are, strictly speaking, *parents*; some schools are scrupulous in discussing *families* or *households* rather than parents. In an age when students may have two mothers or come from blended families with multiple step-parents and half-siblings, assumptions about family structure, like assumptions about any aspect of students' lives, should be avoided.

Acknowledging and responding to socioeconomic diversity poses the greatest challenge for many independent schools. In part this may be a function of the discomfort schools feel about being regarded by many people as "elite" (and elitist) institutions; although many schools make tremendous, even heroic, efforts to make their programs affordable through financial aid, published tuition figures do little to dispel the idea that independent schools are for the wealthy. To teachers, class diversity may be as invisible as diversity of sexual orientation, but students are often more astute in noting who seems able to spend more, or less, for the necessary accoutrements of childhood and adolescence. To teachers who themselves come from economically disadvantaged backgrounds, the shades of class difference may also be readily apparent and may even be sources of some resentment.

The all-terrain teacher must be able both to recognize and set aside his or her own feelings about socioeconomic class, perhaps the most volatile and repressed factor in American society, and to develop an intuition for avoiding situations that call attention to this issue. Do not casually ask a class about vacation plans or experiences, perhaps, and do not assign projects without firmly stated (and low) expenditure limits. Since most schools do not share individual financial aid situations with faculty, teachers are unlikely to know with any degree of accuracy which of their students is receiving scholarship support. When in doubt, the intentional teacher discreetly asks the admission office or perhaps the advisor, and, in the name of confidentiality, neither may provide a direct answer. Wise schools already have in place mechanisms to eradicate differences in opportunity such as access to overseas trips, standardized test preparation classes, purchase of team jackets that might be based on financial status. By the same token, teachers should be extremely wary about assuming that every student will have equivalent access to effective homework support within the household. A school which recognizes that its students come from households in which languages other than English are spoken should be a school whose teachers are alert to inequities that can arise when some students can receive abundant academic support from families that are present, affluent, and educationally advantaged, while other parents or guardians are struggling with multiple jobs, fiscal limitations, and only modest skills in English or academic subjects. What support schools and individual teachers may be able to offer will vary, but the point is to offer as much support, based on knowledge of real needs, as a student requires to participate in the educational experience on a level playing field. The all-terrain teacher will bring his or her skills to bear in smoothing that landscape.

What teachers most need to know about diversity in their school community and in the world at large is that issues surrounding diversity permeate every aspect of school life. A number of researchers have written on the importance of teachers recognizing the many different ways students and families may approach the entire learning process, based on cultural or ethnic background. In many cultures school is a profoundly serious and important, almost sacred, enterprise, and sometimes families are surprised by a teacher's seemingly casual or even humorous approach to some aspect of the learning process. The family may feel as though their child's learning process has been slighted or disrespected when a teacher takes an informal, understated, or apparently flippant approach to a problem. Some children are brought up to recognize teachers as worthy of great respect but in that regard also as frightening; the child asked to come for extra help may regard him- or herself as being in mortifyingly deep trouble. The ramifications of culture are enormous and sometimes unexpected; that "disturbingly quiet" student may just come from a culture in which it is unspeakably rude for children to interject themselves into conversations controlled by adults, as typically happen in a discussion-based classroom. Other children come from cultures in which collaboration is an essential value and who find the competitive nature of independent school classrooms baffling and repellent. Intentional teachers need to learn as much as possible about their students and their worlds and to give explicit consideration to different cultural approaches to education that may be present, if not always evident, in the school community.

The very best way to go about this consideration and to support its growth as a school value is to be clear from the beginning that no aspect of a children's learning experience matters as much in the long run as the personal relationships they establish with teachers. Furthermore, these relationships must go well beyond superficialities toward an open recognition and discussion of the truly hard parts of building relationships, especially across boundaries.

Effective relationships between teachers and students are founded on respect, but equally they must reflect the teacher's positive belief in the student and the teacher's self-disciplined understanding that the adult in such relationships must define and maintain clear boundaries. More is said elsewhere in this book of personal and professional boundaries, but in the matter of negotiating boundaries across differences the watchword is *circumspection*; never has the adage that to understand a person one must take a journey in his or her shoes been more important than in the matter of teachers and students understanding one another from entirely different perspectives. In this case, of course, it lies with the adult to do most of the walking.

Diversity, respect, and high standards

That teachers must respect their students has been said elsewhere, but the point bears repeating. Just as teachers demand respect from students, students must experience school as a place where they are respected, individually and collectively. A school without a culture of such respect will be a poor place, Dickensian and angry, and in order to bring about real progress this culture must be established at the top: board, head, and administrators.

This respect is sometimes hard-won, and every teacher encounters in a career a few students for whom sincere respect is hard to generate; the intentional teacher will rise to the challenge, working hard to overcome negative feelings. In some cases this does not involve the student so much as it does some serious and even brutally honest self-examination on the part of the teacher: What is it that seems so repugnant here? What biases, prejudices, areas of sheer ignorance, or anxieties does this student represent? The teacher's sometimes daunting task, once the self-analysis is done, is to look hard at the student, to find the smallest positive thing or the most remotely perceived glimmer of something good and wonderful.

The work of developing frank respect for every student is not easy; sometimes fellow teachers exacerbate the situation by building a "party line" on the student. Neither is the respect of a teacher for students just a matter of being objective; the teacher must, MUST, find that glimmer and build around it a set of conditions that will allow the student to succeed and even to become worthy of a less hard-earned respect. A teacher can experience almost no better feeling than to find that his or her pessimism about a student was flat wrong. Sometimes, of course, it does turn out the other way; so it goes, but the teacher must be able to look him- or herself in the eye and know that his or her faith never faltered, no matter how severely tested.

As important as respect are standards and expectations. A trap into which many well-meaning educators have fallen over the years is to respond to the struggles of students from historically disadvantaged or oppressed groups by lowering the bar. No message could be clearer to students: you cannot succeed against the standard to which I hold others. No understanding could be more devastating and more likely to produce even further failure. The all-terrain teacher works hard to let every student know that success is possible and that the work, no matter how hard, is doable. Standards alone are not enough, of course. The teacher must also be willing to go to great, even heroic, lengths to support students in meeting these goals. Insisting on the early morning extra-help session, the review of several drafts, and teacher-designated study groups complements the teacher's refusal to listen to silly excuses and his or her tough grading standards. Such demands, coupled with the teacher's own obvious extra efforts, send the message that all students can do great work and that the teacher is willing to show them how.

Earlier we addressed the issue of teachers' need to track down elusive students for extra help. I have known any number of white teachers reluctant to follow up assertively with students of color in order to go over work, teachers who wrote "See me" atop students' papers but did not go to great lengths to track every student down and make them do the extra work that would bring real success. The teachers' fear was that they would be perceived as abusing their positions of authority by singling out or even "picking on" certain students. Nothing, in fact, could be further from the truth, and, once convinced that such tracking down was tough love and would ultimately be understood as such by students, these teachers have become effective in supporting student success in the multiple terrains of student experience.

I have not yet gone into the matter of curriculum. Good cross-cultural curriculum design is based on a comprehensive knowledge of how children learn and a clear understanding of what matters in the material being taught. The more completely the teacher understands the cultural capital and expectations that students bring to the classroom, the more effectively the teacher can reflect on how to build on or compensate for cultural differences so as to create learning experiences in which every student can succeed, in which every student learns what is intended to be learned.

In the matter of curriculum content, the intentional teacher spends more than a little time exploring ways to introduce students to a multiplicity of cultural perspectives on the material. Some will read this as a call to accept all viewpoints as having equal weight and thus to abandon standards and expectations; this is the criticism that has been hurled at multicultural education for half a century, and it misses the point. Of course students need to learn some specific things and to solve certain types of problems in commonly understood ways to succeed in both the educational and vocational parts of our society. There is, some conservative commentators propose, an identifiable body of common cultural knowledge that children and adults must possess to make their way successfully in our world. The most narrow of conservative perspectives cleave to a notion that the assumed Eurocentric narrative will continue to provide the underpinnings of all aspects of our society. Those who hold to the extreme versions of such perspectives argue that to clutter curriculum with other perspectives or to suggest that non-Western perspectives are of equal significance in training our children is a dangerous diversion from that story.

The multicultural perspective, rather than being a distraction that is somehow both free of expectations and judgment or just plain soft, is actually more rigorous. In an era in which the globalization of the economy is in reality the globalization of information, the more one can understand and appreciate different perspectives, the greater one's chances of achieving one's goals. Multiculturalism is not about junking Shakespeare or Jane Austen but rather about understanding Chinua Achebe and Toni Morrison as well, about understanding how algebra came to the West from Baghdad and how internationalization came to China. It is neither wrong nor shortsighted for a school preparing students for American adulthood to teach them Western Civilization, but it is myopic to teach that course as students' *only* window into the past interactions of the world's societies.

Here the intentional teacher should be seeing opportunities to take not simply an active role in expanding his or her own multicultural capacity but in finding ways to enact a commitment to an ever-expanding idea of diversity within the school community. Diversity or multicultural committees are to be found in virtually every independent school, and many schools maintain an administrative office through which this work is developed and coordinated. The all-terrain teacher will be a natural volunteer at the door of this office, if it exists, and a natural center of gravity for the work where an office does not yet exist. Teachers who are not only allies but also active proponents of a community's diversity work will find every aspect of their lives both enriched and somehow a bit easier. Their students will return the respect they feel, the students' families will do the same, and colleagues will in time look to them as leaders on the side of a cause that is as just as it is venerable. Most of all, they will feel a part of the community in a deep and meaningful way, not just as teachers but as forces for change that is good in all ways—as inheritors of the best aspects of the utopian spirit in which independent schools came into being.

CHAPTER X

Other Classrooms:
Advising and Supervision

*"Education is that whole system of human training within and
without the school house walls."*
— W. E. B. DuBois

Inevitably, independent school teachers find themselves called upon to perform service in areas outside the classroom. Whether this work involves
coaching an athletic team, guiding a club or extracurricular activity, supervising a dormitory, leading a school trip off campus or even abroad, or
advising a group of individual students, the teacher must develop, or discover, new sets of skills and new understandings of both the nature and
the purposes of these activities. The teacher finds that he or she is, in fact,
teaching, figuring out how to apply what he or she is learning about curriculum, about students, about organization, about classroom culture, and
about motivation to a new, perhaps alien situation.

What remains constant whether one's classroom is a first-grade homeroom, a middle school soccer field, or a yearbook office, is the nature of
children and, just as importantly, the nature of the teacher. What works
or doesn't work in the classroom is likely to have about the same result in
other venues, and the advice to "be yourself" holds every bit as true for the
coach preparing a team for a long season or the dormitory "parent," as
some schools designate them, putting a hallway to bed for the night. While
at times the teacher wishes to "channel" a respected coach or even an angry
father or mother, those moments must be from the heart, as it were, and not
donned like an ill-fitting costume.

The advisor role

Many teachers, particularly those at the middle and high school levels, will find themselves assigned as advisors to students. Depending on the school and the students' grade levels, the advisor's job may range from a weekly check-in with occasional conversations to being the "one-stop shopping" source for information on everything from scheduling to personal issues. Sometimes the parameters are less than clear, and the advisor has to feel his or her way into the role; the advisor's place in the great scheme of things may be equally vague to students and families.

Not every school uses the *advisor* nomenclature to describe this role, and in the case of younger students, the work of advising students is often embedded in the job description and the work of a pre-elementary or elementary-grade homeroom teacher. Sometimes a formally designated advisor may not be a teacher at all, which can make some aspects of the work more challenging but which schools can address by a thoughtful program of training and orientation for all advisors. In the absence of such a program, the novice or non-teaching advisor is entitled and strongly encouraged to ask for any help that may be needed.

At the very least, an advisor's role in an independent school is to monitor the student's academic life and to offer guidance in planning that life. To this end, the intentional teacher works hard to understand as much as possible both about the school and its programs and about the student, delving perhaps more deeply into the student's file and story than would a classroom teacher. The effective advisor may not necessarily have an active give-and-take relationship with each advisee's family, but he or she should make himself or herself known to parents or guardians as someone who can play a helpful role in the child's life. If the teacher's knowledge is limited (of the whole college admission process, for an older student, perhaps, or of specific resources for helping a child struggling in a class), then the teacher should also be willing and able to help the family or student connect with those who can offer assistance. The advisor should never have to feel or pretend as though he or she has all the answers, and "I'll get back to you with more information on that" or "I'll have the head of that program give you a call" are responses that will satisfy a family or a child that the advisor is trying to provide the best possible help.

The role of advisor is deeply personal to the student, however, and the effective advisor also assumes the mantle of advocate for the student; just as much as classroom work, advising requires the teacher to develop an active and enthusiastic commitment to the success of each advisee. Families expect advisors to be always "on the kid's side," and occasionally they even may wish for the advisor to offer up answers or advice that run counter to institutional goals or the recommendations of colleagues. This can be a real challenge when the advisee's decisions have not been entirely productive or positive or when one suspects that an advisee is being treated unfairly, but part of good advising is the willingness to engage in "tough love." The advisor must be willing to express disappointment and disapproval (always in company with equally forceful statements of the student's potential) and publicly to stand by sanctions that another teacher or the school might impose. Even in such cases the advisor must play the role of professional optimist; the point is to help the student reflect on and learn from past behavior in order to move forward. The advisor must also sometimes help a family through these episodes.

Advisors can fall into a number of traps, however, and the wise teacher learns to self-check in order to keep advising on a professional level. The first of these we have mentioned, which is the difficulty of supporting a student and often a family in the case of a disciplinary or academic performance problem. Another is the temptation to overstep the advisor role and to identify, probably unconsciously, as the *one* person who truly understands and can help the student. At its worst, this attitude can become a "savior" complex and actually cut the student off from more helpful resources or avenues of support. The advisee may truly be misunderstood, or suffering, or struggling with a course or issue in which the teacher has real expertise, but the advisor's desire to protect the child creates a barrier. If this barrier becomes oppositional toward a colleague, the school, or even the family, the advisor has crossed a serious professional boundary. This boundary has also been transgressed when an advisor mistakes him- or herself for a child's therapist and allows the child to share inappropriate confidences or to become emotionally dependent; the advisor seeing this happen to him- or herself or suspecting that it may be occurring with a colleague needs to find resources within the school to quickly correct this situation before it worsens. In Chapter XII we will also detail the requirements on the advisor, or any other school employee who works with children, relating to situations in which the child is at real emotional or physical risk.

Primarily, it is the task of the advisor to stand beside the family as a cheerleader for the student, one whose professional knowledge and judgment serves as a resource for family and student alike and who is able to offer advice, wise counsel, or just a sympathetic ear in the case of bumps in the road of life and to offer thoughtful, informed, and honest feedback—the dependable reality-check—when appropriate, whether the cause be wonderful or troubling.

Clubs, student organizations, and publications

Although they are often called advisors, teachers who are assigned the task of mentoring or monitoring clubs, publications, and other student activities take on a different kind of role, with different parameters and different needs. The greatest challenge in doing this work is not always just keeping a group of students focused on particular goals (which may be difficult enough, drawing upon skills the teacher has used in the creation of a productive classroom culture as well as on those of the coach, outlined in the next chapter) but also understanding, in the context of the school's culture and aspirations, what is expected. While the essential goal for a yearbook staff is self-evident, traditions of quality and content must be sustained or advanced; the appointed advisor of the brand-new Environmental Club may have far less to go on.

The point, after all, is that students in an activity learn something and that they enjoy their participation. If a product is expected—that is, a yearbook, magazine, newspaper, dramatic performance, competition, or act of service—then this product should be of a quality that makes the students feel as though their work was worthy and worth their effort; they should be able to look back on the product with a sense of accomplishment and pride. They should also be confident that the school, as represented by the faculty advisor to the enterprise, provided active and adequate support.

The teacher may have little initial idea what the work is all about, but a few questions and several basic principles should be considered. The first thing to be established is the matter of student leadership. Who are the leaders, how were or are they to be selected, and what are their aims and purposes? In a world driven by the notion that a club presidency or an editorship will be a highly valued line item on a college application, not a few students seek out these roles for reasons rather than a burning desire to put out a great literary magazine or to invest peers in a deeper understanding of child labor issues in the developing world. This is not necessarily a disqualification from doing this work, but it means that the advisor to an organization led by a student more interested in résumé-building than the matter at hand will need to focus extra attention on that matter in order to make the club or activity experience meaningful for all students.

Some monetary costs may also be associated with the group's work; the occasional pizza to fuel a late-afternoon meeting has its price. The intentional teacher finds out what budgetary limitations constrain the activity or whether the group is expected to raise funds on its own. Some schools carefully control low-level fundraising on the theory that it short-stops the larger-scale ambitions of the school's development office, but in other schools no week seems complete without a car wash, bake sale, raffle, or other activity in support of a student group. It may be that students are expected to manage the budget in all respects, but it will nonetheless be important that the teacher understands the finances in some detail.

Above all, it is probably important that the teacher have an idea of how the club or activity fits into the overall institutional culture of the school. In some schools certain activities have "flagship" status, with the school newspaper, the Debate Club, or the Model United Nations group a center of excellence within the school and a regular source of public recognition for the school through local, regional, or even national competitions. In schools where arts performances are not part of the curriculum, the most valued work of music or drama teachers may actually be on after-school or extracurricular productions. If, on the other hand, the club has been gathered informally by a group of like-minded students—the Harry Potter Club, say—and the teacher is either a volunteer or a willing assignee, the expectation may simply be that the students find ways to hold regular, decorous get-togethers, with little beyond that. The teacher will need to explore these questions and then figure out how to use his or her presence and expertise to further the work of the group, aware on some level of the larger issues in play.

The student organization may have a persuasive purpose—arts awareness, political partisanship, issue advocacy, cultural or sexual identity support—and the advisor will need to be expert in the complex work of helping students with strong, often passionate points of view make their voices heard in ways that honor their passion while at the same time adhere to community standards of balance and fairness in a safe environment; a deep understanding of institutional culture can be especially helpful here. This kind of work can be a challenge in the heat of student excitement, but extraordinary stories are told of the power of students to accomplish great ends by thoughtful campaigns of persuasion involving planning, organization, well-crafted communication, and effective presentation—in other words, involving the application of important learning skills and dispositions. Here will be an opportunity for the teacher to experiment with a new skill, one that will also effect wonders in the classroom: the art of leading, and guiding, from behind, allowing students to prevail by gently helping them make productive decisions and plans. The key is to be the quiet but persistent voice of circumspection: "Did you think about this? Did you consider that?" No matter what the age level of the students in the group—kindergarten through high school—these questions can help the Harry Potter Club, a group of third-graders demanding better recess snacks, or the Mock Trial Team achieve aims of which they can be rightfully proud.

In the dormitory

Quiet persistence, along with consistency of manner and expectation, is the hallmark of the effective dormitory supervisor. Here, too, it is important for the teacher to understand the culture and expectations of the school, for a too-strictly supervised dormitory can be as deleterious to the school as the one too loosely guided. Although popular literature set in boarding schools implies that dormitory life has something primal and even Darwinian about it, with cunning students working subterfuge upon hapless teachers, circumventing rules under the very noses of adults with gleeful impunity, dormitories in real life are rather like…real life. Teenage students will indeed break rules and not be caught, but so, too, will students agonize over homework, relationships, grades, and their hopes and dreams. Students will come to the teacher in the dormitory seeking solace, seeking advice, and seeking free food; a generous baker with an open door at the end of the hallway can leverage a few tubes of slice-and-bake cookies into the first steps toward a culture of mutual respect and shared purpose. A dormitory supervisor must simply be ready for anything, alert to subtleties and vigilant in understanding and enforcing the rules in both word and spirit. At the very least the students and teacher or teachers need to establish a *modus vivendi* in which the forms are observed and civility predominates, and at best they can become something approaching a family, with trust, fairness, expectations, occasional grumpiness, and even a kind of collegial and appropriate love in play.

A half century ago, independent schools, and especially boarding schools, were able to enforce their wills based on the doctrine of *in loco parentis*, in which the school acted "in the place of the parent" with its judgments and sanctions absolute. Several decades of anti-authoritarianism later, however, schools and teachers occupy less firm legal ground, and so dormitory supervision, in particular, has become a bit more about the art of negotiation, and certainly about the art of observation, than it once was. The teacher may be armed with rules and a quiver of enforcement strategies ranging from demerits to the withdrawal of privileges; the "nuclear option," patently unfair but not unheard-of, is collective reprisal. Frowned on by the Geneva Convention, it is alive in today's dormitories (and often in large study halls), where the misdeeds of one may result in the loss of benefits for the many. But the wise supervisor rejects such sanctions and builds the desired behavioral structure in the hallway or building around the masterful and delicate interplay of interests, students and teacher. Sometimes the cooperation or conciliation of a few student leaders will do the trick, but at other times the teacher will need to sit in council with the whole group, working toward a viable solution to the problem of living in a group of diverse adolescents. The work is not always easy, but a dormitory united, more or less, in their support for the culture established by their faculty supervisor can be a powerful engine of satisfaction for all concerned—truly, a happy home.

The dormitory supervisor's best friend is his or her supervisor, usually a dean of students who can explain the school's residential culture and provide a first line of defense in the event of a challenging situation. However alone the teacher may sometimes be in the dormitory, he or she should never feel isolated in the role. Above all, the dormitory supervisor should be supremely and keenly aware that his or her work with students in such a setting is extremely sensitive; students away from home may feel everything from elation to anger to liberation to dislocation, and any one student may experience all of these within a single evening; the teacher, who may sometimes be just a few years older than the students, must be sympathetic, firm, just, and above all aware, adult, positive, and professional. Homesickness is best dealt with by acknowledging its reality and then keeping the student busy; conflicts must be talked out and mediated; relationships whose exclusivity or physicality threatens the social order or the bounds of acceptable behavior must be addressed; illicit substance use (alcohol is included in this, as are cigarette smoking and the misuse of prescription as well as nonprescription drugs) must be spotted early and addressed directly. Most teachers, especially those new to the profession, find it terrifying to confront students who are breaking or suspected of breaking major rules or engaged in private behavior that is unacceptable, but the alternative—for the teacher to look away—is far worse, as this sends a clear message to students that teachers do not care. Even if this is utterly untrue, what else are children and adolescents supposed to think? Even in schools whose policy is that the first response to such behaviors is therapeutic, not disciplinary—intervention rather than suspension or expulsion—the response must first occur in order to invoke and initiate the education and counseling intended by the policy; never should the teacher intervene in serious matters in a way that circumvents the school and its policies.

Although the sort of confrontation I am talking about tends to happen by surprise, the teacher is likely to have more than an inkling that something is amiss. Here is where the intentional teacher loses no time in finding a supervisor or school counselor with whom to share suspicions and concerns and to strategize ways to approach the students involved. It may be that the evidence is vague and that simple steps can be taken to eliminate or drastically alter the circumstances under which misbehavior might be taking place, but it may be that a team approach is desirable.

The final thing for dormitory supervisors to consider is their own behavior. Some schools offer teachers wide freedom in how they conduct their lives in a dormitory, while others are explicitly restrictive. Whatever the case, the teacher should at the very least be exceptionally wary of ever appearing on duty having consumed alcohol, and never should he or she be doing anything that is either prohibited to students or that the teacher would not be willing to do in the presence of the students' parents or guardians. Some schools will have alcohol policies less strict than what is recommended here, but the bottom line is that the teacher should always, always be able to make swift and correct decisions with judgment unimpaired. Fires, accidents, and worse occur in dormitories as they do anywhere else, and the teacher in charge of students must be able to respond to sudden emergencies with all faculties intact. The teacher is accountable for his or her response, which if clouded by alcohol or drug use can turn accountability into blame—correctly.

Equally, the dormitory supervisor should be aware that his or her behavior toward individual students will be observed by students as if under a magnifying glass, and proper decorum in word and gesture must be observed on pain of misunderstanding and worse. Those of the old school may try to avoid any physical contact with all students, at all times, and not just in the dormitory, beyond a handshake and perhaps a gentle shoulder slap; some schools go further in their rules on this matter while others may not, but no teacher wants to face the suspicion or an accusation of improper contact with a student, and so caution, even at the risk of denying authenticity of feelings, is the best policy. Extreme tragedy or extreme joy may, once in a blue moon, prompt a hug, but the byword should be, *Never in private, and never repeated.*

Although we are discussing non-classroom activities it would not be totally out of place here to mention that principles regarding physical contact with students vary depending on the age of students. In many early childhood and elementary programs, soothing or reassuring adult contact with the student is an important, even critical, part of classroom culture.

Even with these caveats, the dormitory can be a place of great happiness and great feelings of accomplishment for the teacher. A hallway or building culture of authentic, positive pride, common decency, and intellectual responsibility can be a point of great satisfaction to a teacher who has helped students find the strength and energy to create such a culture, and the friendships made in those halls, even between teachers and students, can be sustaining and life-long; within 20 years, those age differences will have shrunk to insignificance as reminiscences at reunion dinners turn back to school days and dormitory nights. Many boarding school graduates will happily recall that the most important learning that they did was in the dormitory.

The off-campus chaperone

The basic principles governing the work of the teacher taking students off campus, whether to a local coffee shop or half a world away, are based on common sense. The students may not see the trip as being "school," especially if they are far from campus, but the teacher needs to be able to act with the authority of the school at his or her back. On day-school field trips or Saturday nights in town away from the boarding school campus, the teacher must act not only responsibly himself or herself but also help students understand that they are each encased on a small extraterritorial bubble in which the school's jurisdiction is as clear and palpable as if it were the teacher's classroom. The teacher and the students need to have a clear understanding of this authority and how it might be wielded before setting foot off campus with students.

Off-campus trips can be powerful learning experiences, and they can be even more powerful bonding experiences among groups of students, groups of adults, and between students and adults. Whether the scale of the journey is small or large, good planning, anticipation of risks or difficulties, and thoughtful scheduling can create a positive, if not necessarily smooth-as-silk, experience that may catalyze lifetime interests and lifelong friendships. Indeed, sometimes the inevitable problems that seem to arise on such trips are the most potent bonding and teachable moments; the missing bus, the terrible meal, or the insect swarm puts everyone at equal mercy, not only revealing whose resilience and leadership can buoy the group but also challenging everyone, when there is no alternative, to work together to make the best of a bad situation. Indelible memories come from such experiences, and the intentional teacher will learn to take the ups and downs of being a chaperone or trip leader in stride.

As part of the responsibilities of being in charge, the teacher will also need to make certain that all legal or paperwork requirements for off-campus travel are met, from parent/guardian permission to insurance coverage to passports, inoculations, and visas for international travel. Double- and triple-checking transportation arrangements for any travel—even downtown—is a good idea, as is an almost obsessive counting of students (starting at the back of the bus) or taking of roll. If more than one teacher is involved, it is important for them to communicate and deploy sensibly so as to provide the best supervision and support; the last person in a line of hikers, bikers, or walkers should always be a teacher, never a student, to make sure that the group does not progress far ahead of a member forced to stop for health or equipment reasons. Any time that students are swimming, even wading, or involved in any potentially dangerous activity—rock-climbing, high ropes course, backpacking, boating, flying, skydiving, horseback riding—there must be *certified* lifeguards or other knowledgeable instructors or supervisors present; first aid and CPR knowledge is always in order. Some states have extremely specific regulations as to the safe conduct of swimming or sporting activities, and these must be followed to the letter. Similarly, if there are seatbelt laws or rules, teachers need to make sure these are observed by all.

Evening supervision, especially for day-school teachers, can pose questions. Students need clearly stated expectations about where to be, and when; in-room and lights-out times should be specified and enforced. Teachers in student sleeping or bathroom areas should be careful not to intrude on students' personal expectations of modesty, but neither should teachers allow students enough privacy to get into mischief. A good rule of thumb is that students should be given warning of a teacher's presence: "Teacher on the floor!" or a firm knock on a door, followed by a brief—but only a few seconds—wait before entering a room. The teacher-observer must ever be alert to issues of a "what's wrong with this picture?" sort; if something appears amiss, turning a blind eye is bad policy.

Some may sputter about the fussiness of these recommendations, but cutting corners in matters of safety or potential serious student behavioral issues can have catastrophic consequences, with ripple effects that go far beyond immediate risk. The intentional teacher will not wish to be explaining to authorities, to administrators, or to families what went wrong, especially if strict observance of prudent supervisory procedures might have averted misadventure.

In short, the various duties and responsibilities of the advisor or supervisor of students can promise enormous rewards, but not without their share of concerns of which the intentional teacher must be aware. In the absence of set curricula or the guiding structure of a schedule, this work is likely to present teachers with more novelty, but also more opportunity to be creative, than classroom teaching. Relationships with students take new forms, and the teacher's role in the school evolves in unanticipated ways. Common sense, a bit of courage, maturity of outlook, and an open heart and soul will make the "other" classrooms as exciting as a real one.

CHAPTER XI

Other Classrooms: Coaching

"It's not my job to motivate players.
They bring extraordinary motivation to our program.
It's my job not to de-motivate them."
— LOU HOLTZ

For many, many independent school students, the so-called "outdoor classroom," the world of athletic competition, provides some of the most enduring learning. This is also an area that for most schools represents a high level of institutional investment, both financial and psychic. The role of coach in an independent school can be one of the most important parts of a teacher's job, one into which the intentional teacher puts as much energy as into the classroom.

Having the opportunity to manage, teach, and inspire a team in a sport can be an extremely important part of a teacher's development as a flexible and engaged motivator of students, and most coaches find enormous satisfaction in the relationships with students they develop while coaching. Frustrations will come along, but these can be minimized as the coach attends to a few common-sense principles and learns to draw upon the support of the school's athletic department.

As in other non-classroom settings, the coach must fully understand the school's expectations for the team in the larger context of its athletic philosophy, mission, and values. If the school places great value on winning and the coach finds himself or herself in charge of a "marquee" team, then it will be critical to pin down the precise nature and extent of the coaching role and to work quickly to identify and engage the resources necessary to conduct a successful program.

Values of the effective coach

The thoughtful coach knows his or her players and approaches each season, each practice, and each contest with a plan. He or she also understands the immediate needs and desires of players and families and looks for opportunities from the first day of the season to make the following weeks into a positive, exciting learning experience for every player. Along the way, they might even win some games.

Effective coaches are not just experts on the rules, skills, tactics, and strategies of their sport. They are also committed to the value of sharing their expertise with their players and to helping players build competence and confidence as athletes, competitors, and team members. The athletic department at my school suggests the following ways for a coach to build player confidence and team solidarity:

- Be yourself *(Once again the number one guideline for the teacher!)*
- Be consistent and be fair; make decisions for players as you would wish others to make them for your own children
- Know your players' physical and mental abilities, and know their temperaments and personalities
- Learn to critique, discipline, and compliment; feedback is the key to excellent coaching
- Always insist that players give their best effort
- Maintain open lines of communication with players and their families
- Maintain open lines of communication with players' teachers and advisors
- Set a proper example by your own conduct, attitude, sportsmanship, and language

The school will also expect from a coach other basic behaviors, which are likely to include maintaining a professional knowledge of the rules and practice of the sport; keeping and communicating appropriate records, both attendance and sport-related; and taking proper care of equipment and facilities. While the record- and equipment-keeping aspects of coaching may be the least scintillating parts of the job for most coaches, managing these well will keep the coach in the good graces of the athletic department.

Most effective coaches are also compulsive goal-setters, and before the season begins the intentional coach sits down with the athletic director to discuss long-term, seasonal goals. These should go beyond a win-loss wish list, and even if the coach is not going to be formally evaluated on this aspect of his or her work, he or she should request this meeting if only to avoid misunderstandings or disappointment as the season unfolds. Clearly, assistant coaches should also be brought into discussions of this kind. If the team is at a high competitive level within the school—varsity, perhaps— or if the school culture embraces the concept of captaincy as a leadership opportunity, the coach might also sit down to talk about goals with captains or perhaps the players in the highest grade represented on the team. The coach can enlist the active participation and support of student leaders by asking them to think about things they would like to see happen during the season and what they might do specifically to further these aims.

Planning as a key to effective coaching

Setting shorter-term goals, whether for a week, a game, or even a single practice, that are specific, measurable, agreed-upon, realistic, and time-bound ("SMART," using the acronym from leadership and project training) should involve players as well as the coach. Daily written practice plans, which can be posted in advance for older players, should specify these goals as well as time for warm-ups, diagrams and durations of conditioning exercises and skill and tactical drills, and time for cool-down; a list of required equipment and who will bring this to the practice areas should be included. Working toward specific goals can be a powerful motivator for students, with rewards both intrinsic—personal satisfaction and improved skill and knowledge—and extrinsic—points scored, victories achieved, team treats or dinners "won" on the basis of goal-driven performance. Team traditions, cheers, meals, and game-day special dress can also be effective aspects of team-building, but all of these must support an authentic desire of team members to work and play together for common, worthy goals.

It is possible that the teacher may be assigned to coach a sport in which his or her expertise or experience is limited, and perhaps nil. Rather than panic, the coach-designate should rummage the school library, the internet, any local resources, and the athletic offices for coaching guides, rule books, coaching videos, game films, and any other useful information. "Head" coaches at the school should plan on mentoring and guiding novice coaches, and the school should be more than happy to have any coach attend local or regional coaching clinics. In a sport where expertise is not available at the school, the coach might seek to establish a tutorial relationship with an experienced local college or club coach; any guidance the coach can receive will enhance his or her confidence and ability.

A few basic principles apply to almost all coaching situations. Practices should include time for warm-up and stretching, conditioning, specific skill development, small-scale skill drills or full-scale, match-condition drills or exercises ("scrimmages"), and cool-down at the end of practice. Players should be told what they are to do and the purposes of each exercise, and clear transitions should be made between segments—perhaps a water break, perhaps a few minutes of team talk. The coach will need to be visible as a demonstrator and observer, audible, and attentive, ready to offer immediate feedback using a simple, defined process:

- Observe players in action, and have in mind a clear (and preferably specific and limited) set of performance goals for each activity
- When necessary, stop the activity and explain to the player(s) how their technique or execution can be improved
- Demonstrate the skill, action, or play yourself, or by having selected players perform it slowly or broken down into discrete steps
- Rehearse by having the players imitate the demonstration in real time until you are satisfied that the players understand and are capable of satisfactory execution
- Resume activity, beginning at a point where the skill, action, or play must be repeated.

Playing and being safe is a coach's primary goal for players. It is important that coaches know, understand, and act upon the school's policies and procedures with regard to athletic injury, travel safety, and game and practice safety. The wise coach may want additional training in such areas as first aid and cardiopulmonary resuscitation. The Red Cross offers specific first aid training for coaches, and CPR courses are generally easily found; CPR certification generally expires after a year, and the coach will want to remain current. The school may also want coaches and other faculty and staff to be versed in the use of epinephrine injection devices or defibrillators. Even if the school employs a nurse or an athletic trainer, it is advisable that coaches and other teachers have a clear idea how to act as first responders in medical emergencies.

In all his or her work in "other" classrooms beyond the academic, the intentional teacher will actively enjoy the ways in which these aspects of his or her job are bolstering and adding to his or her skills and habits of thought and action. The work of the advisor, supervisor, and coach increases both awareness and understanding of students and overall capacity to motivate and direct students in ways that are immediately apparent. As exhausting as many of these roles might sound, each reinforces the other and gives those energetic and fortunate enough to get to know students in so many ways unparalleled insight into and experience with the ways in which children learn, interact, dream, and grow.

CHAPTER XII

Continuing Education: Cognitive and Social Development in Children

"The function of the child is to live his own life."
— A. S. NEILL

With a bit of luck the intentional teacher's school offers a rich and varied menu of professional development opportunities, with many chances to refresh professional knowledge and to build skills, knowledge, and habits of mind to expand professional capacity. Even if this is not the case, however, every teacher should make a point of adding, even incrementally, to his or her professional knowledge whenever possible.

A teacher can never know or understand too much about two important areas. The first of these is child development, a field that increasingly includes elements of cognitive science, social psychology, and sociology. The other is the field of curriculum and assessment, which we touched on in Chapter IV and about which we will have an extended discussion in the next chapter.

All teachers need to understand a handful of fundamental concepts and essential paradigms about human development if they are to connect with students and create appropriate learning experiences and expectations. Topics with which teachers should be familiar include how children develop conceptually and morally, the ways that learning takes place in the brain, and how growth changes these processes. The study of child and adolescent development has yielded an identified group of age-level characteristics with which anyone who works with young people should be familiar, and the related study of how children can respond to ethical and moral challenges can help teachers understand the struggles of young people working to build personal value sets in a world of enticing offerings and difficult choices.

Child development: An essential history

Many cultural historians in recent decades have been fascinated by the history of childhood: the many and varied ways that societies through the ages have conceived of the nature of children and nurtured their young. From seeing children as inherently wicked and thus in need of structure and regular punishment to romanticizing their "blessed" innocence and purity to simply seeing children as small but increasingly capable and exploitable laborers to simply allowing children to grow amid the love and constant informal tutelage of a clan or tribe, societies past and present have worked to integrate their observations of the nature and development of children into their overall conceptions of the meaning and purpose of existence.

It was not until the late 18th century that Western philosophers and educators began to systematically apply their ideas of how children grow intellectually and morally to the design of schools with programs intentionally designed to foster desired traits. Whatever intuitive grasp of such matters that the great and for the most part unknown teachers of the past might have had, understandings began to become systematized in the work of the Swiss philosopher Jean-Jacques Rousseau; the German thinker and educator Friedrich Froebel; Johann Heinrich Pestalozzi, another Swiss educator whose schools became models for student-centered education; Thomas Arnold, the reforming head of Rugby School in England in the 1840s; and later the brilliant Maria Montessori, whose ideas about early childhood have profoundly affected education today. Such individuals began to look at schools not simply as places for the inculcation of knowledge and behavioral norms in an atmosphere of unyielding discipline but rather as systems capable of infinite purposeful adjustment to nurture specified ideals of character and intellect.

As the field of psychology took form in the latter 1800s, so did ideas about how children grow and children *are*. By the 1950s, this work had focused on the concept that children and even adults pass through identifiable stages of intellectual, social, and moral development, with stages differentiated by expanding capabilities and more or less clear-cut *in*capabilities. No longer was the will of young children believed to be deficient when unable to perform certain tasks, nor were they to be regarded as obtuse for their inability to make certain judgments. Just as the brain itself grows as an organism—and recent research has debunked the notion that the brain undergoes a finite growth period and then, at a point in early adulthood, begins to shrivel away, bit by bit—so too do its capabilities expand not just to learn facts and skills but also to analyze complex issues from ethical perspectives.

Theories of cognitive development and learning

The most influential of developmental theorists is another Swiss, Jean Piaget, who developed a range of simple experiments and then observed carefully to produce an enduring paradigm of human growth. In Piaget's formulation, individuals pass through four stages of cognitive development, with the brain at each stage demonstrating distinct perceptive and integrative capacities.

Piaget's Stages of Cognitive Development are these:

1. Sensori-motor (from birth to approximately two years of age). The child understands the difference between himself and external objects, knows that he or she can be an agent—i.e., is capable of initiating cause-and-effect sequences—and also understands that things can exist even when they are not immediately visible.
2. Pre-operational (from ages 2 to approximately 7). The child learns to use language and understands that words and images can represent objects. The child is egocentric and may not be easily able to see things from another's point of view and tends to classify things by single features.
3. Concrete operational (ages 7 to approximately 11). The child is capable of logical thought and sequencing and can understand equivalencies between like objects with different characteristics—e.g., that a tall, thin container and a short, wide container may have the same volume (a trait Piaget called "achieving conservation"). The child can also classify things by multiple characteristics.
4. Formal operational (ages 11 and beyond). The child can apply thought to increasingly complex abstractions and can think logically and with increasing sophistication about hypothetical and future situations and ideas.

It must be remembered that Piaget's stages are generalizations, and that many children develop at rates outside those he observed and described. In all events, the theories of Piaget offer teachers a reasoned and evidence-based understanding of, for example, why not to expect high levels of abstract reasoning from second-graders or why middle school students are excited by their "newfound" abilities to perform certain kinds of analysis.

Following on Piaget, the Danish-American researcher Erik Erikson proposed a complex and layered model of what he called human "psychosocial" development. Erikson's work focuses on the abilities of the individual at each of eight stages from birth to late adulthood not only to effectively achieve his or her own needs but also on what ideas, perceived needs, and relationships are central to the individual's understanding of his or her place in the world. In Erikson's formulation each stage—infancy (birth to 18 months); muscular-anal (ages 18 months to 3 years); play age (ages 3 to 6); school age (7 to 10); adolescence (10 to 18); young adulthood (18 to 40); middle adulthood (40 to 65); and late adulthood (65 onward)—must be fully experienced or "passed through" to maintain healthy development. Along the way the individual achieves increasing independence and autonomy, capacity for trust, moral reasoning ability, flexibility in problem-solving, empathy, and sense of responsibility. The theory has great relevance in psychotherapy, but teachers should understand the basic characteristics of and issues critical to the age group they teach; they might well want to have an understanding of their own place on a developmental continuum. It is largely from Erikson's work that the idea of the **adolescent identity crisis** derives, a concept that enriches class discussions about Holden Caulfield and that plays out in real adolescent lives in many ways as they work to discover who they are in a sometimes perplexing and disturbing world.

Also notable for ideas on development and learning are Jerome Bruner and Lev Vygotsky, whose theories focus more heavily on social and environmental factors than do those of Piaget and Erikson. Bruner's work, which began in the 1950s, has been extremely influential in the development of the constructivist theory of learning and has provided foundational ideas about curriculum and pedagogy.

In the past several decades Urie Bronfenbrenner, the founder of the Head Start program, has been influential in the development of an "ecological" or "systems" approach to development, in which social and other contextual features of a child's environment are considered as interactive aspects of the child's developmental "ecosystem." This approach, now expanded upon by Margaret Spencer and others, seems especially promising in guiding practitioners toward a more full and sophisticated understanding of how the totality of each child's environment—including social and cultural factors—affects development as well the child's ability to function effectively both within that environment and when confronted with novel situations. "Systems theory" also moves away from what some call the deficit model implicit in the work of Piaget, Erikson, and others, in which human development is seen as a gradual accumulation of "missing" elements, eventually leading to fully realized, and by implication deficit-free, adulthood.

Another school of psychology, the **Behaviorists**, also proposed models for learning that have had great, though perhaps now waning, influence in education. To oversimplify, Behaviorists regard the brain as a "black box" whose processes remain opaque and are in some ways irrelevant. Learning, in the Behaviorist model, takes place when the brain perceives a positive effect—a reward, in the simplest terms—from a particular behavior. Desirable learnings, or desired behavior, can be reinforced by rewards, and undesired behavior can be "extinguished" by withholding reward or, in some Behaviorist models, by inflicting punishment. The application of Behaviorist theory in schools spawned the widespread practice of "behavior modification" as a moderately effective teaching and disciplinary tool, and it lives on today in aspects of the Direct Instruction methodology, several classroom management programs, and a few very specialized methods for teaching students with specific cognitive disabilities, often in the autism spectrum, or with social or emotional disabilities.

University teacher-training programs today include coursework in educational and developmental psychology, for the work of Piaget, Erikson, Bronfenbrenner, and even the Behaviorists has profound application in the classroom. Such work suggests both specific teaching tools and also ways in which teachers can capitalize on known characteristics of children in a particular grade to maximize learning. For example, Piaget found that young children had difficulty making accurate comparisons of the volumes of vessels of different shapes ("conservation," referred to above); this, for Piaget, signified a mental property that indicated the achievement, or rather non-achievement, of a developmental plateau in the deep structure of a child's brain; some see this as yet another example of a "deficit model." Awareness of this mental property has inspired teachers to create lessons on "size"—including mathematical operations—using manipulative materials that can help children perform their own experiments and create their own mental models. "Hands-on" or experiential learning draws much of its power from the ways in which well-designed learning experiences of this sort resonate with and reinforce—and then expand—the understanding models already present in the neural fabric of students' brains.

Moral development

Along with cognitive and emotional growth, researchers also focused on other aspects of learning and development. Lawrence Kohlberg put forward in 1958 the theory that moral growth occurs in discernible patterns that are more based on age and brain development than on the external inculcation of moral principles. Kohlberg's research discovered that children progress in the ways that they are able to conceptualize moral issues and that at certain stages most children are virtually unable to analyze moral complexities beyond a developmentally determined level. Subsequent research has suggested that many adults seem not to pass through all of Kohlberg's hierarchical **Stages of Moral Development** but rather become fixed at less sophisticated levels. While these findings may explain many aspects of the world we live in, for teachers the parts of Kohlberg's work on the moral development of children that matter are those that explain why children's approaches to certain dilemmas and responses to situations sometimes seem shallow or self-serving; knowing that such responses may be developmentally appropriate can help educators craft analytical tools and learning exercises that help children become more sophisticated in their experience of and effect on the moral world.

The least sophisticated moral stage in Kohlberg's hierarchy is what he calls "Obedience and punishment orientation." In this orientation an individual's judgment of right and wrong is based on the consequences for the individual: if the individual is caught and punished, the act was bad. The next level is that of "Self-interest orientation," characterized by moral judgments based on the notion that if it serves the individual well, it must be right. Neither of the first two stages involve the individual taking into consideration the point of view of others, and so these might be associated with the earlier developmental stages identified by Piaget or Erikson. Kohlberg calls levels one and two "pre-conventional."

The third level of Kohlberg's model, "Interpersonal accord and conformity," involves the individual meeting the expectations of others in his or her role. For children, this is the stage of wanting to be a "good boy" or "good girl" according to conventional formulations of those roles; a "bad" child is bad because he or she steps out of the role and fails to live up to expectations. His fourth level, "Authority and social-order maintaining orientation," is the law-and-order mentality in which adherence to clearly stated rules and authority figures is the basis of right and wrong, thus keeping the social order intact. To break a rule is wrong because the cultural consensus says so. Many highly restrictive communities function on this moral level, and neither the third or fourth levels admit of much in the way of analysis or situational discrimination. Kohlberg labels level three and four as "conventional."

Kohlberg calls the fifth level "Social contract orientation," in which the needs and perspectives of individuals are seen as taking precedence over rules. This is the level Victor Hugo was exploring in *Les Misérables* when his character Jean Valjean is condemned to prison for life for stealing bread to feed his starving family. It is also the essence of the idea of trial by jury, where extenuating circumstances may bring acquittal even when the act is admitted. The sixth level, "Universal ethical principles," involves the individual's holding and applying principles of conscience that drive all action. Morality is intrinsic, and supersedes laws and rules that restrain those at lower levels. Kohlberg has acknowledged that individuals who operate consistently at this level are extremely rare. Unfortunately, the sixth level can be claimed by the exclusively self-interested—those at a preconventional level, perhaps, but earnest in their belief in their own moral superiority—whose actions might be seen by others as amoral; thus, this is a difficult level to fully grasp. Kohlberg has designated levels five and six as "post-conventional."

It is easy to see how Kohlberg's work gives educators a set of developmental pegs upon which to hang their expectations for the moral behavior of children; the exasperated fourth-grade teacher at least knows that a child's understanding of his or her own wrongdoing may not get much past the "I'm sorry because I did this, and I know it was wrong only because I got caught" level not because the child is stupid or stonewalling but because that is where the child *is*, from the standpoint of moral development. The high school teacher hearing the same plea from a tenth-grade plagiarist knows that the student's moral education is incomplete; "I'm sorry, but I was under a great deal of stress and I cut a corner" would have been a more developmentally appropriate, if equally indefensible, position. The student able to offer the latter explanation can be educated on a sophisticated level about intellectual responsibility and life's priorities, but the student stuck on the first explanation will need far more instruction.

From the work of Kohlberg and others has grown the field of "**character education**," an attractive idea to many in which educators attempt to design learning experiences that will promote the development of high levels of moral reasoning, and consequently better behavior. In conservative circles character education is based almost entirely around behavioral standards and principles and often creeds, secular or faith-based, while more liberal educators, many in faith-based or creedal schools, it must be said, have connected character education to such ideas as community service, social justice education, and teaching around global issues such as environmental sustainability.

The 1970s witnessed a brief but intense interest in what was called **values clarification**, a variation on character education in which students were asked to understand complex moral issues. Conservatives tended to dislike values clarification intensely, claiming that the exercises (many of them of the "How should resources be apportioned in a lifeboat?" or "Should a person who stole medicine to save his dying child be punished?" variety) promoted moral relativism over fundamental precepts. It must also be said that the situations and the discussions in values clarification exercises tended to be anything but uplifting.

Cultural and gender factors

It should be noted that none of the developmental theories cited here, like the theories of intelligence or neurological development mentioned in Chapter V, were presented in their original forms with a cultural or gender context. If the work of Piaget, Kohlberg, and others is perceived as "universal," the thoughtful teacher will bear in mind that all of them were working in a distinctly Western and primarily white context. Bronfenbrenner and the "ecological" or systems theorists have explored development through a broader lens.

Their work is complemented, however, by work in areas of racial identity development that has been referred to in Chapter IX, and it is worth noting that several researchers, notably Claude Steele, have identified discernible developmental patterns in the educational path of students representing marginalized or historically oppressed identity groups. "Stereotype threat" has been noted by Steele as a tendency for students from traditionally underperforming groups to do poorly, purposely or unconsciously, in anticipation of being judged by stereotypes in which underperformance is expected. Thus, a student capable of outstanding work may do mediocre work because, in a sense, he or she is resisting the challenge of defying the stereotype, a resistance that may even feel like an act of will to the student and the unaware teacher. Researchers are only beginning to fully understand the complex developmental factors in the underperformance of historically oppressed and marginalized students and to suggest ways to counteract these factors.

Other researchers have worked to link leading theories to the practical problem of educating students in the classroom and to understanding the lives of children in their environments. In Chapter IX we made reference to late 20th-century work on the lives of girls and young women, and recent shifts in educational attainment patterns might suggest that female students are at last surmounting the historical barriers to achievement and speaking out loud in what one important researcher, Carol Gilligan, termed "a different voice." Even so, other researchers and writers have explored a few of the darker issues accompanying the emphasis on achievement for girls.

Behavioral disorders and illnesses—and fierce debates surround the classification of many of these—such as anorexia nervosa, bulimia, and cutting persist, and they are seen to be growing; the rate of attempted suicide among girls outstrips that of boys. Furthermore, gay and lesbian students and students struggling with gender identity and gender expression have the highest aggregate suicide rate among teens, even with barriers to social acceptance less prevalent, and these same students report an alarming level of bullying and violence directed at them that has been underscored by several high-profile murders of gay students.

Considerable concern has been raised of late about the state of boys, especially as girls have garnered both more attention and more educational laurels. Whether a "boy crisis" exists, or whether boys have been systematically left behind in schools' rush to acknowledge and empower girls, it is probably true that the educational research onto how boys learn has lagged. A number of writers and educators, notably psychologist Michael Thompson and research supported and cited by the International Coalition of Boys' Schools, have suggested that the education of younger boys has increasingly omitted opportunities for physical movement and kinesthetic learning that may be inherent to male learning and to the behavior of male children. In addition, research has suggested that reliance on traditional models of manhood and male identity as emotionally contained may not be effectively preparing students for schoolwork increasingly involving discussion, reflection, and collaboration. If traditional conceptions of masculinity have favored aggressiveness and competition over emotional intelligence and access to one's emotional self, boys may indeed be at a disadvantage in 21st-century schools that have not worked to respond to their needs.

The intentional teacher should also be aware that K–12 teaching, historically a field populated largely by women, is once again, after several decades in which men were joining the profession in ever-larger numbers (not including administration, where males have always held an edge), becoming more and more feminized. The reasons for this may be teaching's relatively low pay, low prestige, and limited chances for great advancement—all factors that seem to work against the recruitment of males into many professions, given the traditional expectations on males. Young women choosing to teach in hopes of being role models in the empowerment of girls must also be aware of the needs and characteristics of boys—to know Thompson's work as well as Gilligan's—so as not to disempower them. Despite the charges that some of the most passionate advocates for both boys and girls have leveled at one another, education is for all, not a zero-sum game in which one group's success militates another's failure.

The social context of 21st-century childhood

This discussion must end with a survey of the particular social issues with which children and adolescents in our time must grapple as they make their way toward adulthood. Some of these must simply be issues of background awareness for teachers, but others may challenge the individual teacher, who must be mindful of the issues and prepared to act effectively in trying circumstances. The issues are many, and depressing to consider: rampant materialism; the commodification of childhood and the market exploitation of children; the sexualizing of childhood down into the elementary years; violence, sexism, and racism in entertainment; fear of climate change, terrorism, and global catastrophe; the intense focus on admission to prestigious schools, from pre-school to college; the persistence of drugs and alcohol as risk factors in the lives of children. Teachers must come to terms with the fact that all of these are part of the world our students inhabit. The curtains with which adults once hid many of these issues from children have been torn down in the last several decades, and so—at least on superficial levels—children seem wiser, more worldly than they once did.

But consider what we can learn from Piaget, from Kohlberg, and from others. Children may know and experience unsettling things, and their alertness to sexual nuance or their apparent jadedness toward violence in their computer games may shock us. But they are still governed by the rules of child and adolescent development, and their apparent knowing wisdom is often just a pose in which they parrot but do not understand what they hear. They may be more frightened, or at least more concerned, than they seem, or they may be far less so; this would be neither wrong nor unusual. It is the job of the school and its teachers to provide as much safe space as possible for airing, analyzing, and allaying, if possible, these concerns. It is also the teacher's job not to spend time being alarmed at responses that are developmentally normal or perceptions that might not even be real. The teacher must understand the developmental factors at work and try to discover, through listening, through observing, through knowing the student and all that can be appreciated about him or her, what the realities of any situation are.

It will be easy for teachers to become angry and indignant when students misbehave, and it will be easy for teachers to fret when the latest social phenomenon—a new game, a musician, a film, a gadget, a fad—drains money from students' pockets and seems to have them obsessed with violent or anti-social behavior. Teachers are, after all, supposed to be guardians of an established social order and of high-mindedness and even intellectualism. Independent schools set out to be utopias, driven by their unique missions and selecting their governors, educators, and students with an eye to fulfilling these missions. Teachers can be indignant, and they should fret, and the best schools will find ways to cope. But sometimes, things just are what they are; the misbehavior will end and the fad will pass. If the school has stuck to its mission and its values, little lasting harm shall have been done. A misbehaving student may have been separated from the school against the wishes of some teachers, or maybe the student remains, while other teachers think that he or she should not. Perhaps Kohlberg's stages of moral development apply to schools, as well.

When the teacher must act

Idle musing is out of place, however, in one area where the intentional teacher is obligated to act. At any time when the physical or emotional well-being of a student is at stake, a teacher must act quickly and decisively to prevent further harm. In many jurisdictions, if not all, this is a legal obligation, with teachers in the role of "mandated reporters" required to inform the appropriate government agency of any situation in which a child—usually defined as a person under the age of 18 but perhaps best understood by teachers as any student who has not yet graduated from high school (yes, the age distinction is real and it is legal, but it is best to err on the side of caution)—is at risk.

What is risk? It takes many forms, but typically this would involve physical or sexual abuse (both defined extremely broadly in the case of children under 18) but also extreme emotional abuse and neglect. It may also include the risk of committing or being the victim of an act of violence, including suicide.

Such risk is often made manifest to a teacher in the form of a secret. Either the student or a friend of the student will confide in the teacher that something is amiss, sometimes first having tried to extract from the teacher a promise of confidentiality. Or else the student may simply let something drop and then hurry to cover it up or deny it. But the teacher's duty is not changed either by that promise or the denial; experts will advise teachers never to promise confidentiality to a student, but others will advise a more Machiavellian but equally well-intentioned course—to promise whatever might be necessary in order to extract information that could save a life. Whatever the situation, if a child is at risk, the teacher must act.

In most schools the teacher's course of action is clear: find a school counselor, if one exists, or find an administrator. This should be done today, and if violence or harm seems imminent, now! It may be that matters are already in hand, or that the school wishes to investigate a bit further, but in the case of a reportable issue, 24 hours is the maximum legally allowable time for delay, and in a serious situation the school that takes that long may wish it had acted more quickly. In general, one individual at the school, often the head, is responsible for making the call to report. The teacher, in other words, is not alone, but in some cases confidentiality considerations may prevent the school from saying more even to the reporting teacher. In the unimaginable case in which a school refuses to act, the teacher is on his or her own. Shield laws in most jurisdictions protect a mandated reporter from any retribution or blowback from the person reported or, presumably, the reporter's employer; a quick anonymous call to the agency involved might yield this information, but if the teacher knows a child to be at serious risk, the civil risk to the teacher might have to be worth it.

What about a promise? What about the delicious power of sharing a special, serious secret with a student? If the promise has been made—and I am on the side of those who think it should never be—the breaking will just have to be explained, because the teacher's role is so clear, but there will be pleas and tears and anguish and perhaps a loss of ability to trust. Others would ask, Why was the secret shared in the first place, if not because the student needed help? Such situations are extremely difficult, but fortunately extremely rare.

As to sharing secrets with students, if the secret involves risk to the student, legal matters, or serious school rules, the teacher who keeps such secrets, or who even knowingly lets them be told to him or her, is dancing on very thin ice. It is true that a few teachers, often relatively young and new to the profession, become repositories for social gossip and party stories, often told by students wishing to ingratiate themselves with the teacher. These teachers need good mentors to help them turn their role as adults and advisors to better purpose. Remember Piaget, Erikson, and Kohlberg: the student, even at 18, is not fully developed as an adult; brain growth is not complete, and moral judgment and social integration have not set into adult patterns. Being the adult, for the intentional teacher, is maintaining one's own course of development.

While experience is the very best teacher when it comes to understanding the development of one's own students, the intentional teacher will try to keep up with new developments in the understanding of how children grow and learn. He or she will also not turn a blind eye or deaf ear to developments in the culture—in the worlds that children occupy—that may have an impact on their learning and their lives. The best of "old school" teachers, those who remain effective and admired but never seem to change despite the shifting currents of the world, are paying close attention to these and making subtle adjustments to their ways even as their course remains steady. Above all, the very best teachers find reasons never to pass summary judgment on their students or their world but instead seek and utilize resources to help them engage positively, and always optimistically, with vicissitudes and challenges.

CHAPTER XIII

Continuing Education: Curriculum, Pedagogy, and the Professional Community

"What we are after is an awakened consciousness, differing in each individual, an excitement in thinking, reading, and writing for their own sake, new discoveries, new enthusiasms, the casting off, or the retention with better understanding, of the old...How we do these things matters not at all. The numberless ways of their accomplishment reside in the numberless personalities of those of us who teach."

— MARY ELLEN CHASE

In Chapter V we provided a whirlwind lesson in curriculum design and lesson planning, but the intentional teacher works hard to think more deeply and more precisely about how children learn and how to create circumstances that facilitate learning. The human story in our Information Age is very much about how we teach and how we learn, with new theories of education arising and new purposes for schooling itself being offered and debated.

More than 2,000 years ago Socrates engaged his students with a program of focused questions designed to elicit responses that would become steppingstones to enlightenment, and the notion of dialogue as a path to learning was born. Apprentices through the ages have watched and assisted their masters in order to learn complex skills, and young men were sent off to sea in order to learn the trade of sailor; experiential learning is perhaps as old as humanity itself. In parts of Asia, young men studied and memorized sacred texts in the form of tomes on civic management to become adepts; in China a rigorous system of examinations determined the future prospects of the most assiduous scholars, a class of mandarins who became the world's most expert bureaucrats, leading and administering by word, precept, and above all precedent. Talmudic and Islamic scholars excavate the meanings of ancient texts as meticulously as archaeologists uncover antique cities, and their commentaries have become written discussions that have lasted for centuries. History does not lack for examples of great learning and the great application of learning.

Education in the modern era

When the schooling of large portions of the population became a political and social goal of Western society in the 19th century—not that long ago—new methods had to be devised to effect the education of millions, most of whom came not from scholarly traditions but from villages, farms, and newly developing cities where learning had previously been the province of a privileged and usually powerful few. For most of that century and a good part of the next, the focus was on content: What did modern workers need to know in order to contribute to the growing industrial democracies where they lived? It was an unstated assumption, or perhaps rather just an idea that permeated the atmosphere of the times, that the best methods of delivering this content would follow the methods of industry: standardized texts and standardized pedagogy, with economies of scale to be achieved wherever possible. The expectations of a class system were mirrored in the tracking of students based upon further assumptions of their optimum utility in the society: vocational, business/secretarial, standard, and college preparatory. There was to be a place for every student, and every student in his or her place.

With the stirrings of the Progressive Education movement in the early 1900s, a few educators realized that the focus ought to be on individual students and drawing upon understandings of their characteristics to determine how best to teach them and what should be taught. For this many of the early Progressives turned to psychometric testing, trying to tease out of the data from the still-fledgling tests some ideas as to how teaching could be tailored to student needs, although this usually meant that student sorting—in the form of tracking, only a bit more scientific—continued.

Independent schools multiplied and flourished in this era, not so much because of educational advancements but because a growing upper middle class sought exceptional opportunities for its children and found them by establishing new day schools for children of all ages wherever they lived. Many of these were "country day" schools in leafy suburbs, featuring comfortable campuses and progressive or progressive-tinged programs that included outdoor play to ensure that students would absorb enough vitamin D to escape rickets, the scourge of poor urban youth. A new generation of educational visionaries established small boarding schools based on new and occasionally idiosyncratic principles—some progressive, some not—and the established boarding schools and prestigious urban day schools that had been founded to educate the children of the very rich grew and adapted to the possibilities of a world at once more "democratic" and even more affluent. While the Great Depression and World War II killed off some of these schools, many are going strong today. In past decades the establishment of new schools—some faith-based, some ideological, and some focused on fulfilling social or educational needs—has continued.

Educational historians and educational zealots would argue as to whether the development of pedagogical and curricular ideas has kept pace with the growth of schools or changes in society. In recent years great public discussions have taken place about standards, the importance of a college education for all students, failing urban schools, the quality of teaching, and the need for reform. Little consensus has been achieved, and the national solution, at least for public education, has been to bind schools and students to a system of standardized tests intended to measure the yearly progress of children and the quality of schools. Many educators excited by the ideas of constructivist teaching discussed previously in this book have had to shelve their ambitions and their ideas in favor of teaching for a test whose results drive everything from school funding to the teacher's continued employment. The yeasty world of pedagogy and curriculum has remained for many teachers an ideal and not a reality.

This background is important for an independent school teacher because it illuminates the forces behind trends in our field and also the stakes for which the intentional teacher may be playing. If independent schools are to preserve their independence and their economic and academic viability, their faculties will need to be superb and their work clearly distinct from that of their tax-supported peers—a level of quality that will require teachers to engage energetically and enthusiastically with their profession and to understand and appreciate the context of their own work.

Influences on contemporary curriculum

In the previous chapter we made reference to Jerome Bruner, a psychologist and educational theorist and the author of several seminal books on education and teaching. It is perhaps as much to the influence of Bruner as to anyone that we owe the development of constructivist thinking. In

Bruner's work we can trace the shift away from teaching focused on select-ing the right content and demanding that students master as much of it as possible to a focus on "the process of education," the actual title of a 1960 book by Bruner. For Bruner and his successors, the central effort must be to fully understand the ways that students learn and to tailor learning experi-ences that allow them to master content by constructing understandings in ways consonant with the functioning of the brain. An early example of a fully articulated constructivist curriculum is the famous *Man, A Course of Study Program* (MACOS), an interdisciplinary middle school humanities–science program that became popular in the early 1970s. MACOS was built around essential questions ("What is uniquely human about human beings?") and multicultural content and based on active learning involv-ing role-plays, research, and considerable other hands-on activity. Bruner also promoted the **spiral curriculum**, in which teaching and learning keeps returning to designated skills and concepts as learning progresses, reinforc-ing and building upon those skills as concepts and challenges become more complex.

Any teacher seeking to understand curriculum in the context of learn-ing theory ought to spend time with Bruner, but so too should he or she look to the works of Howard Gardner, whose theory of multiple intelligences we discussed earlier and who worked as a student with Bruner on the MACOS curriculum. Gardner's work ranges over much of the educational spectrum, and he has put considerable energy into what might be called the correc-tion of misapprehensions of his work. Erroneously regarded by some as a guru of promiscuous interdisciplinary learning, Gardner has been clear in his writings that he is a staunch advocate of disciplinary mastery and that M-I theory supports this position. True multidisciplinary thinking in fact requires deep mastery of the modes of thinking and understanding that are associated with traditional disciplines, a point of view that does not detract from Gardner's deep interest in the relationship between creativity and learning and in what we have referred to in Chapter V as intellectual character—the dispositions that support active learning.

Gardner's work led to the establishment of **Project Zero**, an educa-tional think tank within Harvard's Graduate School of Education that has been extremely influential in the world of curriculum. Along with other groups, Project Zero has put the idea of curriculum design as a funda-mental pedagogical art on the map; "planning backwards," assessment for understanding (rather than simply for content mastery), performance assessment (assessing by asking the student to demonstrate the application of learning rather than by answering questions about it), "authentic assess-ment" (assessing by the application of learning to real-world or practical problems), and indeed the term "intellectual character" itself comes from Project Zero and its members. Project Zero members also laid much of the groundwork for the **Looking at Student Work** approach to understanding the relationship between curriculum and learning, in which extremely focused and disciplined observation and analysis can yield deep understandings of how children learn.

Another source of important ideas in curriculum and pedagogy has been the **Coalition of Essential Schools,** a consortium of schools organized along principles set forth by Theodore Sizer in his *Horace* books on the state and future of education. Although a number of independent schools have been affiliated with the Coalition since its establishment in the late 1980s, many of the Coalition's most vital members are public chartered and pilot schools, and the organization's strong focus on equity issues has become the educational tenet for which it is best known. From the Coalition comes the notion of "**teacher as coach**": seeing the role of the teacher not as the font of all knowledge to be pumped into the heads of students but rather as a knowledgeable, caring guide helping students to discover or construct understanding through structured inquiry and personal interaction with content. Sizer also introduced to the educational conversation the idea of school as a place of **unanxious expectations,** with emphasis on learning and not achievement for achievement's sake.

The intentional teacher might also want to become familiar with the ideas of E. D. Hirsch, Jr., whose influential 1996 book *The Schools We Need and Why We Don't Have Them* inspired a backlash in conservative quarters against some versions of Progressive practices and as well as the **Core Knowledge** curriculum. Core Knowledge educators focus on students' mastery of defined bodies of knowledge deemed essential to **cultural literacy** (being able to "read" the culture for information on which to build a meaningful life) and thus educational and life success. A number of independent schools have embraced the Core Knowledge idea, which, if not strictly constructivist and presented by Hirsch as anti-Progressive, in fact focuses on the need to actively draw connections between factual learning and deeper concepts; the alert teacher might have noted stacks of Core Knowledge-derived flashcards on sale at bookstores, along with *What Your ___ Grader Needs to Know* books purporting to provide the baseline knowledge on which the program is based.

A few other movements within independent education continue to have great resonance, including the **Waldorf schools** concept, an experiential and developmental curriculum established by the German educator Rudolf Steiner in the 1930s, and **Montessori education,** originally an early childhood and elementary curriculum devised by Maria Montessori in the

1910s based on close observation of individual developmental patterns and now used by scores, perhaps hundreds, of schools in North America. The **Reggio Emilia** concept, another highly successful developmental curriculum from northern Italy, has also been extremely influential among North American early childhood educators in recent years.

At the secondary level, the **International Baccalaureate** (IB) curriculum, with its elementary and middle school precursors, claims to set an international standard of excellence within a traditional curriculum framework, and a number of independent schools in North America, particularly those with large transient international populations, have embraced the IB. Originally developed by international schools in Europe, the IB has also become popular with ambitious American public school systems that wish to establish academic credibility for their programs along the lines of the College Board's **Advanced Placement** curricula.

Essential knowledge: Bloom's Taxonomy

Beyond the sweeping concepts embodied in movements and specific organizations, one established idea with which teachers ought to be familiar in their individual work as curriculum and assessment designers is Benjamin Bloom's famous "Taxonomy of Educational Objectives in the Cognitive Domain." First published in 1958, **Bloom's Taxonomy** details in hierarchical form the types of learning that students are asked to do, drawing distinctions between low-level and high-level learning. Educators have found the Taxonomy to be a powerful tool in the development of assessments, and numerous versions of "teaching with the Taxonomy" can be found in educational literature, in print and online. It should be noted that Bloom also identified two other domains associated with learning, the affective and the psychomotor, but his description of aspects of the cognitive—intellectual, thought-related—remains most influential today.

The levels in Bloom's Taxonomy, here presented with suggestions on how each might find its way into the organization of curriculum and a trajectory of assessments, are as follows:

- **Knowledge:** The ability to recall facts, terms, dates, procedural steps, definitions, and basic knowledge. *Assess knowledge* by means of quizzes on facts, definitions, basic processes/causality, and definitions. Multiple-choice, fill-ins, and simple quiz structures are apt.
- **Comprehension:** The understanding of how factual information or basic ideas relate to one another or to larger concepts. *Assess comprehension* by asking students to arrange, compare, re-state, inter-

pret, and describe. Question sets, short-answer written tests and quizzes, and asking students to produce timelines, cause-and-effect maps, or flow-charts are a few ways to do this.

- **Application:** The ability to utilize or apply learning of concepts or processes. *Assess **application** by means of laboratory experiments, demonstrations, writing exercises focusing on explanation or persuasion, and student-created dialogues or role-plays.* Ask students to use knowledge to solve more abstract problems, to write paragraph-length essays, or to perform prediction-test-response experiments (even thought experiments) to assess learning on this level.

- **Analysis:** The ability to break learning down into understandings of relationships between component parts or causal links and to identify evidence that supports the analysis and generalizations that may follow from it; this also involves making inferences based on evidence. *Assess **analysis** by means of essays focusing on analytical questions and asking the student to give supporting evidence and to show the connections between the evidence and the thesis, complex laboratory experiments in which the evaluative balance is tipped toward interpreting results rather than proper procedure, essay tests or non-verbal explications or expositions, and research reports.* Question prompts that ask for analysis include *why, how, differentiate, compare, explain why, compare and contrast, explore,* and *prove.*

- **Synthesis:** The ability to connect understandings and knowledge in novel ways to produce new understandings, new ways of considering information, or alternative theses or solutions. *Assess **synthesis** by asking students to design new plans or to create persuasive presentations or persuasive communications.* Students will be excited by being asked to demonstrate their ability to synthesize by applying their learning to authentic or "real-world" problems in designing their own experiments, producing complex dialogues or role-plays, or making multimedia presentations, but essay tests and examinations and other complex assessments are also appropriate; students can even be asked to propose their own answers to one of the essential questions of the study.

- **Evaluation:** The ability to form and support opinions and to make informed judgments about validity or quality of assertions or work based on knowledge and understanding. *Assess **evaluation** ability through critical studies, writing op-ed essays, or engaging in critiques on work or performances.*

Bloom's work has pervaded education in numerous ways, including the design of textbooks; many conventional textbooks are divided into sections in which concepts are introduced in stages that correspond with the Taxonomy, and question sets at the end of sections in many textbooks are organized precisely along Taxonomic lines. A teacher could do well to base the sequence of assessments in a unit or study along these lines, and a "classic" test structure features short-answers corresponding to knowledge and comprehension, longer answers corresponding to comprehension and application, and essay questions seeking evidence of analysis, synthesis, and evaluation. A model of this can be found in Appendix III.

We mention Bloom here not only for the utility of his ideas but also as an example of the ways in which educational research has yielded eminently useful practices; the trick is for the intentional teacher to know where and how to look for such ideas, which seldom come up in the course of a liberal arts education that does not involve coursework in educational theory or human development.

The next wave of technology

It is somewhat beyond the scope of this book, but the intentional teacher will want very much to consider the need to maintain his or her personal technology skills and interests in technology at the forefront of his or her thinking about curriculum and pedagogy. While computers in the first decades of their use in classrooms have been increasingly useful as teaching tools and have had even more impact as tools to automate and make more efficient many of the tasks teachers must perform, interactive online resources and user-developed content are bringing about great changes in the way teachers incorporate technologies, including technologies yet to materialize, into their work. From communication to data-gathering and research to collaboration across vast gulfs of space and culture, contemporary and emerging technologies offer the promise of a revolution in pedagogy and assessment. What are known as Web 2.0 technologies along with ever-smaller and more powerful laptop computers and smartphones have the capability to connect people, enable complex research and data development, foster communication in many modes, and even create large-scale multimedia and multigenre products. Teachers are beginning to push the technology envelope in terms of asking students to do work that is not just more easily done using digital technologies but simply impossible without them. Educational and economic futurists are calling creativity and collaboration the essential skills of a globalized economy, and comfort with technology will be critical for students entering the 21st-century workforce. Schools are beginning to move from a cautious approach to technology and mistrust of the digital tools with which students fashion their personal lives toward an enthusiastic and increasingly sophisticated embrace of all the potential of technology. It may even be that many of the instructional models on which this book is based will in time be infused and enhanced by complementary instruction in digital or virtual form.

Professional organizations

The teacher who is in need of self-education in the course of building a career has available a wealth of resources for learning about teaching and learning, and at a bare minimum the intentional teacher will wish to join one of the many professional organizations related to his or her field of study or age level taught. For example, North American teachers (and others, of course) can join the National Council of Teachers of English, the National Council of Teachers of Mathematics, the National Council for the Social Studies, the National Council for History Education, the American Council on the Teaching of Foreign Language, the American Classical League, the National Science Teachers Association, the International Association for Jazz Education, the National Art Education Association, the National Association for Music Education, the Educational Theatre Association, the National Middle Schools Association, the National Association for the Education of Young Children, and the National Association of Early Childhood Educators. Specialists will find the American Library Association, the International Dyslexia Association, Teachers of English to Speakers of Other Languages, and the National Association for College Admission Counseling, along with a host of organizations serving those with focused interests in aspects of special education. All of these organizations publish regular magazines or newsletters, and most sponsor annual conferences for the sharing of new ideas, concerns related to the field, and best practices. Many also sponsor multiple online listservs and forums where teachers can share questions or ideas. Most schools will support a teacher in joining at least one of these organizations, and in any case annual fees for one of these non-profit organizations are often either tax deductible or can be claimed as an unreimbursed business expense. Every teacher should become part of the larger professional community through membership in one of more of such groups.

And these are just the groups devoted to PreK–12 education. Teachers can dig more deeply into their fields as members of the Modern Language

Association (MLA), the Organization of American Historians (OAH), the American Association for the Advancement of Science (AAAS), the International Society for Technology in Education (ISTE) or similar organizations primarily for college-level educators or practitioners in the field but which also take an active interest in matters related to pre-college teaching; the AAAS, for example, has developed and promotes Project 2061, a challenging and radical approach to K–12 science curriculum, and the OAH *Magazine of History* features teaching modules suitable for middle and high school classes. The ISTE not only promotes technology proficiency standards for students and teachers of all ages but even maintains an active ISTE group in the virtual world of Second Life (www.secondlife. com) where educators can explore issues relating to technology. (Second Life is itself the home of a number of curriculum-related projects and supports a number of resources for teachers, including a listserv for those who use Second Life in—or in some cases, as—their classrooms.)

Along with professional organizations, a number of think tank-type organizations produce curricula and promote ideas about teaching and learning. As a few among many examples, the Thomas Watson Institute at Brown University publishes low-cost curricula on various topics in modern and current history, the Concord Consortium offers compelling ideas in mathematics and science education, and The Education Research Consortium (TERC) has published influential science and mathematics curricula for many years. Many industry and commercial advocacy groups also publish curricula and offer resources to educators; some of this material may be useful, and some is egregiously biased. The intentional teacher can look carefully through these and perhaps use them not only to teach the intended content but also to educate students about how to evaluate the value of sources.

Several important umbrella organizations also publish materials and magazines for educators and those interested in education. The Association of Supervision and Curriculum Development (ASCD) publishes books, monographs, and the important monthly magazine *Educational Leadership*, and its annual conference and regional conferences are venues for the presentation of ideas on the cutting edge of pedagogy and curriculum. The National Association of Independent Schools maintains a useful website that includes a section devoted to exemplary school practices, and its award-winning quarterly magazine, *Independent School*, is the publication of record in the independent school world; its annual conference and the annual People of Color Conference are the professional gatherings from which the best of new ideas flow out to schools. *Education Week* is the essential trade publication in K–12 education, and its op-ed "Commentary" section has long been a source of compelling ideas. The Coalition of Essential Schools newsletter *Horace* offers insights and ideas from Coalition educators and those interested in contributing to the body of knowledge related to Coalition principles. *Teachers College Record*, from Columbia University, publishes excellent research reports and book reviews both online and in paper, and the *Harvard Education Letter* (brief, bimonthly) and the *Harvard Education Review* (long, quarterly) both offer both research results and good ideas; the *Review*'s actual reviews amount to an industry standard. The two largest teachers' unions, the American Federation of Teachers and the National Education Association, both publish magazines, albeit primarily with a public school focus, and hold politically important annual meetings, and at the other end of the spectrum the Hoover Institute at Stanford University publishes *Education Next*, a quarterly journal of relatively conservative educational thought. *The Independent Teacher*, a high-quality online journal published semiannually at the University of Chicago Laboratory School, offers practical advice, program reports, and reflections and musings by teachers. *Phi Delta Kappan*, the magazine of the educators' honor society Phi Delta Kappa, is highly readable and often presents extremely useful ideas.

Along with the increasing array of online university and professional development courses available for teachers, the online world contains a number of virtual communities for teachers and in particular independent school educators. Along with listservs maintained by professional organizations for teachers at specific levels or in specific disciplines, a number of regional groups unite school technology specialists. The grandaddy of professional listservs is the ISED list, which allows members from independent schools around the world to seek and share ideas in a frank and friendly community, and the newer Independent School Educators "ning" is a professional-social network on which members can share and discuss ideas, concerns, and personal information.

Closer to a teacher's home, regional and metropolitan independent schools associations offer varying amounts of professional development support for teachers in member schools, and the intentional teachers should be alert to what might be going on in their own. In a few metropolitan areas groups of teachers from different schools meet to discuss issues and ideas, and any teacher can contemplate initiating such collaboration; even where independent schools may see themselves in fierce competition for students or resources, or where inter-school rivalries threaten to get ugly from time to time, teachers must recall that the students are their central concern, and that sharing ideas or posing problems about teaching and learning is our work, the work of professionals.

Even within a teacher's own school, whether the professional development program is thriving or languishing, the intentional teacher can find resources for personal growth. Most educators would attest that collaborating with colleagues in the development of curriculum and assessments or simply in tackling institutional or classroom problems can be the most inspiring kind of professional development. To work systematically with other professionals toward a defined goal, allocating and utilizing specific resources, is to become a part of the work and traditions of the field of education, as physicians on rounds or collaborating in the analysis of laboratory results are engaging in the fundamental work of medicine. The teacher excited by ideas related to pedagogy, curriculum, or school culture might even consider regularly inviting a few like-minded or curious colleagues to an occasional informal colloquium on a compelling reading or essential question or to view and parse an interesting video relating to education; good food, good talk, and good fellowship will remind everyone involved that they are part of something bigger even than the important work they do in their classrooms every day.

The highest call to the intentional teacher is to be a professional, to understand that his or her work derives from ideas, from principles, from practices, and even from traditions that are themselves intentional and that are inherently worthy and inherently important. The fact is that independent schools and their faculties have long practiced a kind of self-imposed isolation (sometimes proudly called autonomy) from one another that would be unthinkable among universities, hospitals, or even groups of attorneys. Education, like the law, like medicine, and like professors' disciplines, has a defined body of knowledge and practice that is constantly growing for the broad and noble purpose of making the world and its future better. The best teachers know that professional development prepares them to be even more successful in playing their own critical role in that work.

CHAPTER XIV

Professional Behavior

*"The true teacher defends his pupils against his own personal influence.
He inspires self-trust. He guides their eyes from himself to the spirit
that quickens him. He will have no disciple."*

— BRONSON ALCOTT

We have thus far compiled a formidable list of things that an independent school teacher must know, think about, and do, and along the way we have implied the existence of a kind of code of conduct. The code is real, and although its tenets may vary from school to school and region to region, it is firm and, at its outer edges, unyielding. The first article of this code is that the students are a teacher's first concern, and the second is that teacher be intentional in all things—that is, that he or she be considerate of the possible outcomes and repercussions of each act contemplated or performed and each word uttered in a professional setting.

This concept ought to be daunting. While I do not mean to suggest that the teacher must at all times be "Caesar's wife," appearing pure in thought, word, and deed, I very much do mean that teaching carries some great responsibilities. If the values and practices of independent schools are intended to shape student behavior toward certain ideals, then teachers, who carry out these practices, need to subscribe to and support these values and practices. While they will experience moments of backsliding, doubt, and outright rebellion, teachers need to work hard to put their best feet and best selves forward as at least passable examples of lives lived according to the school's ideals. This may be terribly old-fashioned and out of step with the aspirations of Generation X and the coming crop of so-called Millennials, but as one reads about their great desire to find meaning in their working lives, I would put it forward that educating young people is not a bad way to find such meaning.

The values proclaimed by independent schools represent both enduring principles and wonderfully mutable ideas of how these principles might
best be enacted. The reader can parse for him- or herself the classical mot-
tos with which schools enunciate their essences and perhaps come to the
conclusion that perhaps things have changed since the schools' establish-
ments—strident, militant, or absolutist creeds might have been intended
in these ways a century of more ago, but most schools seek to have them
interpreted now in a kinder, gentler light.

Schools and educators have not been at liberty to think of themselves
as unassailable at least since the social revolutions of the 1960s and 1970s,
when the failings of the entire enterprise of education were summed up in
book titles like *Death at an Early Age* and when even the most august independent schools were forced to make their curricula "relevant" and their
communities "equitable."

A personal code

Independent school teachers inherit a professional code of conduct that is at
times both rigorously formal and humbly personal and self-reflective, and
each teacher must fashion of it a personal code. Yes, teachers must behave
well and adhere to standards of behavior that are a bit higher than those of
the culture at large. But simultaneously teachers must be open to the notion
that this is all far less vital to the future of the world than the sometimes
joyful, sometimes agonizing struggles they share every day with children.
Like the children, great teachers are energetically skeptical of anything that
smacks of the absolute or the perfect, and yet they understand the need for
guideposts and ideals against which humans can measure the quality of
their existence.

At times this duality of vision may feel as though it lands the teacher
in a parallel universe, not quite like that of adults and yet neither childish
nor childlike. Many teachers in the company of adults from the worlds of
commerce or the like are amused to find themselves far less tendentious and
grave than their peers; teachers tend to keep a needle of humor at hand to
burst balloons of arrogance or dogma, even if they do not always use them
publicly, for they understand that arrogance and dogma are the enemies of
learning. Teachers also tend to seek one another out, and if they can't find
other teachers, they are often happy to talk to children, who, granted, may
not always be so eager to be chatted up by teachers.

The code for teachers is not so much a list of do's and don't's, although
there are a few obvious but absolute ones involving personal behavior in
the presence of students or when a sudden emergency could put students at

risk. Rather, the code is a set of professional principles that will enable the teacher to shape a long, successful, and estimable career. The point is not so much to avoid impurity of thought, word, and deed as to avoid an issue much more troubling to the young: hypocrisy.

School rules

A teacher needs to be very aware of the rules that govern the behavior of both faculty and students at his or her school. This may be as small as the need for a parking sticker and as large as a prohibition on certain kinds of dress. Whatever the rules of the school may be, the teacher should make a point of following them, not just in the letter but also in the spirit. Even if the culture of the school seems to permit teachers certain liberties unavailable to students, if the rules are intended to apply to all, the intentional teacher tries his or her level best to avoid participating. Teachers may be permitted a handful of actions, such as drinking coffee in a classroom, that students accept as being the natural and distinct privilege of adults beyond the special and necessary permissions required to do their jobs, but beyond this, the wise teacher should not venture.

The purpose of this perhaps narrow and puritanical-sounding proscription is not just to deny oneself what students may not have but rather to keep one's footing in the community on a solid base of right behavior. Students watch faculties intently, and although some students may envy as cool a teacher who places himself or herself above a rule or two, ultimately an arrogation of privilege undermines a teacher's work even as it undermines the school's ability to sustain its culture. A teacher who really objects to a rule or practice of the school can work to change it or find ways of minimizing its impact on his or her life, or he or she can look for another position. The most pusillanimous approach, roundly to be condemned, is for the teacher to "work" students on behalf of an issue, using the righteous energy of students to accomplish his or her own goals. It is one thing for a teacher to share students' dismay and even to suggest ways for students to act on their concerns, but it is quite another for a teacher to whip students into a frenzy on a matter of personal interest that would not otherwise have excited student opinion.

Presence and punctuality

It should also be a matter of professional pride to the intentional teacher to appear when and where presence is required and to meet all deadlines, including, if the school legislates this, the return of student work. One teacher's face might not be missed in an assembly or chapel, but if the school expects the teacher to be present, the teacher should be. Some schools are casual in regard to enforcing such matters, while others will have an administrator designated to track such things, but if the school is to be a functioning community, all of its members must take part in community gatherings and share alike in its experiences. Even if no one is officially keeping tabs on the teacher's whereabouts, someone, student or colleague, is vaguely aware of who is missing, and in time a teacher with a tendency to play hooky will acquire a reputation, if not as a shirker, at least as someone who has not fully bought into the school's essential work. Independent school teachers are generally not expected to "work to rule"; those choosing to stick to the minimum are not only doing a little less than their jobs but also losing an opportunity to put their stamp on the community as active contributors.

With regard to deadlines and due dates, the intentional teacher makes a positive effort to be on time with comments, grades, paperwork, library book returns, and personal paperwork for the business office or other non-academic functions of the school. One does this in order not to inconvenience others—to ensure that parents will receive quarterly reports in a timely fashion, for example—but also to establish oneself as eager to keep the wheels of the school moving and capable of managing the business of life efficiently. We have already addressed the importance of giving students timely feedback on their work, and similarly we have suggested one business day as the outside window of time for returning a parent telephone call or e-mail. Even when the teacher is unable to provide a full response within that time, a quick message to the effect of "I'm on it" will establish the teacher's commitment.

Teachers finding themselves regularly in default with regard to deadlines at many schools will land in hot water, but fear of consequences should not drive punctuality. If the teacher feels in danger of being overwhelmed and inundated, the first step is to make a plan to resolve the issue and the second is to inform the prospective recipient of the potential problem; just as we prefer students to alert us in advance of a missed deadline, so do schools dislike being surprised when they are in expectation of a report or other important information. The worst course of action is to go underground, to withdraw from sight or contact in the hope that the issue will just go away. Until the work is completed, the issue will not go away, and the only thing that does disappear when a teacher seeks to wish away a problem is credibility.

Boundaries

For many teachers one of the most difficult areas to manage is the matter of boundaries. These can be the subtle dividing lines between personal and professional life, delicate relations between colleagues or between the teacher and a supervisor, or the sometimes perilously permeable space between teacher and student. Independent schools have a host of events requiring attendance, and even more at which attendance is desirable. Regardless of a teacher's age or experience, the challenges of maintaining self-possession and balance amid these demands can be great, but the consequences of losing either can be disastrous.

There will be times when school seems to pervade every aspect of a teacher's life. Lessons must be planned, work graded, telephone calls returned, new messages in the e-mail in-box attended to, books ordered. Worries over a single student may keep the teacher awake, or a great idea may inspire an extra evening of fevered planning. At times the minutiae of school may crowd out family, pets, roommates, friends, and lovers. When these times occur, the teacher needs to just put his or her head down and plow through.

But...

The wise teacher finds a way to keep hold of a little bit of time, even on the busiest days, to manage life and to acknowledge the demands that come from places other than school. Whether it is to read a few pages from a non-school book before going to sleep or going for a run, row, or a bicycle ride, the teacher will find that erecting an impenetrable barrier between school and at least a small part of each day will do wonders for the teacher's (and his or her household's) state of mind.

Technology has created greater challenges for teachers than just e-mail and the telephone. Social networking websites represent the social milieu in which young adults reside, but these websites—more or less universally accessible—provide their own set of challenges. The teacher whose site contains material that is in any way questionable runs the risk of being questioned. A 2008 article in the *Washington Post* detailed a reporter's cursory search through one site for pages belonging to members who identified as teachers and the rather shocking results; any parent, student, or supervisor could have found the same material. Teachers the reporter contacted were horrified to learn that they had been "discovered," and the reporter did find instances in which public schools had instituted disciplinary proceedings after being alerted to professionally inappropriate material online. Rumors persist that employers do occasionally troll these sites for evidence of employee misbehavior, and although a handful of schools have landed on the side of discouraging teachers from exploring student's sites, schools have only begun to address the question of teachers' pages. All these sites remain fair game for public perusal; teachers are urged to keep their virtual presence at least rated PG-13, or perhaps PG for those working in early childhood, the lower elementary grades, or especially conservative schools. Certainly, using these sites for casual communication with students would be inappropriate, and some schools actively forbid this. Others are experimenting with using social networking sites as a curriculum resource, with results yet to be seen.

The teacher needing to communicate with students electronically should stick to the school e-mail system, if possible, so as to leave a clear and recoverable record of any contact with students. "Instant messaging" or texting students should also be avoided, unless the school e-mail should offer a chat function, and, as in any communication with students, the teacher should be scrupulous in avoiding anything that could be taken as suggestive, professionally inappropriate, or even double entendre.

Relations with colleagues can become dicey at times, as well. Sometimes one is simply involved in a spat, but in the small and emotionally intense world of a school, small issues can be magnified, and word spreads. Professionalism dictates that teachers keep their issues with colleagues confined; sharing one's woes in a search for allies or sympathy usually backfires.

Romantic entanglements can pose great challenges, even when the cause is true love and the lovers young and free. Professional behavior between community members—cordial, friendly, but not overly affectionate—is the expectation. If the entanglement is extremely thorny, threatening marriages or established relationships, or if it is ending in a notably distressing or public way, the participants' friends and colleagues will find themselves in a social minefield for a while amid the inevitable side-taking and recrimination. The actual parties involved (who should have known better) should not be surprised—although they are likely to act both surprised and indignant—when the school administration expresses concern. The death of a student may be the only thing more upsetting to the equilibrium of a school than a romantic affair between colleagues that destroys a family, and those who have been in schools that have experienced either will attest to the trauma involved; the impact is redoubled in a boarding school. The intentional teacher would be advised to steer as clear as possible of such situations, either as a participant or as a confidante or active ally, but, alas, advice is easier to give than to accept in these cases.

It is worth mentioning that the intentional teacher ought not neglect the people who actually make a school function: administrative staff, receptionists, buildings and grounds crew, custodial staff, food service workers, and all other employees at the school who may not teach but who provide essential services for teachers and students. The congenial assistance of school staff behind the scenes can make a teacher's life infinitely more easy and pleasant, and these people often encounter enough impersonal treatment in their work to truly appreciate those who express genuine gratitude and support for their efforts and who approach them with a natural, polite, and cheerful demeanor; good teachers make clear to students that treating staff with respect is the right, the only, way to behave, as well. No matter what the circumstance—even dealing with students—teachers who make a difference in their schools also tend to be those who never forget to say "please" and "thank you."

Boundaries in relations with students can also be extremely hazy. Friendly relations between a teacher and students should be the norm, and the teacher who finds himself or herself coming to feel dislike for a student should realize that this, too, is a dangerous boundary. The best course of action, as noted earlier, is to lean into the discomfort by working to understand the student and his or her situation and needs more deeply as well as to examine the sources of the teacher's own antipathy. If a deeper acquaintance can be established in a school-related situation, this might prove helpful. Often the most difficult of students are those whose personal backgrounds include stresses or challenges that, when known, evoke at least understanding, if not empathy, allowing dislike to turn into something more positive. A difficult student may suddenly surprise the teacher by an unexpected act of character excellence or creative ebullience, and the dark spell is broken. But it is the teacher's duty to ameliorate matters.

The uncrossable line

Emotional entanglements between teachers and students are not unknown, but here again the intentional teacher's task—and sacred responsibility, perhaps beyond any other—is to make sure that these do not occur in his or her life. The teacher must turn away from the student, which is difficult and itself at the outer limits of professional behavior, and figure out a course of action. If the student seems to be pursuing the teacher, either romantically or to fulfill some other vague emotional need, the teacher must immediately take the situation to a supervisor or counselor (and not just a friend) to make sure that the school is both alert to the situation and working to build the necessary firewall between the student and the teacher as well as to help the student. If the teacher feels emotionally attracted to the student, the teacher must put professional and personal distance between himself or herself and the student; counseling is probably in order, but stronger measures may ultimately be required or, worst of all, imposed.

The much more elusive middle ground occurs when the relationship between a teacher and a student, or a group of students, passes beyond a very subtle boundary in which casual give-and-take begins to involve personal content that in some way privileges the students over others, including other teachers. The teacher who finds himself or herself freely sharing with students a critique of a supervisor, a colleague, or the school has crossed a line, and the teacher who attempts to manipulate a situation by courting student opinion is on the far side of this line. In the same way, the teacher who shares or simply agrees with students' critiques of peers or other teachers has passed over the border of unprofessional behavior. The teacher who lets students in on his or her personal secrets or those of colleagues has also crossed a line. The teacher who needs to be "in" with students and who uses meanness or secrets to achieve some warped version of coolness has, at the least, a great deal of growing up to do.

The charismatic teacher

Here lies the danger of the charismatic teacher. Most of us have experienced at least one of those: the teacher with the personality, charm, and ability to make students feel special, all somehow *entre nous*. Often these teachers are devastatingly effective in the classroom with many students, able to wrap a class around their little fingers and make the most mundane of subjects exciting. Schools can make great pets out of such teachers, exploiting their charm and popularity for promotion and fundraising. The teacher becomes, or at least seems to become, indispensable.

There is often another side of this coin, showing up frequently enough to be recognizable as a pattern. Sometimes the charismatic teacher has wormed his or her way into the love of students by allowing little excursions, in both directions, across professional boundaries. An offhand comment about another teacher here, a smile as the student carps about an annoying classmate there, a little privilege for a favored student or a tiny public snub of an unpopular community member—these small expressions of a need to cultivate approval may add up to popularity but eat away at the integrity of the community. Strangely, it is probably this same need for approval that makes some of these teachers so effective in the classroom:

they pour their hearts into making learning exciting in order to make themselves seem exciting. Unchecked, the charismatic teacher may transmute popularity into a kind of power within the community that awes and even frightens away some students and not a few colleagues; others will want to be drawn into the teacher's circle in order to bask in his or her aura. In any case, barriers grow between segments of the community, the in-crowd and the rest. Perhaps something will occur that causes the school to take note and try to sort the situation out, but it may persist for years.

The intentional teacher might well envy the charismatic teacher in a way, and it is altogether possible that the intentional teacher might in fact toy, even subconsciously, with becoming that figure of grace and power. I think, however, that the wise teacher will know when he or she is at risk of falling into this role, and with luck he or she can redirect all of the things that make the charismatic teacher wonderful—at least at first—so as to take his or her work to a new level of true and balanced professional excellence. It has been observed that charismatic teachers have a high likelihood of reaching a stage of "burn-out" or sudden dissatisfaction with their work and their career. Dependent on personal magnetism and popularity, they may have never had much incentive to develop a sustainable relationship with all aspects of their profession, and when the magnetism weakens or more popular newcomers steal the scene, they flounder.

The redirection begins with the realization that a teaching career may more easily be made authentic and meaningful by working hard to better one's craft just as one works to be authentic, to be oneself. Far better to improve the substance and quality of one's teaching than to seek the adulation of students through manipulation. The energy of the prima donna is all emotional, dazzling the crowd with swoops and leaps of classroom pyrotechnics, but in the end the work is done to serve the teacher more than the students. The intentional teacher, no less passionate and no less skilled, focuses on students and on reaching every one, including those for whom the showmanship of the charismatic teacher might have missed its mark.

A teacher just entering the profession, looking over a sea of faces who are predisposed to like what they see and hear, can make a choice: play to the crowd, cash in on youth and coolness, and be the flavor of the year, or maybe two. Or, use those same qualities to build strong teaching relationships with each student—planning ever more stimulating curriculum, building an impressive and inclusive classroom culture, and mastering the art of teaching—for a lifetime's worth of satisfaction and efficacy.

The teacher who understands the nuances of what it means to be "the consummate professional"—the highest praise a teacher can receive, in the minds of many educators—is not going to have to give the matter of professional behavior a great deal of thought, because it will come naturally. Yet another challenge is left, however: to use skill and wisdom to make a difference not just in the lives of students but in the school as a whole, and perhaps even in the profession. As a collaborative field, teaching needs practitioners who understand that great teaching is the foundation on which great schools are built and who want to make a contribution to that undertaking.

CHAPTER XV

The Teacher in the School

"Leadership and learning are indispensable to each other."
— JOHN F. KENNEDY

The intentional teacher may indeed be the consummate professional, a wizard in the classroom and a dynamo of efficiency and spirit around the school. Respected by colleagues and administrators, beloved of students, and a favorite of families, he or she takes what it means to be an effective educator to the highest level. He or she is a student not only of his or her teaching field but also of the art of teaching itself. Curriculum, assessment, and pedagogy are grist to his or her mill, and students are excited to enter the classroom each day.

Even if this rosy picture does not quite describe every independent school teacher, sooner or later the teacher finds him- or herself in the groove, able to manage professional and personal life and even, as time goes on, to take on a few new responsibilities in both. New challenges loom, and new experiences lead to greater confidence and, as often as not, a desire for more.

Within the profession of teaching, there are limitless opportunities for personal growth and the expansion of professional capacity. A school, however, may seem to be of finite size; soon a teacher with energy and ideas may begin to feel a few constraints. The wise teacher will take that feeling and respond to it by exploring ways to dig more deeply into the culture and purposes of the school and to begin the process of making his or her mark on the school not just as a fine classroom teacher but also as a passionate exponent of the school and a believer in its possibilities.

The teacher and the administration

If the intentional teacher is fortunate—and I believe this kind of luck comes to a majority of independent school teachers—he or she will have experienced an open door to the offices of power. Department heads, division leaders, deans, and even the head of school will have welcomed the teacher into their offices for a few words, to discuss a child or an idea, and just to further an acquaintance by chatting about life and work. Perhaps the teacher has had an idea and has dropped in to seek support or permission to carry it out, or perhaps the teacher has had a serious concern about a student or even a policy of the school—a point of disagreement, even.

Any teacher ought to be curious about the individuals who guide the school; in most schools, talk about "the administration" consumes a fair amount of faculty energy, whether the topics are positive musings or grousing. A point comes, though, where such talk becomes unproductive, and even unprofessional, and at that point—where the group begins to express idle speculation or speak in terms of futility around some aspect of school life, the teacher has a choice: add to the chatter, or step up and act.

The drop-ins with administrators, however brief, will have introduced the teacher to the inner life of the institution, to the points of contact between the school's mission and the challenges of defining it in practice. It would be my hope that the intentional teacher, having put so much into his or her own work, would not be intimidated or put off either by talking to administrators in the flesh or by the tenor of the idle chatter but rather intrigued by the idea of people making a difference in the school.

Quite possibly a teacher could spend the better part of a career paying little heed to administrative matters that did not affect him or her directly. Although some schools require all teachers to partake of some form of committee work, some teachers have no great interest in matters of policy or governance, preferring to focus on their own work, their own students, and their own growth. Others are uncomfortable dealing with the decision makers who set the pay scale or decree the mission. The intentional teacher may be among these, although I hope not. If so, there is no harm in a teacher demurring from work or responsibilities from which he or she is disinclined, even if it means a loss of opportunity to make another kind of difference.

But for other teachers, even from the outset of their careers, there will be something exciting about the idea of contributing to the policies and ideas that drive the institution. In part the teacher will live the differences he or she makes—a new or modified policy or practice will alter in some way the nature of the teacher's work. To participate in making change is to exert some small control over his or her working life. Many teachers will find that to be asked to do this work is a gift and an acknowledgment that their wisdom and their concern for the school transcends the classroom.

It is probably not the norm in independent schools for a teacher relatively new to the school to be invited to participate in significant work
beyond the teacher's job description. To a degree this is a matter of mercy,
but at the same time schools may be losing valuable contributors; after all,
they did hire the teacher, presumably to make an immediate difference in
the academic and extracurricular life of the school. But a number of schools
will welcome the new teacher into the school's work not just as a teacher
but as a participant in the deliberations of the institution. Where active
discussion of school policies and practices is part of the culture of faculty
or department meetings, the new teacher will be drawn into thinking about
areas perhaps outside his or her immediate frame of reference but nonetheless important to the school in carrying out its mission. Perhaps he or she
will find him- or herself on a standing or ad hoc committee, looking into
some matter and reporting back to the faculty, the administration, or even
the governing body. This will be a golden opportunity for the teacher; a
bit of extra work, yes, but a chance to collaborate, to influence, and then
to present ideas that he or she had a part in creating—a chance to make a
mark, right away!

But for most teachers such opportunities will come more slowly.
The teacher who is interested, however, should be direct in sharing this
desire, probably directly with a senior administrator or certainly with a
department head, and discussing the nature of his or her interests and
predilections.

The teacher and the governing body

The intentional teacher, even if uninterested in larger issues in the school,
ought to be aware of the structures by which the school is governed and
administered. Independent schools vary in their governance, although the
vast majority are operated, at the most formal level, by a self-perpetuating
board of trustees (or governors, or overseers; nomenclature varies), volunteers who oversee the management of the school and, at the least, hire
and evaluate the head of school, set the school's mission, and determine,
or at least approve, the school budget, including tuition levels. Members of
the board serve for set terms, and there is usually an executive committee
made up of the board officers. The head of school may sit on the board,
and certainly the head attends and reports at all meetings. Board members
at most schools are a mix of current and past parents, former students, and
"friends" of the school. The traditional role of board members is to contribute one of the "3 W's": work, wisdom, or wealth, but oftentimes board

members are experienced in such positions and have plenty of work and wisdom to offer, even if wealth may be their most obvious qualification. In some schools, boards meet frequently and board members are well known in the school, while in others meetings are less frequent and board members more remote. Whether the board is familiar or formidable, its primary and legal responsibility is the well-being of the school, and the policies it sets are directed toward that end. A number of independent school boards include elected faculty members who participate as constituent representatives to the board; a few even include students. A few academic administrators, the chief financial officer, and the chief development officer may attend board meetings regularly, and college or next-school counselors and the admissions director may report on occasion.

Boards are most likely to interface with faculties through committees that include groups involved with academic program, student life, buildings and grounds, and sometimes even salary and benefits. But there is a wholly appropriate firewall between the faculty and such committees, which do not participate in the *administration* of the school but rather make recommendations on board policies to *support* the administration. In many cases these committees invite classroom teachers to sit either as regular committee members or to report on specific issues. These teachers may have a voice and even a vote on committee matters (although they probably do not attend full board meetings unless a special committee report is to be made), and in the work of the committee they both become known (and occasionally are auditioned for further leadership roles) and play an indirect but significant role in the governance process.

While seniority is often a factor in deciding who is chosen for committee work, interest or particular expertise can also matter. Because trustees are volunteers with limited time, committee work tends to be intensive and focused, with little time for on-the-job training of members. Teachers on board committees tend to be those who are respected for the informed nature of their opinions, their tact and finesse, their record of hard work, and above all their obvious commitment to the school and its mission. While a teacher with original ideas may be invited to join, a teacher known to be at odds with the school's administration or basic values is unlikely to be tapped.

If board committee positions are beyond the teacher's grasp, other opportunities to become actively involved in school issues are always in the offing. Small committees, even within a department or a division, may be exploring ways to improve or streamline practice or to institute new programs, and there may be standing advisory groups with defined agendas that meet regularly with administrators. Perhaps the teacher has an original idea of a scale beyond the capacity of a single person to manage; he or she may enlist the assistance of others, becoming at once a potential innovator and a leader.

What matters is that the teacher with an abiding interest in the way the school works and in the conditions in which he or she is expected to perform his or her duties find outlets for this interest. In a sense the teacher must find his or her voice within the school, both a timbre of professional and positive energy that resonates with the larger aims of the school and a pitch on key with that of both leaders and potential collaborators. The teacher must also discover, perhaps through trial and error or perhaps because of excitement about a newly discovered idea or a deeply held conviction, the issues and areas on which he or she wants to work.

The teacher is likely to find, after embarking on the work of making the school a better place, that his or her stature begins to rise. The teacher may not be very ambitious, or he or she may not actually welcome a bit more attention, but most teachers discover that involvement with institutional issues is refreshing if only because, after spending days and nights in the land of children and teenagers, working with adults and being regarded as having adult things to offer is both a change and a validation. One feels "professional" in ways that are not always present even in one's classroom.

There are, of course, other ways for a teacher to contribute to the overall life of the school besides committee work. Many schools appreciate the willingness of teachers to act as admission tour guides and interviewers, and the development office may have vast needs for volunteers that teachers can fill. A growing number of schools have discovered the value of relatively recently hired classroom teachers as ambassadors in the recruiting of faculty; that a school would select a first- or second-year classroom teacher to conduct preliminary interviews at a job fair is a powerful statement of the esteem in which teachers are held and sends an equally strong message that teachers are invited—indeed expected—to play an important part in the life of the school from their first days on campus.

A place to make a difference

There are of course often extra duties that need to be performed. Some schools assign dance chaperones or monitors at athletic events, but others depend on the kindness of faculty volunteers for this work. Those who do step up and cheerfully take on these responsibilities are admired for their attitude and appreciated for the work, and every teacher should make a point of performing these unglamorous but necessary chores frequently enough both to understand their nature and to observe students in yet other milieus.

If the teacher's skills and dispositions tend toward curricular innovation, venues for sharing and testing new ideas are plentiful. A division or department meeting may include "teacher show and tell" segments for offering up new or particularly successful practices for peer review, and exemplary work may find itself on display at events for families or governing bodies. Beyond the school, the teacher might approach the staff at the regional independent schools association to find out whether it sponsors meetings or conferences at which presentations or workshops by teachers at member schools are on offer. On a larger scale, many disciplinary and age-level professional organizations like the National Council of Teachers of Mathematics and the National Association for the Education of Young Children have regional as well as national conferences at which presentations by educators are the main order of business; umbrella organizations such as the National Association of Independent Schools, the Coalition of Essential Schools, and the Association for Supervision and Curriculum Development do the same. Websites of such organizations regularly feature conference CFPs (calls for presenters). If a teacher has an idea or a program that has worked well, packaging the idea as a presentation to a group of peers is both an excellent kind of professional development and terrific personal and professional reinforcement.

Along with presentation, the teacher who enjoys writing can find publication opportunities that range from school magazines to personal blogs to professional journals, online and print. Many of the latter are open to thoughtful opinion pieces as well as being in more or less constant need of book reviewers, and a few are eager for straight reportage on issues and events. While "the wonderful thing my perfect school does" articles sometimes need to be refocused as "here's an idea that has worked well for us that might have utility at other schools," great ideas or successful programs and practices ought to be shared, and the intentional teacher will probably be eager to do this, in whichever ways best suit him or her. A few teachers take great delight in monitoring newspapers and pouncing on opportunities to write incisive—and frequently published—letters to the editor.

The teacher who finds himself or herself out in the world, sharing ideas in person or in print, will of course enjoy the recognition and sometimes notoriety that come with this public status. But the intentional teacher should not lose sight of the far greater value that his or her contributions have for both the school and the profession. A school whose faculty is known among educators as having and sharing worthy ideas will perforce find its reputation enhanced; if the school becomes identified with a particular practice or idea, this is a permanent institutional asset. As for the profession, the throwing open of the doors behind which independent school teachers have practiced their craft alone for so many years will benefit colleagues, and above all students, forever after. As grandiose as this claim may seem, open dialogue among teachers is every bit as important as that same dialogue among scholars and physicians.

Becoming a teacher-leader

The teacher who has become involved in some or all of this work will find himself or herself in increasing demand as a voice and a presence within the school. A source of ideas, wisdom, and work, he or she will have evolved into a teacher-leader, a professional category seldom seen noted as a job but understood by all as a valued class of adults within a school. With the role come the rewards of respect and perhaps an expanded job description along with certain responsibilities, unstated but profoundly important, both to the school and the profession. While it may seem crass to mention it, independent school salary scales often afford considerable latitude for what is sometimes referred to as "merit pay," and the active and positive teacher-leader may find his or her efforts materially rewarded, as well.

As one whose ideas and efforts have influenced the course of the school and perhaps the work of those at other schools, the teacher-leader is to a degree identified with the school and all it stands for. A real obligation goes with this identification to uphold the school, its faculty, its administration, and its students. Presumably this upholding comes easily to the teacher-leader, but there will be moments of friction or dissonance. As others within the school will be looking to the teacher-leader for guidance as a role model for other teachers and perhaps as a beacon for students, he or she must handle delicate situations, including his or her own doubts, judiciously. As a leader of the faculty, of the school, and of students he or she must be careful to weigh in only after thinking through not only the issue but how his or her stance or attitude will be received and will affect others. The teacher-leader's status may have been gained inadvertently, and at times it may be uncomfortable, but he or she will understand the mandate to serve the school and its students even beyond personal feelings. A situation may call for debate, even active dissidence as an advocate for the faculty, but the teacher-leader will need to conduct him- or herself with all the positive energy and grace that brought the mantle of leadership in the first place. Others may wish to make trouble, but the teacher-leader's role in the fray must be statesmanlike even in dissent. Fortunately, such circumstances are unusual.

Perhaps no one else at a school is in a better position to interpret and internalize the best values of a school than the classroom teachers, and true teacher-leaders, invigorated by the prospect of working with others to realize these values more fully, can be among the school's most precious assets. If they can sustain the enthusiasm and commitment that brought them this status, and if they can continue to find ways to contribute to the school that are meaningful to themselves and to the community, their careers will pass smoothly and honorably, their impact felt by generations of students and colleagues and seen in the luster on the reputation of the school.

As to personal satisfaction, teachers will find this where they can, but few of us are immune to the pleasures of being held in some regard in our schools and in our fields. Our families and friendships may matter more, but to see one's contributions and efforts bear fruit in a workplace we love is a truly wonderful thing.

CHAPTER XVI

A Teacher's Path

"Every place you have been is on the road to where you are."
— MIMI HARRINGTON

The teacher setting out on a career can have little idea of what is to come, intentional as he or she may wish to be. Polishing one's craft and making one's presence felt do not guarantee a smooth or straight path through life. What the path will become for an individual teacher is both a mystery and a challenge, with periods of unalloyed joy and moments of anguish. But as the path unfolds, the key will be for the teacher to remain intentional—to know his or her strengths, his or her needs, and above all to have a purpose. Few professions offer more opportunities than teaching to build a meaningful life; the ever-changing panorama of students, colleagues, and families guarantees that a teacher will touch, and be touched by, the strivings, plights, and joys of many.

I ended the first chapter of this book by urging the newly fledged teacher not to be afraid to say yes, either to opportunity or to responsibility. Generally I would regard this as good advice in life: When intriguing ideas present themselves, even when the outcome is utterly unpredictable, embracing opportunity is a pretty good way to make a rich, interesting life. Truly intriguing ideas do not come along every day, for teachers or for most other people, but when a new school is looking for faculty or the teacher is offered a chance to write or present or a chance to serve as part of a group doing interesting work, think hard. Consider the alternatives, consider the benefits; consider, if you will, the regrets.

"Ages and stages"

The needs of the intentional teacher will change with the passages of life, from young adulthood to middle age and beyond. Family relations will alter as partners, parents, and perhaps children demand attention in new ways and as one discovers new things about oneself. As this happens, so will the teacher's relationships with his or her profession and school change; new priorities and changing conditions may make it desirable or even necessary to move from one school to another. At each one even the finest teacher will need to re-establish himself or herself as a respected professional, or even as a teacher-leader.

For many teachers there comes a need in life to take time out, often to devote energy to rearing a family or to obtain an additional degree. This might be for a semester or even just for the statutory time allowed under the federal Family and Medical Leave Act after the birth of a child or the illness of a parent, or it might be for a decade or more. Reentry will pose its challenges, whether for the parent of a newborn who is juggling sleeplessness, feeding, and child-care issues with all the requirements of teaching, even with a reduced job description, or for a teacher whose skills may feel rusty and who must rebuild confidence in his or her own instincts or perhaps prepare to climb a new learning curve as a school changes. But "timeout" teachers bring back with them to the classroom life skills and worldly understandings that are likely to make them better, stronger professionals.

At some point in their careers most teachers consider leaving the profession. Many teachers ponder cashing in, they might hope, on their organizational, creative, collaborative, and motivational skills to work in a field perhaps related to, or perhaps very far from, their teaching. Others are tempted to leap the other way, following a path of service that might promise extraordinary personal satisfaction if little financial reward. Curious by nature, many teachers would like the opportunity to travel and experience new places and new cultures, either as part of a new profession or as the central focus of retirement years.

Some teachers respond to restlessness by moving to new schools. The motivations for changing are many, from wanting to try a new region, to being near family or friends, to remaining with a partner who is relocating, to looking for a school with a more congenial culture or philosophy; we have written as if all is always well for the intentional teacher, but sometimes schools fall short of their promise, and sometimes teachers do not fit in quite so well at a school. People change, and so do schools; it is not uncommon for a school to have an uptick in faculty turnover in the year or two following a change of head as teachers and leaders adjust to alterations in a school's course or ways of doing things. The search, the move, and the adjustment to new schools all become part of the experiences that shape the teacher, each one adding in its way to the teacher's stock of wisdom and perspective.

For many teachers the way to shake off feelings of being in a rut is to make their summers as much of a change of pace as possible, either by finding stimulating or high-paying jobs in fields unrelated to teaching or by saving their pennies during the school year for travel. Some are fortunate enough to be able to sign onto their own schools' summer programs, life-guarding, leading student travel, or just working with a new age group of students. Others hightail it for the wilderness or the beach, finding jobs as wait-staff, guides, guards, or instructors. For travelers there is the promise of funding; a number of Federally funded summer study programs include generous stipends, while many schools offer their own travel-grant pro-grams for teachers. Some teachers connect their travel to curriculum and work the tax code to discount aspects of their journeys.

To take advantage of such opportunities presupposes that the teacher has the summer "off," and most teachers will only grudgingly allow others to use that word. Many schools require faculty to do summer reading, while others have occasional or regular requirements for summer meetings about curriculum or other topics. E-mail and voicemail connect the teacher more tightly to the world of work than in years past, and so things may come up that require the teacher's attention, even as he or she is bent on lounging by the shore and catching up on reading, friendships, or family matters.

The administrator's path

Moving from the classroom to administration is something that most teachers consider, sometimes because an offer is at hand, sometimes just because the money and prestige seem better, and sometimes because they are ready for a major change but do not wish to leave the familiar ground of the independent school world. A few teachers enter the profession with a plan and even a timetable that reaches its climax in the chair behind a head of school's desk, but most administrators seem to have arrived in their positions by longer and more circuitous paths. Oftentimes the route was purely accidental, as one responsibility grew, led to another, and another, until the teacher was no longer actually teaching, and instead of children, adults were coming into the office.

As often as not, the gateway to administration is either a department headship or leadership of a major committee in the school. Sometimes the teacher has embraced and then become identified with an issue or cause at the school, and over time the work around the issue grows to take up the equivalent of a class or two. At that point, other related administrative duties may pop up as if by magic, and suddenly the teacher finds him- or herself dealing with one of two things: an active desire to lead but limited possibilities within one's school, or an opportunity too good to pass up.

The first is more of a challenge, because it may not admit of an easy solution. The teacher-leader, department head, or committee chair who finds himself or herself enjoying administrative work in some area or areas may discover administrative ambitions within. Perhaps these are also being encouraged by a senior colleague or a mentor, who urges the teacher on. The teacher may enjoy working with the big picture or organizing things to make them run smoothly. Matters of curriculum and pedagogy may excite even greater interest when the person considers them on a departmental, divisional, or school-wide scale. The more he or she is around ideas about how to do things in the school, the more ideas he or she seems to have. At some point, the daily work in the classroom does not seem quite as compelling as meetings of the department heads, the committee, or the working group. Maybe, just maybe, being an administrator could be as interesting, or even more so, than teaching or heading a department. The problem is, there may not be a position readily available to the teacher at the school. Stay and wait? Cool it, and just stay the course? Change schools?

If, on the other hand, the person is not so compelled by his or her own ambition as by a kind of pressure exerted by events that seems to be driving him or her toward administration, the problem is, how to respond? Perhaps the school does have an opening, a division directorship or a deanship that looks interesting but would mean giving up sufficiently satisfying work in the classroom or the department. But colleagues keep saying, *Go for it! Apply! You would be great!* And in fact he or she cannot really make a compelling case for *not* going for it. There are some challenges in the position that he or she feels confident to meet, and the less visible but perhaps harder parts of the job are certainly within one's power to handle. The children are going to be heading to college in a few years, and this would probably mean more money. Summer vacation would be shorter, but it would still be four weeks. Well, why not?

In this case, an administrator is born, translated from teacher-leader, department chair, or the like to an administrator. Along with the office and administrative support, the new administrator will find that some relations with colleagues will have changed; some will feel strained, others more formal. Along with respect, there is occasional awe, and there may be fewer wide-open conversations with old friends. The administrator wears team colors picked by the head of school and must support that team publicly through thick and thin. Mostly this is easy, but occasionally there are twinges of discomfort. Fortunately, the administrative group is congenial and able to air issues frankly and honestly; consensus is easy. The change is a success. Even occasional problems—having to confront a long-time colleague about some issue, being part of major disciplinary decisions—are manageable, and the person realizes that he or she is good at the work. Working with a mix of students and adults regularly is stimulating and occasionally really exciting. As much as the person might miss having his or her own classes, administration feels good.

But in the first case, when ambition stirs but there is no way to honor it within the school, the stakes are higher. To seek an administrative position will mean leaving a school in which one has thrived and grown. With luck, wise counsel will present itself in the form of a friendly head, or perhaps the teacher has been lucky enough to find another mentor in the profession. The person may take tentative steps—updating a résumé, arranging an informational interview with a headhunter who specializes in administrative searches—just to test the waters. Magically, an interesting position opens up at a school that seems to be a potential match and, with his or her head's blessing and encouragement, an interview is arranged. If the vibe is good, the process advances. If not, there is no rush. It is still early in the spring, before notice must be given. In time the right job appears and the candidate is successful. He or she is delighted to find that the new school actually pays part of moving expenses; this is not uncommon. The teacher bids a sad and fond farewell to the current school—he or she will be missed!—and off he or she goes, to make a new home in a new community, with new surprises and a whole new cast of characters to be learned. In some ways it is back to the beginning, but now the person is an new administrator in a new school. He or she knows that listening well and truly understanding the culture—remembering how PIG'S EAR helped before—are going to be the keys to success, and that to suggest or impose sudden changes (even though part of the job may be initiating and leading some work that has been handed down by the board of the new school as a strategic priority) will undercut effectiveness, as will too many references to "my old school." But the new administrator has seen it before and is ready for the challenge.

Some administrators will continue to rise toward headships, while others will find themselves permanently happy as division directors, academic deans, or in other positions. Headship seems to require boundless energy, tremendous vision, a real interest in the business and development side of schools, and a thick skin. Fortunately enough people seem to possess these qualities to ensure a good supply, although great headships, where a leader's vision, philosophy of education, and personal qualities so perfectly mesh with the identity and needs of a school that the match seems made in heaven, are not quite so common.

Administrators, including heads, are as prone to seeking new schools as teachers are, often simply looking for new challenges. This may involve an upward trajectory with regard to position, to school size, or even prestige. (While we have not addressed the latter issue, to some independent school educators this matters very much, and teachers as much as students and families are happy to be associated with a place that is particularly old, august, beautiful, selective, or wealthy.) Along the way they may have good experiences and less successful ones; the question of match between a school and a senior administrator tends to be more visible and important than for a classroom teacher, as the administrator will interact with all quarters, making decisions that affect the large parts of the school community, if not all of it. Sometimes the perfect match is made, and the administrator grows old and gray happily carrying on the work of a school that grows and changes even as the best of administrators, like the best of teachers, continue to grow and change.

It is not unknown for a successful administrator, even a head of school, to determine at some point in his or her career that the attractions of the classroom outweigh those of the office. Moving back into a teacher's role in a school where one has been in authority is not easy for many reasons, but it has been done, and done well. It is easier, perhaps, to shift schools and to start fresh as a classroom teacher in a place where one is not required to explain oneself or be the subject of questions that are seldom asked directly. Those who have made such a move find that their delight in once again being able to focus directly on students makes whatever material sacrifices might have been involved more than worth the hassle of the process. They are likely to fall quickly into the role of teacher-leader, with experience and wisdom that are valuable to colleagues and to the school in many areas.

The teacher at mid-life

Educators, like other people, are prone to mid-life crises, periods of doubt and anxiety that come along just when they are needed least. They may have the person yearning for change, even cataclysmic change, in order to validate some vision of the self or to take one last crack at capturing a youthful dream just before it threatens to recede out of grasp. The educator who sees this happening in himself or herself will need to confront it; there is no good that can come from denying it until it bursts out in some startling or damaging way. With luck he or she will have loved ones or good friends who can name the issue and help the teacher through; a good therapist may be a better choice, and some schools may even make such help available through an Employee Assistance Program. Mid-life or mid- or late-career restlessness can be accompanied by a loss of effectiveness, or rather of the will to be effective—a feeling that the whole enterprise, whatever it may be, is futile, and that the person has no place in it anymore.

The answer to mid-life blahs of this sort is change. A full-blown change of school or career may be in order, but generally the intentional teacher or administrator, reflective and skillful, can find new challenges in his or her current school or perhaps new avenues for self-expression. A number of national and international teacher exchange programs, including Fulbright Fellowships, offer the prospect of a year or half-year of work in a new and invigorating setting. Taking a sabbatical to travel or study away from one's home is another option; even changing classrooms or buildings can be a tonic. The school, it is to be hoped, will understand and support this process, as the teacher or administrator has already demonstrated his or her worth. In the most extreme case the school might even suggest a sabbatical or paid leave of absence as a vote of confidence and an expression of its willingness to be patient.

Sometimes a very fine teacher will go off the rails. This may seem to have been inevitable from the teacher's personality or personal circumstances, or it may be that the school has quietly, even without intending to, withdrawn its respect and support for the teacher. In either case, it is a tragedy to be avoided; the wisdom and all the inner resources of the intentional teacher should be devoted to averting such an outcome in his or her own career or in that of a colleague.

A fine end

For the vast majority of teachers and administrators whose early years are marked by success, the later years of a career will bring more of the same. With developed habits of seeking professional development, leaning into discomfort when it arises, and pursuing professional and personal interests, these intentional educators will find that life continues to serve up delights along with the inevitable sorrows. Schools that recognize, foster, and honor the continuing value and vitality of experienced faculty can count on their contributions for the full length of a career.

At some point, the intentional teacher will conclude that the time has come to bring an end to the career. Perhaps this will be the time to pursue those dreams of service, travel, or yet another career. The curious mind of the teacher will seek new adventures and new opportunities to make the world a more interesting place, and whatever the new enterprise, quiet retirement or the passionate pursuit of new goals, it will surely be worthy and satisfying.

James Hilton's Mr. Chips, to whom both readers and moviegoers have said good-bye several times over, is often regarded as the most cloyingly sentimental of literary schoolteachers. But like our intentional teacher, Arthur Chipping built a career around his belief in children and his belief in the nobility of education as an ideal and as a practice. As his story concludes, the names of former students pass through his mind, each an individual, each a story, and each an integral part of his life. For our intentional teacher, it will be the students whose lives have been touched in the course of that career that will indeed form the core of lasting memories of a life well and purposefully lived.

Resources

CHAPTER 1: *One A Teacher's Will*

Some of those interested in or at least intrigued by teaching come via literature; the better novels set at least partially in independent schools provide a great way of journeying inside a teacher's mind. The class of the field includes *This Side of Paradise* by F. Scott Fitzgerald (Scribner's, 1920; little of St. Regis's School, to be honest, and a great deal more of Princeton), *A Separate Peace* by John Knowles (Macmillan, 1959), *Saying Grace* by Beth Gutcheon (HarperCollins, 1995), and *Old School* by Tobias Wolff (Knopf, 2003). *Goodbye, Mr. Chips* by James Hilton (Hodder & Brown, 1934), although set in a British school, is a moving (if possibly over-the-top to modern readers) portrayal of a very intentional teacher through the course of his career. Ethan Canin's story, "The Palace Thief" (1995; later filmed as *The Emperor's Club*) is also worthwhile.

Most "school" books are written from a student point of view, and for those who enjoy lighter fare P. G. Wodehouse (*The Gold Bat* stories, c. 1902–1908), Rudyard Kipling (*Stalky & Co.*, 1899), and Owen Johnson (*The Lawrenceville Stories*, 1909–22) evoke boarding school life a century or more past. More recently, Curtis Sittenfeld's *Prep* (Random House, 2005) offers a disquieting view of boarding school life in the late 20th century. *The Catcher in the Rye* by J. D. Salinger (Little, Brown, 1951) is another must-read, not so much for the view it provides of Pencey Prep as for its portrayal of the quintessential preppy "lost boy."

While the myriad films set in independent schools are designed to please a public conditioned to a stereotypical view of such schools as bastions of extreme wealth and privilege, most fall woefully short of presenting a true picture of life as it is (or was) in such schools. On the other hand, they often feature moral dilemmas that ring somewhat true to real teachers; *The Emperor's Club* (Michael Hoffman, 1998) and *School Ties* (Robert Mandel, 1992) are good samples. *The Dead Poets Society* (Peter Weir, 1989) captures a poorly run school in a bad moment, as does *Finding Forrester*

(Gus Van Sant, 2000), but both are reported to be inspirational in their way. Other films about school tend to focus on miracles putatively wrought by teachers; *The Blackboard Jungle* (Richard Brooks, 1955), *Conrack* (Martin Ritt, 1974), *Wildcats* (Michael Ritchie, 1986), and of course *Teachers* (Arthur Hiller, 1984). *The Prime of Miss Jean Brodie* (Ronald Neame, 1969) fits into this category, and the dramatization of the formidable Jaime Escalante teaching Advanced Placement mathematics in the classic *Stand and Deliver* (Ramón Menéndez, 1984) put a handle on lecture-based teaching even as it revealed the role a great teacher with high expectations can play in student success. *A Smile as Big as the Moon: A Teacher, His Class, and Their Unforgettable Journey* by Michael Kersjes (St. Martin's, 2002) is the moving story of a special education teacher who takes his class to NASA's Space Camp.

Inspirational and just plain helpful books on teaching tend to focus on specific aspects of the enterprise, but Theodore Sizer's *The Red Pencil: Convictions From Experience in Education* (Yale University Press, 2004) and *The Students Are Watching: Schools and the Moral Contract* (Beacon Press, 1999), the latter written with his spouse, Nancy Faust Sizer, address the great questions of teaching, as does, in a very compelling way, Parker Palmer's *The Courage to Teach: Exploring the Inner Landscape of a Teacher's Life* (Jossey-Bass, 1997). Frank McCourt's autobiography *Teacher Man: A Memoir* (Scribner, 2005) entertains as much as it reveals the soul of a teacher who fell into teaching and then could not bring himself to leave—the teacher's will at its most potent.

CHAPTER 11: *Finding a Teaching Job*

When the aspiring teacher has decided to explore career opportunities, the number of resources available to job-seekers in education is quite amazing. The guidebooks listed in the text—*Peterson's*, *Bunting & Lyon*, and *Porter Sargent*—provide addresses and information on individual schools for initial contacts and more information as the search process continues. The Association of Boarding Schools (TABS) and the National Coalition of Girls' Schools list member schools on their websites and also provide information on member schools' interests and missions; the NCGS site also lists some school position openings.

The prospective teacher can check out Karen Stabiner's *All Girls: Single-Sex Education and Why It Matters* (Riverhead, 2002) for background; not for everyone, single-sex schools have passionate advocates, and a number of successful schools have withstood the pressure to coeducate.

A number of teacher recruitment agencies contract with independent schools and place thousands of teachers each year. In all cases, placement fees are paid by the school, so candidates need not be concerned about having to pay money out front to obtain a teaching position. Many of these agencies sponsor fairs, and there is always a huge agency presence—with scheduled interview times—at the National Association of Independent Schools annual conference.

The largest of the agencies is Carney, Sandoe & Associates, headquartered in Boston but doing business nationally. Cal/West Educator Placement, led by the redoubtable Lee Miller, specializes in West Coast placements, while Educator's Ally, Independent School Placement, and Manhattan Placements focus on the New York City-tri-state area. Southern Teachers Agency has been placing teachers in the American South since 1902. Other well-regarded firms include The Education Group and Search Associates, which specializes in overseas teacher placements.

A handful of agencies specialize in placing candidates from underrepresented minorities. Both StratéGenius and The National Employment Minority Network (NEMNET) offer career services and consultative services for schools and have established extraordinary reputations; NEMNET also runs several job fairs each year.

The National Association of Independent Schools, through its Career Center, and virtually all regional independent schools associations (some of which are listed on the NAIS website under "accreditation"; others can be found by searching "independent schools association" plus a city, state, or region) post job listings for member schools on their websites; NAIS also allows candidates to register.

Education Week, a national publication for precollegiate educators in both public and private schools, offers a comprehensive career resource at its TopSchoolJobs.org website; other education-related publications and organizations have similar services. United States military personnel and veterans can become part of the Troops to Teachers program, as well.

Job-seekers can develop successful strategies by exploring how schools go about hiring. Two short volumes written for schools to guide them in the matter of hiring for diversity are *The Colors of Excellence: Hiring and Keeping Teachers of Color in Independent Schools* by Pearl Rock Kane and Alfonso Orsini (Teachers College Press, 2003) and *AISNE Guide to Hiring and Retaining Teachers of Color* by Michael Brosnan (Association of Independent Schools of New England, 2004—available by download at www.aisne.org). The early chapters of the author's own *An Admirable Faculty: Recruiting, Hiring, Training, and Retaining the Best Independent School*

Faculties (National Association of Independent Schools, 2005) could also be helpful.

Many independent schools offer internship programs for beginning teachers, including Shady Hill School in Massachusetts (whose program leads to a master's degree from Lesley University) and Punahou School in Hawaii, notable for the care with which teaching interns are selected, placed, and trained; candidates should inquire of any school of interest whether such a program is offered. The McMurry Fellows program places minority candidates in independent schools for one-year internships. A further resource for candidates and new teachers of color is Michael Brosnan's *Thriving in Independent Schools: A Guide for Teachers of Color* (Association of Independent Schools of New England, 2004), also referenced in the Resources section for Chapter IX.

CHAPTER III: *Knowing Students*

A tremendous resource for teachers wishing to know more about their students and their experience is *Fires in the Bathroom: Advice for Teachers from High School Students* by Kathleen Cushman and the Students of What Kids Can Do (New Press, 2003); the book even includes templates for teachers to collect data, and its high school focus does not diminish its power and utility. Almost any of the resources suggested in relation to Chapters VIII, "Families," IX, "Diversity," and XII, "Continuing Education: Child Development," could also illuminate aspects of students' lives for teachers.

A cottage industry has lately grown up around "exposing" the severe pressures on contemporary students and the various ways students have adapted. Many are frankly alarming, akin to the annual flow of frightening college admission articles in newspapers and magazines. The original of these is *The Hurried Child: Growing Up Too Fast Too Soon* by David Elkind (Addison-Wesley, 1994), and a more recent take is *The Pressured Child: Freeing Our Kids from Performance Overdrive and Helping Them Find Success in School and Life* by Michael Thompson (Random House, 2005); several books written for popular audiences that offer even more dire portraits of contemporary adolescence, at least, are *Doing School: How We Are Creating a Generation of Stressed-Out, Materialistic, and Miseducated Students* by Denise Clark Pope (Yale University Press, 2003) and Alexandra Robbins's rather lurid *The Overachievers: The Secret Lives of Driven Kids* (Hyperion, 2006).

Two works of non-fiction have been frequently cited in independent school circles as cautionary tales regarding the need for teachers to know and understand the experiences of students from nontraditional backgrounds. *Best Intentions: The Education and Killing of Edmund Perry* by Robert Sam Anson (Random House, 1987) tells the story of a New York City student at a northeastern boarding school and the double life he led—a street-wise city kid and a model scholarship student; in the end, the incompatibility of these roles spelled his doom. In *Black Ice* (Knopf, 1991), Lorene Carey recounts her difficult experience at a similar school and points out the ways that racism, institutionalized and individual, is still a powerful part of many students' lives in schools with, as the first title suggests, the best of intentions. Activist-comic Steven Tejada has turned his experience living in two worlds—his tough South Bronx neighborhood and an upscale progressive independent school followed by a prestigious liberal arts college—into a performance called "Boogie Down Journeys," a thought-provoking experience for students and teachers alike that should not be missed if the opportunity avails.

Cognitive theory in the past half century has made enormous strides. New breakthroughs in brain research, especially as imaging technologies enable "real-time" viewing of what thinking and learning look like in the brain, have confirmed some basic assumptions but promise more nuanced understandings as time goes on. The intentional teacher might want to pay attention to the cutting edge of neuroscience at least by checking out such popular (and sometimes self-consciously hip) science and technology magazines as *Seed*, *BBC Focus*, or *Wired*; those with more hardcore science backgrounds or interest may want to read *Scientific American* or even the American Association for the Advancement of Science's *Science* magazine or its British equivalent, *Nature*.

More practically, perhaps, teachers can find out a great deal about how the mind works from Steven Pinker's *The Language Instinct: How the Mind Creates Language* (HarperCollins, 1995) or his very accessible and engaging *How the Mind Works* (W. W. Norton, 1997). *Brain Matters: Translating Research into Classroom Practice* by Patricia Wolfe (Association for Supervision and Curriculum Development, 2001) is the book that introduced many educators to the classroom implications of the latest developments in neuroscience; "brain-based learning" (the name might strike the reader is oddly self-evident) and neuroscientific findings are the subjects of numerous conferences and workshops for educators in our time, but Wolfe is a good place to start.

Homing in on practicality, the ideas of Howard Gardner and Robert Sternberg on the complexity and even multiplicity of intelligence has taken us a long way from some of the early theorists of intelligence, whose ideas became uncomfortably tied up with eugenics early in the 20th century. By showing that intelligence comes in many forms in *Frames of Mind: Theory of Multiple Intelligences* (Basic Books, 1983) and *Multiple Intelligences: New Horizons in Theory and Practice* (Basic Books, 1993), Gardner suggested that all people have capacities that can be developed in the service of their own success and that of society as a whole. Many educators grabbed a tight hold of these ideas, which suggested that the sorting and sieving of students that had marked traditional Industrial Age schooling (and which had conveniently enabled the continuing dominance of white, male, bourgeois culture in many social, cultural, economic, and educational arenas), and some rushed to the fuzzy edges of what it means to be schooled, thus prompting Gardner's defense of the need for students to develop true expertise and deep understandings in *The Disciplined Mind: Beyond Facts and Standardized Tests, the K-12 Education That Every Child Deserves* (Simon & Schuster, 1999; note in the subtitle another answer to E.D. Hirsch, Jr., as referenced in the resources section of Chapter XIII, "Continuing Education: Curriculum, Pedagogy, and the Professional Community"). That Multiple-Intelligence theory came to be seen as "radical" and even anti-intellectual by educational conservatives is one of the strange phenomena of our time. Gardner has continued to present his ideas as deeply embedded in the context of the "real world" and its demands, most recently in *Five Minds for the Future* (Harvard Business School Press, 2007) and *Responsibility and Work*, referred to in the Resources section for Chapter XIV, "Professional Behavior."

Hard on Gardner's heels came the work of Robert Sternberg, until recently at Yale. Sternberg also viewed intelligence as multifaceted, or at least consisting of multiple elements, and in his work he has focused on the demonstrable aspects of "applied" intelligence; the titles of his books tell all: *Successful Intelligence* (Plume, 1997); *Practical Intelligence in Everyday Life* (with coauthors George Forsythe, Jennifer Hedlund, Joseph Horvath, Richard Wagner, Wendy Williams, Scott Snook, and Elena Grigorenko; Cambridge University Press, 2000); and the recent *Wisdom, Intelligence, and Creativity Synthesized* (Cambridge University Press, 2007). Lately, as the Dean of the School of Arts and Sciences at Tufts University, Sternberg has been behind efforts to bring the undergraduate admissions process into line with his triarchic theory of intelligence by shaping applications questions designed to elicit evidence of analytical, creative, and practical capacity.

A few years back there was a great flurry of interest in the subject

Emotional Intelligence: Why It Can Matter More Than IQ by Daniel Goleman (Bantam, 1995). Stressing emotional well-being, optimism, perseverance, and self-esteem, emotional intelligence also explains and supports the importance of social interaction and emotional connection to effective learning. The subject of access to the emotional and creative self also plays into Daniel Pink's *A Whole New Mind: Moving from the Information Age to the Conceptual Age* (Riverhead, 2005), a book more about curriculum than individual abilities but which discusses the ways in which creativity and self-awareness are essential to both the globalized economy and personal satisfaction.

In the resources section for Chapter XII, "Continuing Education: Child Development," there is a detailed description of the material from the All Kinds of Minds program that addresses many aspects of student psychosocial development and which provide teachers with excellent tools for knowing students well.

CHAPTER IV: *Classroom Culture: "Management"*

Resources for brand-new teachers are many. Many regional independent schools associations presented beginning teacher institutes, either as pre-service events or early in the school year. The intentional teacher should inquire whether attendance at such a program is a possibility.

A number of books remain very popular among new teachers, notably *The First Days Of School: How To Be An Effective Teacher*, a remarkably comprehensive how-to by Harry K. Wong and Rosemary T. Wong (Harry K. Wong Publications, 2004) that is neither subtle in its prescriptions nor qualified in its advice; a grain of salt is occasionally required in putting the book to use, but the authors cover a great deal of ground. *The Everything New Teacher Book: Increase Your Confidence, Connect With Your Students, and Deal With the Unexpected* by Melissa Kelly (Adams Media, 2004) offers its own store of useful advice. Books covering some of the same ground as the volume in your hand include the very useful *The Skillful Teacher: Building Your Teaching Skills* by Saphier, Hale-Speca, and Gower (referred to earlier), which is something of an industry standard on excellent classroom practice. Subject-specific books abound, with Carol Jago's *Papers, Papers, Papers: An English Teacher's Survival Guide* (Heinemann, 2005) setting the standard. *The Teacher's Essential Guide to Effective Instruction* by Jim Burke (Scholastic, 2008) and *Teachers Change Lives 24/7: 150 Ways to Do It Right*, by Jim Burgett (Education Communication Unlimited, 2007) offer advice from award-winning public school teachers, while Robert L. Fried's *The Passionate Teacher: A Practical Guide* (Beacon Press, 1996) speaks to the need for great teachers to sustain their deep commitment to both their students and their craft.

Classroom management is the subject of a number of useful books, among these *Reluctant Disciplinarian: Advice on Classroom Management From a Softy who Became (Eventually) a Successful Teacher* by "tough love" advocate Gary Rubinstein (Cottonwood Press, 1999) and *The Key Elements of Classroom Management: Managing Time and Space, Student Behavior, and Instructional Strategies* by Joyce McLeod, Jan Fisher, and Ginny Hoover (Association for Supervision and Curriculum Development, 2003). Independent school teachers Richard Eyster and Christine Martin have been offering both short and long workshops on this topic for a number of years, and their not-surprising message—know your students and their needs—is as compelling as their presentation. Similarly, *The Essential 55: An Award-winning Educator's Rules for Discovering the Successful Student in Every Child* by Ron Clark (Hyperion, 2004) addresses issues of student needs and high standards in the context of building productive classroom culture.

A more idealistic—and iconoclastic—take on traditional classroom structures can be found in Alfie Kohn's *Punished by Rewards: The Trouble with Gold Stars, Incentive Plans, A's, Praise, and Other Bribes* (Houghton Mifflin, 1993). Kohn goes one step further by taking on the idea that homework is an absolute good in *The Homework Myth: Why Our Kids Get Too Much of a Bad Thing* (Da Capo Books, 2006).

"Intellectual character" as a construct growing out of contemporary conceptions of intelligence as a matter not only of capacity but disposition, is the subject of Ron Ritchhart's persuasive and original *Intellectual Character: What It Is, Why It Matters, and How to Get It* (Jossey-Bass, 2004). Ritchhart, a Project Zero researcher at Harvard, makes the case for creating classroom cultures that focus on intellectual challenge and engagement rather than rules and policies: inspire students to think, he says, and management will take care of itself.

CHAPTER V: *Planning, Macro to Micro*

The most influential work on curriculum planning and design in independent schools in the past 15 years has been done by Grant Wiggins. His *Understanding by Design*, written with Jay McTighe (Association for Supervision and Curriculum Development, 2005—expanded second edition), is the essential guide to generating constructivist curriculum and assessment, complete with worksheets, templates, and even a supplementary workbook (*Understanding by Design: Professional Development Workbook*, Wiggins and McTighe; ASCD, 2004). If the intentional teacher consults only one book on curriculum and assessment, it should be this one, affectionately known as *UbD*.

That said, there are a wealth of resources on all aspects of curriculum and assessment. *The Art and Science of Teaching: A Comprehensive Framework for Effective Instruction* by Robert J. Marzano (Association for Supervision and Curriculum Development, 2007) is just one of Marzano's many books on curriculum and assessment that contain practical advice for teachers; another is *Classroom Assessment & Grading that Work* (Association for Supervision and Curriculum Development, 2006).

The workbook-formatted *The Skillful Teacher: Building Your Teaching Skills* by Jon Saphier, Mary Ann Haley-Speca, and Robert Gower (Research for Better Teaching, 2008—revised edition) is an exceptionally valuable resource, as is *Checking for Understanding: Formative Assessment Techniques for Your Classroom* by Douglas Fisher and Nancy Frey (Association for Supervision and Curriculum Development, 2007); both have been cited as being among "best books" for teachers.

Harvard's Project Zero and its leading lights, who include Howard Gardner and David Perkins, continue to offer extraordinary services as well as ideas to teachers. The centerpiece of their current professional development programs is the week-long "Project Zero Classroom" summer institute at the Harvard Graduate School of Education. Perkins's "Teaching for Understanding" model, like Wiggins's "Understanding by Design," is built around the idea of setting clear learning objectives for students and applying assessments tied clearly to those objectives. Perkins (an enormously engaging presenter, as well) has also written *The Intelligent Eye: Learning to Think by Looking at Art* (Oxford University Press, 1994), a brief but powerful introduction to his ideas. Project Zero also offers online classes in a number of areas through its Wide World program for teachers, teacher-leaders, and administrative leaders.

One-stop shopping for understanding problem-based learning can be found in John Barell's *Problem-Based Learning: An Inquiry Approach* (Corwin, 2006—second edition), which details how to construct and implement effective PBL cases. Barell is also the author of *Why Are School Buses Always Yellow?: Teaching for Inquiry, PreK-5* (Corwin Press, 2007).

Not to be confused with problem-based learning, project-based learning is becoming an ever more popular and ever-better-understood approach to challenging students to engage deeply with complex subjects. One of the great resources on project-based learning is the George Lucas Education Foundational and its beautifully produced magazine *Edutopia*; subscriptions are free.

Carol Tomlinson is the name to know with regard to differentiated instruction, and she and several co-authors have created practical guides for developing differentiated learning experiences for students at every age level, all published by the Association for Supervision and Curriculum Development: *Differentiation in Practice: A Resource Guide for Differentiating Curriculum, Grades K-5* (2003) and *Differentiation in Practice: A Resource Guide for Differentiating Curriculum, Grades 5-9* (2003), both with Caroline Eidson; *Differentiation in Practice: A Resource Guide for Differentiating Curriculum, Grades 9-12*, with Cindy Strickland (2005). By herself Tomlinson is also the author of *Fulfilling the Promise of the Differentiated Classroom: Strategies and Tools for Responsive Teaching* (2003) and *How to Differentiate Instruction in Mixed-Ability Classrooms* (2001—second edition), both also published by the Association for Supervision and Curriculum Development. Rounding out Tomlinson's highly influential body of work is *Integrating Differentiated Instruction & Understanding by Design: Connecting Content and Kids* (Association for Supervision and Curriculum Development, 2006), written with frequent Wiggins collaborator Jay McTighe.

We have tended to avoid subject-specific resources, but since its first appearance in 1997 Ellin Keene and Susan Zimmerman's *Mosaic of Thought* (now in a second edition, subtitled *The Power of Comprehension Strategy Instruction*; Heinemann, 2007) has become something of a cult classic among teachers looking for effective ways to teach reading comprehension and analytical thinking at all grade levels.

The intentional teacher may find him- or herself with the necessity of creating or using curriculum maps. These incredibly useful tools allow schools to collect information on the "taught curriculum," including content, skills, assessments, materials, and other elements, which can then be analyzed in numerous ways to improve curriculum and instruction. The apostle of mapping has been Columbia professor Heidi Hayes Jacobs, whose influential *Mapping the Big Picture: Integrating Curriculum & Assessment K-12* (Association for Supervision & Curriculum Development, 1997) and *Getting Results from Curriculum Mapping* (Association for Supervision & Curriculum Development, 2004) remain the standard resources. Jacobs is also the author of *Interdisciplinary Curriculum: Design and Implementation* (Association for Supervision & Curriculum Development, 1989). Her consultancy organization, Curriculum Designers, offers workshops as well as online resources—including courses—to help teachers and schools harness the power of this very useful technique.

CHAPTER VI: *Classroom Culture: Teaching with Standards*

"Standards" are everywhere, and content-focused organizations like the National Council of Teachers of Mathematics and the National Council for History Education have been at the forefront of creating bodies of standards based on professional judgment and carefully keyed to student age and educational background. In addition, many states have developed their own standards and frameworks for student attainment in many subject areas at each grade level, and the intentional teacher—in the absence of anything else—might contact both the main professional organization for his or her subject area as well as the state department of education; Massachusetts, for example, published curriculum frameworks in the Arts, English/Language Arts, Foreign Languages, Comprehensive Health, Mathematics, History and Social Science, Science and Technology/Engineering, and English Language Proficiency. While these are intended to help public school teachers prepare students for statewide testing, they are also useful models of comprehensive standards. The College Board publishes its own "Standards for College Success" as well as materials detailing the criteria for success on its putatively college-level Advanced Placement examinations. The International Baccalaureate Organization produces similar materials, aiming at a "world standard" of academic excellence the crosses national boundaries.

Teachers will need to know, understand, and perhaps internalize the standards that obtain at his or her school, and the best way to do this, as stated in the text, will be to sit down with experienced colleagues and do some collaborative evaluation. Still, it will be critical for the intentional teacher to tease out nuance, the subtle differences that separate excellent work from the satisfactory and the shoddy. This type of exercise could easily become the subject of a fruitful and illuminating meeting of a division or department, especially with experienced leaders to guide discussion through the inevitable—and always illustrative—areas of disagreement that are likely to arise, even among long-time colleagues with shared values.

An extraordinarily effective way to clarify standards for students is the evaluation or scoring rubric, examples of which are found in the main text. Rubric design is both an art and a science, but clarity and simplicity are paramount; specificity is also important, but note that too specific a set of guidelines is likely to inspire work that is rubric-driven—and perhaps legalistically defensible—rather than produced to meet high standards; some teachers are skeptical of rubrics because they fear that students will "write for the rubric" and not explore the material more deeply or creatively. There is perhaps a fine distinction between a rubric that implies a kind of prescription and one that merely states standards against which students may do their best using individual approaches. These and other quandaries are addressed in *Introduction To Rubrics: An Assessment Tool To Save Grading Time, Convey Effective Feedback and Promote Student Learning* by Dannelle Stevens and Antonia J. Levi (Stylus, 2004) and *Scoring Rubrics in the Classroom: Using Performance Criteria for Assessing and Improving Student Performance* by Judith Arter and Jay McTighe (Corwin, 2000), just two of the many books on rubric design and application; many books are filled with examples, and the internet teems with even more downloadable and adaptable models.

Important as standards are, they must be embedded in the context of authentic, engaging curriculum, and thus the reader is referred to the Resource sections of Chapters V, "Planning;" VII, "The Give and Take of Feedback;" and XIII, "Continuing Education: Curriculum, Pedagogy, and the Professional Community."

CHAPTER VII: *The Give and Take of Feedback*

Grant Wiggins, cited elsewhere as a towering influence on curriculum and assessment in independent schools, has defined feedback as "information about what and was not accomplished, given a specific goal" ("Assessment as Feedback," on the New Horizons for Learning website, www.newhorizons.org/strategies/
assess/wiggins.htm). Wiggins has made it work in recent years to write and speak compellingly about the essentiality of clear, precise feedback in any system that assesses and then evaluates student learning. His massive but comprehensive *Educative Assessment: Designing Assessments to Inform and Improve Student Performance* (Jossey-Bass, 1998) addresses the feedback question and more; as with any discussion of feedback, all resources and ideas related to "Standards," as in Chapter VI, would be equally applicable to the use of feedback to guide and correct learning and behavior.

Although aimed primarily at administrators, *The Skillful Leader: Confronting Mediocre Teaching* Alexander D. Platt, Caroline E. Tripp, Wayne R. Ogden, and Robert G. Fraser (Research for Better Teaching, 2000) can also be mined for good ideas by teachers. Research for Better

Teaching, which also publishes *The Skillful Teacher* cited elsewhere, offers workshops for teachers and administrators on a number of topics, including observation, feedback, and evaluation.

Steve Clem of the Association of Independent Schools of New England is, as the text states, the leading proponent of truly thoughtful observation and feedback methodologies both in the context of teacher improvement and professional evaluation. His "Eloquent Mirrors" workshops are useful not only for administrators but for classroom teachers who wish take a active roles in the creation of true communities of practice; schools with classroom "open door" policies in which teachers regularly observe other teachers at work are places in which the idea of better teaching is always at the forefront. The Association for Supervision and Curriculum Development offers a comprehensive multimedia kit on observation and feedback titled *The Supervision Series: Another Set of Eyes*, by Keith Atcheson.

It is worth adding that relatively few schools have enunciated "standards for effective teaching" that might be used as the foundation of evaluation based on observation and feedback. However, a number of organizations have attempted to define such standards, most prominently the National Board for Professional Teaching Standards, which has built its standards for the National Board Certification process around its Five Core Propositions:

- Teachers are committed to students and their learning
- Teachers know the subjects they teach and how to teach those subjects to students.
- Teachers are responsible for managing and monitoring student learning.
- Teachers think systematically about their practice and learn from experience.
- Teachers are members of learning communities.

The National Association of Independent Schools offers Principles of Good Practice not only for elementary, middle school, and secondary educators but also for supervisors of teachers; embedded within these are performance expectations for teachers as well as guidance in the development and application of systems of professional evaluation. Most accrediting bodies now expect fair and comprehensive teacher evaluation to be part of a school's operations, as well; gone are the days of extreme inconsistency and haphazardness in the evaluation of faculty.

Finally, Sara Lawrence-Lightfoot's 2000 book *Respect: An Exploration* (Basic Books), explores the role that authentic respect can play in fostering confidence and a sense of true purpose in human relationships and human work. Although not exactly about "feedback," the book is very much about the synergy between respectful interaction and personal growth.

CHAPTER VIII: **Families**

Two short but highly informative resources on families and family dynamics for teachers by the National Association of Independent Schools include Finding the Heart of the Child: Essays on Children, Families, and Schools by Edward Hallowell and Michael Thompson (1997) and Understanding Independent School Parents: An NAIS Guide to Successful Family-School Relationships by Thompson and Alison Fox Mazzola (2005).

Sara Lawrence-Lightfoot, who has written extensively on educational and social matters, turns her brilliant and revealing spotlight on parent–school relationships in *The Essential Conversation: What Parents and Teachers Can Learn from Each Other* (Random House, 2003), which argues for a positive and proactive attitude toward families in the service of the ultimate goal of student success. Lawrence-Lightfoot also touches on these and other relationships in *Respect: An Exploration* (cited in the Resources section of the previous chapter), in which she uses specific cases to explore the subtleties of respectful, positive exchange.

Robert Evans has taken a somewhat more alarmist but ultimately empathetic tack in his *Family Matters: How Schools Can Cope with the Crisis in Childrearing* (Jossey-Bass, 2004). Evans is also a compelling speaker; no teacher should pass up an opportunity to hear him present on any topic.

Teachers as well as parents and guardians can learn a great deal from *The Blessing of a Skinned Knee: Using Jewish Teachings to Raise Self-Reliant Children* by Wendy Mogel (Scribner, 2001), while *Best Friends, Worst Enemies: Understanding the Social Lives of Children* (Ballantine, 2001) and *Mom, They're Teasing Me!: Helping Your Child Solve Social Problems* (Ballantine, 2002) by Michael Thompson, Lawrence Cohen, and Catherine O'Neill Grace might both be considered essential reading for teachers interested in unraveling the tangled webs of children's familial and social relationships and travails.

Alfie Kohn, known for his heterodox ideas relating to many aspects of education, has also addressed family matters in *Unconditional Parenting: Moving from Rewards and Punishments to Love and Reason* (Atria Books, 2005).

In recent years much of the public attention devoted to "the social lives of children" has been about bullying and meanness, and teachers should be aware that there are sources of help available in these matters. The "Teasing and Bullying" project is part of the ongoing work of the Wellesley Centers for Women at Wellesley College (Massachusetts); the project sponsors publications and occasional workshops. The Olweus Bullying Prevention program, brainchild of Dan Olweus, is explained in *Bullying at School: What We Know and What We Can Do* (Blackwell, 1993). Rachel Simmons, the author of *Odd Girl Out: The Hidden Culture of Aggression in Girls* (Harcourt, 2003) also conducts workshops on this topic.

CHAPTER XI: *Diversity: "Getting It"*

Any educator interested in diversity and multicultural education should make a point, if possible, of attending the annual National Association of Independent Schools People of Color Conference, usually held in early December. Workshops, keynotes, and interest groups make this one of the most significant opportunities in education for like-minded people to come together from an astonishing range of schools and organizations dedicated to educational equity. The NAIS website is another great source of ideas and resources, and the organization also sponsors a listserv for diversity professionals in independent schools.

Other organizations that can be helpful to educators include: The Curriculum Initiative, with a focus on Jewish traditions and studies; the National Association for the Advancement of Colored People; Facing History and Ourselves, dedicated to education against injustice and inequality and whose curricula on the politics and sociology of genocide can be found in many independent schools; the Partnership of Excellence in Jewish Education; the Southern Poverty Law Center, publishers of *Teaching Tolerance* magazine; and the Anti-Defamation League: "Fighting bigotry, hate, and extremism." Local agencies and organizations committed to social justice and the elimination of racism can also provide guidance around school policies and practices and may be able to offer curriculum support as well.

The essential reading list on this topic includes Peggy McIntosh's profoundly influential 1988 essay, "White Privilege: Unpacking the Invisible Knapsack," available through her office at Wellesley College and elsewhere. *We Can't Teach What We Don't Know: White Teachers, Multiracial Schools* by Gary R. Howard (Teachers College Press, 2006—2nd edition) also addresses the dilemma of teachers whose experience differs from their students'. Of equal importance are Lisa Delpit's *Other People's*

Children: Cultural Conflict in the Classroom (New Press, 1996), which discusses the role of cultural differences with regard to expectations about education, and Beverly Daniel Tatum's *"Why Are All the Black Kids Sitting Together in the Cafeteria?" and Other Conversations About Race* (Basic Books, 1997). *The Dreamkeepers: Successful Teachers of African American Children* by Gloria Ladson-Billings (Jossey-Bass, 1994) covers much the same ground in a less theoretical way, offering concrete advice for teachers. Other influential writers on the subject of educational equity and minority achievement include Claude Steele, Pedro Noguera, Sonia Nieto, and Jawanza Kunjufu. In *Teaching to Transgress: Education as the Practice of Freedom* (Routledge, 1994), bell hooks exhorts teachers to understand the essentially revolutionary nature of schooling; a similar if broader argument can be found in *Teaching as a Subversive Activity* (Delacorte, 1969) by Neil Postman and Charles Weingartner, a call to arms from an earlier era. Michael Brosnan's excellent monographs *Thriving in Independent Schools: A Guide for Educators of Color* and *From Assimilation to Inclusion: How White Educators and Educators of Color Can Make Diversity Work* (both Association of Independent Schools of New England, 2004 and 2009, respectively and available by download at www.aisne.org) are specifically focused on factors that affect the work of teachers.

Theories of multicultural education in general have been advanced by many, but James Banks has had a particularly strong influence in *An Introduction to Multicultural Education* (Allyn & Bacon, 1994) and *Multicultural Education: Issues and Perspectives* with Cherry Banks (Wiley, 2006—6th edition). A great survey of ideas in multicultural and cross-cultural education can be found in *Toward Multiculturalism: A Reader in Multicultural Education* (Intercultural Resource Corporation, 2004—2nd edition), edited and with contributions by Jaime S. Wurzel; the most recent edition includes the classic story "The Bear That Wasn't" by Frank Tashlin (1946), a superb allegory of how people respond to the expectations of others.

The work of Carol Gilligan has had considerable influence on thinking about the education of girls, in particular her ground-breaking *In a Different Voice* (1993), which is based in part on research conducted at independent schools. *Failing at Fairness* (1995) by Myra and David Sadker, offers up a scathing indictment of what the authors classify as sexist classroom practice but offers ways in which teachers can combat this. The National Coalition of Girls' Schools maintains a useful website, and the American Association of University Women monograph, *¡Sí, Se Puede! Yes, We Can!* specifically addresses academic success issues for Latina/Hispanic girls.

The best resources for teachers on GLBTQ issues can be found at GLSEN, the Gay, Lesbian, and Straight Education Network; founder Kevin Jennings is a former independent school teacher. Both national and local chapters of PFLAG (Parents, Families, and Friends of Lesbians and Gays) can also be useful. A starting point for those interested in reading about a successful approach to inclusivity around sexual identity issues is *When the Drama Club Is Not Enough: Lessons from the Safe School Program for Gay and Lesbian Students* by Jeff Perrotti and Kim Westheimer (Beacon Press, 2002).

Although class seems to be America's dirty little secret, a few organizations have stepped to the plate to provide educators with resources for discussing issues of economic justice. United for a Fair Economy and its Responsible Wealth Project both provide materials and support for educators. Virtually all texts and organizations dedicated to issues of equity and social justice also address this issue, sometimes quite directly. The notorious but nonetheless influential *A Framework for Understanding Poverty* by Ruby K. Payne (aha! Process, 2005—4th edition) presents a controversial version of the forces that cause many students to struggle, but sooner or later the intentional teacher will encounter the book and will need to sort out for him- or herself the strong feelings it has engendered among caring and committed educators.

The many organizations devoted to supporting equity and focused on the needs and issues of minority populations tend to have curricular materials available as well—for example, the Asia Society and the Museum of the North American Indian. The more comprehensive books on the history of academic disciplines—mathematics, the sciences, literature, the arts, history—tend to include valuable information on the global origins of different ways of thinking about and solving problems, and the student of epistemology could happily lose him- or herself contemplating how the multiplicity of ways of knowing in different societies might play out in the educational process of 21st-century independent school students.

For thoughts on leadership in the process of school development in the area of diversity and multiculturalism, the sources are legion, but a useful place to start might once again be programs offered by the National Association of Independent Schools, notably the annual Summer Diversity Institute. NAIS also supports the Assessment of Inclusivity and Multiculturalism, a program by which schools can engage in a systematic and comprehensive review of their own programs and policies in these areas and also receive feedback from their own constituencies. Assessments are led by "Discovery Committees," on which one would expect to find a substantial number of intentional teachers.

CHAPTER X: *Other Classrooms: Advising and Supervision*

The resources presented here for Chapters III, "Knowing Students;" VIII, "Families;" IX, "Diversity: 'Getting It';" and XII, "Continuing Education: Child Development" would all be of great utility and interest for teachers interested in expanding their capacity as advisors to students. The key to successful advising is simply having a keen interest in and awareness of each child and his or her environment, needs, and challenges.

The successful club, activity, or publication advisor is not only clear on the school's expectations but also on what the standards of excellence might be for such work. A number of awards programs for publications exist, including the National Council of Teachers of English Program to Recognize Excellence in Student Literary Magazines, several Journalism Education Association awards (including one for Yearbook Advisor of the Year), and the Columbia Scholastic Press Association, which offers awards and critiques in hundreds of categories for high school yearbooks, magazines, and newspapers. The Columbia Scholastic Press Advisers Association offers workshops for its members as well as many workshops and seminars at which student leaders can hone their skills. The Journalism Education Association sponsors an annual Advisers Institute, as well. Yearbook publishing companies also provide training and support for advisors as well as student staff members.

The United Nations Association of the United States of America offers many resources for Model United Nations advisors and team members that would be useful even when a school's target event is not directly sponsored by the Association. Local bar associations support Mock Trial programs and their members. High school debate coaches and teams can find great resources through the National Center for Policy Analysis Project's Debate Central website, www.debate-central.org. Any activity that involves collaboration, competition, or potential competition with other schools—one thinks of science competitions, National History Day, robotics contests, and the like—will tend to have some sort of governing body behind it, and such bodies will go out of their way to help coaches and advisors learn the ropes to raise the caliber of competition or presentation.

Advising either product-driven or externally focused clubs or simply those with more local or intramural purposes is largely a matter of attending to student interests as well as to matters of goal-setting and team-building; the intentional teacher will find the content of and resources suggested for Chapter XI, "Other Classrooms: Coaching," to be pertinent. As well the website of the Student Leadership Institute at DePaul University, studentaffairs.depaul.edu/sli/resources/index.asp, provides a comprehensive bibliography not only of books on general leadership issues but also of resources, including books, written specifically for student leaders; many of these would be applicable to secondary and even middle school students. The National Association of Student Councils also has resources for student government advisers.

A comprehensive body of thinking on boarding school life and issues can be found in a group of books from Avocus Publishing. The earliest of these, *Casualties of Privilege: Essays on Prep Schools' Hidden Culture* (1991), edited by Louis Crosier, is somewhat unnerving in its student-written accounts of the obliviousness of teachers toward certain behaviors, but the rest, *Healthy Choices, Healthy Schools: The Residential Curriculum* (1994), also edited by Crosier; *Second Home: Life in a Boarding School* (1996), edited by Craig Thorn IV; and *Far and Wide: Cultural Diversity in the American Boarding School*, edited by Thorn and Tim Hillman (1997), provide sensible and sensitive guidance for boarding school teachers wishing to be intentional—and alert—in all aspects of their work.

CHAPTER XI: *Other Classrooms: Coaching*

A search on "coaching books" will yield a world of volumes directed at those interested in developing workplace leadership skills. While many of are very office-focused, no doubt the thoughtful searcher will encounter books with application not only to athletic coaching but also to classroom culture. We leave it to the reader to explore this vast field using personally developed criteria.

Of books focused on athletic coaching, Jim Thompson's *Positive Coaching: Building Character and Self-Esteem Through Sports* (Warde Publishers, 1995) is well-regarded as providing thoughtful guidance in a general sense, but perhaps the most fruitful and readable source of wisdom on coaching is the plethora of coach and play autobiographies on the market. Many can be seen as shameless self-promotion, but as a body they are proof that confidence and a strong belief in the power of hard work and a winning attitude are essential to successful athletic performance—and that these traits are as valuable off the field as on. While the elementary-school basketball coach may find that not all the words of Pat Summitt or Bobby Knight apply, there may be surprising insights into motivational or tactical practices that work; most children, after all, enjoy the activity and camaraderie of organized sport and *want* to be well coached by someone with high (but not impossible) standards. The intentional coach can capitalize on students' predisposition to work hard toward improvement, and suggestions gleaned from any source can be useful.

Sport-specific information and support for coaches is relatively easy to come by, although not every athletic administration is as attuned as it might be to the breadth of available resources. The overall governing body for high school sports, other than state or regional associations, is the National Federation of High School [Athletic] Associations, which publishes official rulebooks and has some jurisdiction on rules and officiating for the most common high school sports as well as general policies pertaining to interscholastic sports. (Note that some leagues or organizations opt to use rules other than those promulgated by the Federation; an athletic director should be able to inform a coach which rules obtain.) The NFHS also offers a Fundamentals of Coaching course that can be completed online, as can their First Aid for Coaches course. For the sake of their players as well as for their own protection, all coaches ought to seek certification from legitimate bodies not only in first aid but in cardiopulmonary resuscitation; the Red Cross offers both, and the American Heart Association offers the latter. Some coaches will wish to become certified either as athletic trainers or as Emergency Medical Technicians. In any event, no coach should engage in anything remotely like injury or medical care unless either certified to do so or in circumstances so extreme that inaction could be fatal.

The national governing body for virtually every sport offers some level of coach training. For example, the United States Soccer Federation and the National Soccer Coaches Association of America offer coaching licensure, with the lowest-level USSF courses being more geared to beginners. US Lacrosse offers coaching clinics; local organizations may also offer courses or clinics, and coaches are usually welcome at players' clinics, as well. USA [Ice] Hockey offers similar programs, as do USA Field Hockey, USA Gymnastics, USA Swimming, and so on (a notable exception being football, which tends to be overseen by state or regional school athletic associations). Search out the analogous group in any sport from cheerleading to archery to learn about similar opportunities. An internet search by sport will also turn up coaching books, coaching videos, and game and performance videos galore, and the coach relatively unfamiliar with his or her assigned sport should make liberal use of such resources.

A few wonderful books have tracked high school teams through entire seasons. *In These Girls, Hope is a Muscle* by Madeleine Blais (Grand Central, 1996) follows a girls' high school basketball team from pre-season to a state championship; Buzz Bissinger's *Friday Night Lights: A Town, a Team, and a Dream* (Da Capo, 1990) looks inside the workings of a successful but pressured high school football team (and inspired not only a film but a television drama); and Pat Conroy's *My Losing Season* (Nan A. Talese, 2002) details the author's experiences on an underperforming college basketball team. Each of these provides insight into the chemistry that binds—or fails to bind—players and coaches into teams. A few films, notably *Hoosiers* (1996; David Anspaugh) do the same; that so many teams still insist on viewing this film together before big games is a testament to its truthfulness about comradeship and the nature of the team experience for young athletes.

The intentional coach is also urged to look into opportunities to build game awareness and coaching expertise through play, either in pick-up games or in the ever-expanding universe of adult summer and evening programs in every imaginable sport. There is also an endless need for coaches in town and regional youth sport programs, which offer not only further opportunities to build coaching skills but the bonus of contact with potential student-athletes for one's own school.

CHAPTER XII: *Continuing Education: Cognitive and Social Development in Children*

For the basics of child development from the giants in the field, the reader should consult *The Psychology of the Child* by Jean Piaget and Barbara Inhelder (Basic Books, 1969) and *Childhood and Society* by Erik Erikson (Hogarth Press, 1964—revised edition), both readable and easy to find, as they are standard college texts. A more general summary that includes a few other treasures can be found in Carol Mooney's *Theories of Childhood: An Introduction to Dewey, Montessori, Erikson, Piaget, and Vygotsky* (Redleaf Press, 2000). For shear utility, Chip Wood's *Yardsticks: Children in the Classroom Ages 4-14* (Northeast Foundation for Children, 2007—3rd edition) is a superb year-by-year look at the developmental characteristics of children especially as these are expressed in school situations; one longs for a high school-age companion volume.

Lawrence Kohlberg's Approach to Moral Education by F. Clark Power, Ann Higgins, and Lawrence Kohlberg (Columbia University Press, 1991) is definitive on the subject of Kohlberg, although books, programs, and other resources on "moral education" abound. The Curriculum Initiative (cited elsewhere) and the Council for Spiritual and Ethical Education both offer programs for independent school (and other) teachers interested in this area. For those curious about "values clarification," the standard volume is *Values Clarification* by Sidney Simon, Leland Howe, and Howard Kirschenbaum (Grand Central, 1995—revised edition). An internet search on this topic will introduce the teacher to the sometimes ugly controversy around this approach.

Technology is not the subject of Daniel Pink's *A Whole New Mind:*

Moving from the Information Age to the Conceptual Age (Riverhead, 2005), but technology will be a significant engine of the movement Pink describes. For detailed information on Web 2.0, the teacher will want both to search (or Google, to use the argot of the times) the internet, but the online Classroom 2.0 site (www.classroom20.com) would be a good starting point. The exponential development of technological capacity and its impact on education is discussed in the author's "Technology and the Culture of Learning," *Independent School* magazine, Summer 2004, but changes in hardware, software, resources, and application concepts have begun to come more rapidly than they can be usefully documented as resources here.

Issues in the social and educational development of girls have been of particular interest in recent decades. Following on the attention given to Carol Gilligan's work, *Reviving Ophelia: Saving the Selves of Adolescent Girls* by Mary Pipher (Putnam, 1994) suggested that social and educational norms were depriving adolescent girls and young women of opportunities to be confident and successful learners. The even more dire issue of eating disorders is the subject of *The Golden Cage: The Enigma of Anorexia Nervosa* by Hilde Bruch (Harvard University Press, 2001—edition has a new foreword by Catherine Steiner-Adair), which explains the complex and persistent dynamics behind an illness that can have devastating effects on students—boys as well as girls—their peers, and their families. The National Eating Disorders Association also sponsors educational programs in support of healthy development for girls and women (and boys and men).

A couple of brief but practically useful resources for educators are *How Girls Thrive: An Essential Guide for Educators (and Parents)* by JoAnn Deak and *A Great Balancing Act: Equitable Education for Girls and Boys* by Anne Chapman (both National Association of Independent Schools, 1998 and 1997, respectively). Girl Scouts USA, an organization that has sponsored considerable research on learning and social development in girls, also offers useful resources through their website.

Michael Thompson's work on boys includes *It's a Boy!: Understanding Your Son's Development from Birth to Age 18* (Ballantine, 2008) and *Speaking of Boys: Answers to the Most-Asked Questions About Raising Sons* (Ballantine, 2000; both books are co-authored by Teresa Barker) and *Raising Cain: Protecting the Emotional Lives of Boys*, with Dan Kindlon (Ballantine, 1999); the latter is also the basis of a compelling 2005 PBS video production of the same name.

Real Boys: Rescuing Our Sons from the Myths of Boyhood by William Pollack (Random House, 1998) explores the "code" that impedes boys' emotional development, while *The Minds of Boys: Saving Our Sons From Falling Behind in School and Life* by Michael Gurian (Jossey-Bass, 2005) looks to the educational system to explain the apparent trend toward poorer academic performance in boys. Christina Hoff Sommers created a stir in some quarters with *The War Against Boys: How Misguided Feminism Is Harming Our Young Men* (Simon & Schuster, 2000); not necessarily a book educators will savor, it has nonetheless sparked considerable heated public discussion. The Boys Project, run by Judith Kleinfeld at the University of Alaska, is a practical attempt to explore and rectify the growing gap in male aspirations relative to those of girls and women.

Most of the diversity-related resources mentioned in the Resources section for Chapter IX would be relevant to an understanding the cultural dimensions of child development. In addition, the reader might wish to consult *Young, Gifted, and Black: Promoting High Achievement Among African American Students* by Claude Steele, Theresa Perry, and Asa Hilliard III (Beacon Press, 2004); Steele is the originator of the theory of stereotype threat.

The neurodevelopmental basis of learning differences is the subject of Mel Levine's *A Mind at a Time* (Simon & Schuster, 2002), which introduced the All Kinds of Minds concept to a broad public audience. All Kinds of Minds publishes books for students that include *All Kinds of Minds: A Young Student's Book About Learning Abilities and Learning Disorders* (Educators Publishing Service, 1992) for elementary-grade students along with *Jarvis Clutch, Social Spy* and *Keeping A Head in School* (both Educators Publishing Service, 2001 and 1994, respectively). All are written to help students learn how understanding their personal development patterns and learning styles can have an impact on social and academic success. Some educators have found Levine's 2003 *The Myth of Laziness* (Simon & Schuster) to be controversial, but the book argues compellingly that neurodevelopmental weaknesses, not character flaws, hold back many students from academic success.

Attention-Deficit Hyperactivity Disorder is explored in detail in *Driven To Distraction: Recognizing and Coping with Attention Deficit Disorder from Childhood Through Adulthood* by Edward M. Hallowell and John J. Ratey (Touchstone, 1995); this is the book that first brought ADD and ADHD to public notice. The intentional teacher is likely to find that several of his or her students are being medicated for this or some other learning issue, and it is well for the teacher to understand something about this "disorder." Anyone having an opportunity to hear Dr. Hallowell speak on the subject should not miss it. The intentional teacher who understands this subject well may find that, like dyslexia and other so-called "learning disabilities," ADHD infuses students with certain compensatory strengths and proclivities that can be extremely valuable to students in their nonacademic lives and that can be harnessed in the classroom to make collaborative work, for example, more fruitful.

Teachers interested in learning more about language-based learning issues can check in with the International Dyslexia Association, which offers dozens of regional events aimed at helping teachers gain skill in helping students who struggle in this area. There are numerous sources of on-site and online coursework in specialized techniques for helping students with reading- and language-related difficulties; the Orton-Gillingham methodology is the oldest and best known, although the Lindamood-Bell and Scottish Rite approaches have also been found effective.

CHAPTER XIII: *Continuing Education: Curriculum, Pedagogy, and the Professional Community*

Jerome Bruner is perhaps too little heralded as a founder of the constructivist approach to learning. In *The Process of Education* and *Toward a Theory of Instruction* (both Harvard University Press, 1960 and 1966, respectively) he laid out a new approach to curriculum and instruction in which the learning characteristics of students, rather than subject matter, take center stage, and his 1996 book *The Culture of Education* (Harvard University Press) completes a landmark revision of the way we think about teaching and learning.

The former head of Phillips Academy in Massachusetts (better known as Andover) and one-time dean of the Harvard Graduate School of Education, Theodore Sizer produced the definitive study the challenges facing America's schools and some ways to meet them in his powerful Horace trilogy; happily, they are as readable as they are influential. *Horace's Compromise: The Dilemma of the American High School* (1984) presents a heartbreaking look at the issues confronting the average teacher in an average school; *Horace's School: Redesigning the American High School* (1992) suggests some specific remedies; and *Horace's Hope: What Works for the American High School* (1997) is a call to action for comprehensive reform. This body of work in part inspired the Coalition of Essential Schools, itself a formidable resource for educators through its publication, *Horace*, and its annual Fall Forum. Most recently, along with publishing a steady stream of books (several of them cited earlier), Sizer and his wife, Nancy Faust Sizer, were founding principals of the Francis W. Parker Charter Essential School in Massachusetts; "The Parker" offers its own professional development program and is very much worth a visit—even the school website, www. parker.org, is a treasure trove.

In *The Power of Their Ideas: Lessons for America from a Small School in Harlem* (Beacon Press, 1995), Deborah Meier demonstrated the value of building a small educational community around habits of mind; Meier's work at Central Park East Secondary School in New York City and her more recent work at Mission Hill School in Boston has been influential in convincing a number of large urban school systems to move toward the establishment of smaller, more autonomous schools in the place of giant comprehensive schools; along with Dennis Littky at The Met Center in Providence, Rhode Island (who documents his beliefs in *The Big Picture: Education Is Everyone's Business*, a 2004 Association for Supervision and Curriculum Development book co-authored by Samantha Grabelle), Meier has become an icon of the ways that high standards plus innovative thinking can yield educational success for all students.

A comprehensive history of North American independent schools has yet to be written, but the story of how early 19th-century European notions of child development and learning were transmuted into the founding principles of what are now some of the most august independent residential schools is well told in James McLachlan's *American Boarding Schools* (Scribner's, 1970). How the social revolutions of the 1960s and early 1970s affected these schools can be discerned in *A World of Our Own* (Coward-McCann, 1970) written by Peter S. Prescott from within a prestigious New England boarding school just as the forces of change were beginning to shake its foundations.

John Dewey, for all his influence on American education, is not the most readable of educational theorists, but by far his most accessible books are *Experience and Education* (Macmillan, 1938), in which he lays out a theory of how individual experience can be integrated into meaningful learning. In *Democracy and Education: An Introduction to the Philosophy of Education* (Macmillan, 1916), Dewey makes the point that a main purpose of education is to create a populace aware of the world and capable of reasoned analysis and judgment.

When E. D. Hirsch, Jr. published *Cultural Literacy: What Every American Needs to Know* (Houghton Mifflin, 1987), his ideas took hold among educators and others who believed that education should move "back to basics." Soon enough the Core Knowledge Foundation had been born to promote these beliefs, and bookstore shelves filled with the books of the *What Your __th Grader Needs to Know* series, from preschool through grade 6 (Delta) and the parallel *Teacher Handbook* series, for grades K to 5. Hirsch followed up with his attack on progressive and constructivist ideas in *The Schools We Need & Why We Don't Have Them* (Doubleday, 1996), and today a number of schools have embraced Core Knowledge principles. As "equity pedagogy," Core Knowledge levels the playing field for all students by bringing them to a shared level of knowledge of basic facts and ideas within the mainstream culture. The Foundation holds an annual conference and sponsors workshops throughout the year.

It should be noted that Hirsch's ideas have not gone unchallenged. In 1999 Alfie Kohn, often regarded as a gadfly but whose sting is often painfully on target, responded with *The Schools Our Children Deserve: Moving Beyond Traditional Classrooms and "Tougher Standards"* (Houghton Mifflin, 1999), an impassioned defense of student-centered, constructivist teaching and learning.

Founded in Switzerland at schools educating international students who would be returning to school or attending university in multiple national systems, the International Baccalaureate purports to mark a global standard of academic excellence, and many North American schools have signed on to one of its several programs. The International Baccalaureate Organization offers the Primary Years program for students ages 3–12, the Middle Years program for ages 11–16, and the Diploma program for ages 16–19; successful completion of the diploma program can lead to advanced standing for students entering university. Although the International Baccalaureate is "all or nothing"—schools cannot opt in for selected portions of the program—the organization publishes a great magazine of global education, *IB World*, and holds workshops and conferences for its teachers (and those interested in the program) as well as online professional development workshops. Teachers interested in learning more about international collaboration should look at Peter Tacy's *Ideals at Work* (Deerfield Academy Press, 2006), an enthusiast's history of the Round Square global consortium of schools with its record of successful exchanges, service-learning and service-travel programs, and genuine global educational programs.

The very student-centered Waldorf schools have attracted a devoted following among families, and Waldorf offers teacher training (required for anyone teaching in a Waldorf school) all over North America. A glimpse into the ideas of its founder, the polymath Rudolf Steiner, can be had with a look at *The Education of the Child in the Light of Anthroposophy* (1909; available in English online at the Rudolf Steiner archive, www.rsarchive.org).

Among early childhood educators, none has been more influential than Maria Montessori. Her book *The Montessori Method* (in English from Shocken, 1988; first English edition, 1912) explains the method from top to bottom, while a comprehensive and updated guide to Montessori techniques is *Montessori Today: A Comprehensive Approach to Education from Birth to Adulthood* by Paula Polk Lillard (Shocken, 1996). The influence of Montessori is felt today in every pre-school, kindergarten, and elementary school, even those who might never acknowledge the connection.

Like the Montessori method, the approach developed in the pre-schools of Reggio Emilia in Northern Italy involves careful attention to the individual child's interests in a multisensory environment designed to spark learning at every turn. *Bringing Reggio Emilia Home: An Innovative Approach to Early Childhood Education* by Louise Boyd Cadwell (Teachers College Press, 1997) is one of many recent books exploring how the Reggio Emilia system might be translated to other school systems.

Those interested in keeping up with role of technology in teaching and education in general could start with the many publications and services of the International Society for Technology in Education (www.iste.org); their annual National Educational Computing Conference is the largest and most highly regarded gathering of educational technology experts in North America. More recently Classroom 2.0 has become the center of the widening movement to expand the reach and utility of interactive technologies to extend and transform the very nature of pedagogy and curriculum. Clayton Christensen's *Disrupting Class: How Disruptive Innovation Will Change the Way the World Learns* (written with Michael Horn and Curtis Johnson; McGraw-Hill, 2008) speaks to the very real potential of new technologies to disrupt, or recast, the way in which schools will work in coming decades.

Several thoughtful and useful revisions and expansions of Benjamin Bloom's Taxonomy of Educational Objectives in the Cognitive Domain have appeared in recent years, drawing upon new understandings of constructivist curriculum theory and of brain function. These include *A Taxonomy for Learning, Teaching, and Assessing: A Revision of Bloom's Taxonomy of Educational Objectives* by Lorin Anderson, David Krathwohl, Peter Airasian, Kathleen Cruikshank, Richard Mayer, Paul Pintrich, James Raths, and Merlin Wittrock (Allyn & Bacon, 2000—revised and abridged edition) and *The New Taxonomy of Educational Objectives* by Robert Marzano and John Kendall (Corwin Press, 2006—2nd edition).

The College Board in Princeton, New Jersey, is best known for the array of standardized college entrance tests it produces, but its resources for teachers include books, online material, and sponsored workshops for teachers, particularly those teaching its Advanced Placement courses. In addition, the College Board in recent years has been paying particular attention to middle school and early high school education insofar as these relate to the Board's interest in high academic standards and college readiness.

CHAPTER XIV: *Professional Behavior XIV*

Unfortunately both the news and literature are filled with examples of bad professional behavior by teachers, but the common thread in all cases is not just bad judgment but the compounding sin of hypocrisy. Making good life choices in the work of educating children is rather like making good life choices in general, with of course the precondition that teachers must follow both the law and whatever institutional rules are in force. The best resource, then, will be the teacher's conscience and whatever handbooks or guiding principles underlie the school's codes of behavior for any and all community members. Legal guidelines, however unnecessary we hope these will be, can be found in state and local statutes and are discussed generally in *The Courtroom in the Classroom: The Law in Independent School Life*, edited by Donald Grace (Avocus Publishing, 2006).

The National Association of Independent Schools publishes a comprehensive group of Principles of Good Practice for its member schools, and its 2007 publication *A Guidebook to the NAIS Principles of Good Practice*, edited by James Tracy, uses case studies to set up detailed analyses of many of the thorny situations that arise in school policy and governance.

Literary works featuring professional behavior that ranges from the appalling to the criminal can be found especially in John Horne Burns's distressing *Lucifer with a Book* (Harper and Brothers, 1949), *Good Times, Bad Times* by James Kirkwood (Fawcett, 1968), the deeply troubling *Academy X: A Novel* by Andrew Trees (Bloomsbury, 2006), and Taylor Antrim's outlandish *The Headmaster Rituals* (Mariner, 2007). Louis Auchincloss offers a more nuanced look at the moral dilemmas of independent school educators in the classic *The Rector of Justin* (Houghton Mifflin, 1964), as does Richard Hawley's sad *The Headmaster's Papers* (P. S. Eriksson, 1983).

Mr. Chips notwithstanding, readers might best look for good teachers in literature at the edges of events more often than in the center: "old Spencer," the one teacher who seems to understand Holden Caulfield at Pencey Prep, and Lupin the werewolf from J. K. Rowlings's Harry Potter series come to mind. A few great real-life stories include Pat Conroy's *The Water is Wide* (the 1972 Houghton Mifflin book is the basis of the 1974 Martin Ritt film *Conrack*) and *Teach Like Your Hair's on Fire: The Methods and Madness Inside Room 56* by Rafe Esquith (Viking, 2007). Sadly, many of the "good examples" are presented as iconoclasts and rebels who must fight against the "bad" constraints of their school structures, and I like to believe that there are plenty of good schools whose cultures foster excellent professional behavior. Literature and film also abound with examples of the charismatic teacher gone wrong: the most outrageous example by far is the Professor Slughorn's Slug Club in the Harry Potter series, but real teachers cringe as *Dead Poets Society*'s Mr. Keating amps up his power over his students under the guise of liberating them.

For a more scholarly look at professional behavior in general, Howard Gardner's *Responsibility at Work: How Leading Professionals Act (or Don't Act) Responsibly* (Jossey-Bass, 2007) details the most effective traits of both successful people and the organizations in which they thrive; this is an extremely compelling book in that it comes from one of the great educational thinkers of our time. Steven Covey's *The 7 Habits of Highly Effective People: Powerful Lessons in Personal Change* (Free Press, 2004—revised edition) might almost be suspect for its extreme popularity, but its ideas are sound for teachers who intend to remain in the classroom as well as for those ambitious for administrative responsibilities.

CHAPTER XV: *The Teacher in the School*

Shaping School Culture: The Heart of Leadership by Terrence E. Deal and Kent D. Peterson (Jossey-Bass, 1999) is a definitive guide to the ways that school communities can work together to develop norms and expectations and the programs to sustain them. Steve Clem and Vance Wilson, experienced independent school educators, also expatiate on the breadth of the curriculum as school culture in their influential *Paths to a New Curriculum* (1991) and *Taking Measure: Perspectives on Curriculum & Change* (1998), in which they are joined in authorship by Karin O'Neil; both books are published by the National Association of Independent Schools.

It has not been a major topic in this book, but collaborative teaching, sometimes in the form of "team teaching" and sometimes just a matter of a shared classroom, has been a common and successful technique in pre-kindergarten through elementary classrooms for years, and more recently it has been introduced in upper-grade classrooms as a part interdisciplinary and project-based teaching. *TeamWork: Setting the Standard for Collaborative Teaching, Grades 5-9* by Monique Wild, Amanda Mayeaux, and Kathryn Edmonds (Stenhouse Publishers, 2008) tells the story of how three outstanding teachers have collaborated to create successful learning even within a rigid, externally imposed curriculum.

Teaching and Leading From the Inside Out: A Model for Reflection, Exploration, and Action by Judy F. Carr, Janice R. Fauske, and Stephen P. Rushton (Corwin Press, 2007) is yet another example of teacher-leaders in action. Whether and how to assume the mantle of leadership is a challenge that all good teachers must face. Leadership books for the business community glut the market, but Michael Fullan, author of *Leading in a Culture of Change* (Jossey-Bass, 2001) and the introduction to *The Jossey-Bass Reader on Educational Leadership* (Jossey-Bass, 2006—2nd edition), addresses much of his work to an educational audience. Jim Collins's *Good to Great: Why Some Companies Make the Leap... and Others Don't* (Collins Business, 2001) was an instant success in the business world, but Collins has written *Good to Great and the Social Sectors: A Monograph to Accompany Good to Great* (HarperCollins, 2005) specifically to talk about leadership and institutional culture in nonprofit organizations and how individuals can help such organizations advance their missions.

A different tack on school leadership, focusing on instructional issues, can be found in *Schooling by Design: Mission, Action, and Achievement* by Grant Wiggins and Jay McTighe (Association for Supervision and Curriculum Development, 2007).

Finally, *The Skillful Leader II: Confronting Conditions That Undermine Learning* by Alexander D. Platt, Caroline E. Tripp, Robert G. Fraser, James R. Warnock, and Rachel E. Curtis (Research for Better Teaching, 2008), though written in the main for administrators, addresses the challenge of maintaining a culture based on high professional and academic standards—surely the main part of the work of the intentional teacher-leader.

CHAPTER XVI: *A Teacher's Path*

The teacher ready to dig more deeply into the profession of teaching or looking to make a quantum leap in his or her knowledge base has a number of outstanding resources available even on top of the world's many excellent schools of education. The Klingenstein Center for Independent School Leadership at Teachers College of Columbia University offers several levels of professional support, from the Summer Institute for Early Career Teachers to the prestigious year- or semester-length Joseph Klingenstein Fellowship programs to the unique Master's Degree for Independent School Leadership.

Harvard's Graduate School of Education also offers several programs for aspiring and sitting school leaders, one of which, the Annual Independent School Institute, is expressly designed for independent school heads. The HGSE offerings for K–12 educators are fairly limited, but they have great scope and depth.

The legendary David Mallery, a former teacher and a professional development guru, offers a menu of tasty annual seminars that bring together educators at similar career stages, including the First Five Years, the Experienced Pro, the Administrator's Life, and the longer, immersive Westtown Seminar. All are known to be life-changing experiences.

For teachers serious about taking on leadership roles, the National Association of Independent Schools offers a one-year Fellowship for Aspiring School Heads program, a summer School Leadership Institute, a summer Institute for Leadership in Sustainability, and a Lessons in Leadership Institute on the Battlefields of Gettysburg (presented by both NAIS staff and a military historian).

A number of regional independent school associations offer experienced teacher institutes of one kind or another, and in recent years the Westtown School (Pennsylvania) has offered a summer program on this topic.

The Gardner Carney Leadership Institute at Fountain Valley School (Colorado) has established a reputation as an outstanding resource for teacher-leaders and middle-management administrators, and Independent School Management, a large consultancy based in Wilmington, Delaware, offers leadership and topical workshops on many subjects each year. Workshops for department leaders pop up regularly, often sponsored by regional associations. The Wallace Foundation's "Knowledge Center" website, www.wallacefoundation.org, also offers resources on school leadership.

When the time comes to move the intentional teacher will probably want to contact one of the agencies mentioned in the resources for Chapter II, but several other placement services, notably Independent Thinking of Newton, Massachusetts, and Educational Directions in Portsmouth, Rhode Island, specialize in administrative placements; Educational Directions also publishes the "Green Sheet," a regular listing of administrative (but non-head) openings at independent schools. Still other firms specialize in head-of-school searches, and many headhunters spend years cultivating a stable of potential school heads—so aspiring heads might wish to contact one of these. Educational Directions (which also published a "Blue Sheet" listing head-of-school openings), Wickenden Associates of Princeton, New Jersey, and Gregory Floyd & Associates of Kennebunk, Maine, are among the most prominent names in this field, although every agency mentioned here also offers head-search services; Wickenden also conducts administrative searches.

More temporary—and usually lateral—changes of scene can be arranged via teacher exchange programs. The Fulbright programs are the best known and most prestigious, but schools that are members of the Round Square international consortium or the North American Network of Complementary Schools can work exchanges within these organizations. Various cultural organizations also have the capacity to orchestrate exchanges or even temporary placements.

Although written for schools more than for individuals, Sarah Levine's *Promoting Adult Growth in Schools: The Promise of Professional Development* (Allyn & Bacon, 1988) remains a standard in the field. Robert Evans's *The Human Side of School Change: Reform, Resistance, and the Real-Life Problems of Innovation* (Jossey-Bass, 1996) is also written for schools but offers illumination for the teacher, as well; a teacher conscious of what is happening may be able to manage the forces of change in his or her own life so as to make change exhilarating and not painful or threatening.

And of course there are books too many to name on changing careers; *What Color Is Your Parachute? 2008: A Practical Manual for Job-hunters and Career-Changers* by Richard Nelson Bolles (Ten Speed Press, 2007) is the best known and most frequently cited. There are also a number of spin-offs and copycat books including one by Bolles focusing on retirement planning.

Speaking of retirement, it is probably never too early for the intentional teacher to seek out financial planning advice, whether for life post-career or working out some ideas for managing educational costs. Some schools make planning available through the school's business office or one of its insurance or pension-plan providers, but in any case it is a very good idea. Teachers in boarding schools who do not own a permanent residence should consider these issues especially carefully; the costs of housing and meals can come as a jolt to those who have never had to bear them fully, year-round.

At this point I had better mention two great books about the totality of a teaching career. I was referred to *The Sage of Petaluma: Autobiography of a Teacher, by J. Abner Peddiwell* by Harold R. W. Benjamin (McGraw-Hill, 1965) in a terrific evening course in curriculum at Rhode Island College, but I did not read it until several decades later. Sensitive and sage, indeed, the fictitious Mr. Peddiwell has a great many wonderful and true things to say about teaching; thank you, Professor Crocker.

I encountered Eric W. Johnson's *Teaching School: Points Picked Up* (Association of Independent Schools of New England, 1996—revised edition; originally published in 1981) relatively early in my own career, when it made a strong impression. It had an even greater impact years later when I encountered it with the wisdom of experience and middle age. I owe to Eric Johnson the idea that one can write well about teaching in independent schools as well as the Abbie Hall epigraph used at the start of Chapter V; I happily pass Ms. Hall along to yet another generation.

A "Backwards Planning" Template for a Unit or Course

(adapted from copyrighted work by Grant Wiggins and Jay McTighe and the Association for Supervision and Curriculum Development, 1998/2005; used by permission)

Unit Design, Backwards

I. IDENTIFY DESIRED RESULTS

What is the main topic or the "big idea" of this course or unit?

_____

_____

_____

What are the big, guiding, "essential" questions that this course or unit is trying to get at?

_____

_____

_____

_____

What will students understand as a result of doing this course or unit?

_____

_____

_____

_____

II. DETERMINE EVIDENCE OF UNDERSTANDING

What evidence will show that students understand _____ ?

Performance tasks, projects, presentations, exhibitions

_____

_____

_____

_____

Quizzes, tests, question sets, writing assignments

_____

_____

_____

_____

Other evidence—e.g., observations, work samples, dialogues

_____

_____

_____

_____

Student self-assessment, reflection

_____

_____

_____

_____

III. IDENTIFY CONTENT, PLAN INSTRUCTION

By the unit's end, students will need to know...

_____

_____

_____

_____

To succeed, students will be able to or know how to...

_____

_____

_____

_____

_____

What teaching and learning experiences and materials and resources will equip students to demonstrate the desired understandings?

_____

_____

_____

_____

_____

_____

_____

_____

IV. DESIGN FOR ENGAGEMENT

What will you do to help students see what they must do to achieve the goals of the unit—how will they know assignments, expected performances, and criteria by which work will be judged?

_____

_____

_____

How will you hook students? What engaging, intriguing, and thought-provoking experiences, materials, and data will address their interests and proclivities?

_____

_____

_____

What tasks and content will inspire students to explore the "big ideas" and essential questions of this unit? What will need to be taught to connect the content and concepts?

_____

_____

_____

What opportunities will there be for students to reflect on the big ideas and understanding goals? What ways will there be for students to revise and refine work as their understandings become more sophisticated?

_____

_____

_____

What kinds of work products and performances will students produce to exhibit their understandings? How will these be evaluated, and how will students be able to self-evaluate to identify their own strengths and weaknesses?

_____

_____

_____

V. DESIGN FOR INTERACTIVITY/TECHNOLOGY

What aspects of the unit or course will lend themselves to collaborative student work?

_____

_____

_____

_____

Where will there be opportunities to take advantage of interactive technologies to gather or present information?

_____

_____

_____

_____

_____

Where might there be opportunities for students to publish work in digital or other form, either to seek feedback or to offer information or entertainment to an audience beyond the classroom?

_____

_____

_____

_____

_____

What aspects of the unit will provide opportunities for students to establish collaborative or informational connections outside the boundaries of the classroom, the school, or the country?

_____

_____

_____

_____

_____

VI. DESIGN FOR MULTIPLE-INTELLIGENCE LEARNING

What tasks or performances will address

LINGUISTIC intelligence?

_____

_____

LOGICAL-MATHEMATICAL intelligence?

_____

_____

SPATIAL intelligence?

_____

_____

MUSICAL-RHYTHMIC intelligence?

_____

_____

the intelligence of THE NATURALIST?

_____

_____

INTERPERSONAL intelligence?

_____

_____

INTRAPERSONAL intelligence?

_____

_____

BODILY-KINESTHETIC intelligence?

_____

_____

VII. DESIGN FOR DIVERSITY

How will the unit or course address or acknowledge the contributions or alternative viewpoints of other cultures with regard to the content or the procedures of the subject under study?

_____

_____

_____

_____

How will the tasks students perform in the unit address or acknowledge differing cultural perspectives and approaches to the learning process? How will different voices be heard in the classroom?

_____

_____

_____

_____

How will the presentation of content in the unit or course address or acknowledge differing or heterodox cultural perspectives?

_____

_____

_____

_____

How will the assessment of learning reveal evidence of acknowledgement and understanding of multiple perspectives, including cultural perspectives?

_____

_____

_____

_____

VIII. DESIGN YOUR RUBRIC(S)

How can you break down the unit so that you balance the things you are assessing against your important goals?

_____

_____

_____

_____

What are the meaningful categories for evaluation in this unit? What do you really want students to be good at and to know at each stage of the unit?

_____

_____

_____

_____

What will satisfactory work look like? What will excellent work look like? What kinds of work will fall short of the mark? What words will describe the characteristics of the very best work on each stage or section of this unit?

_____

_____

_____

_____

What can you ask students to allow them to help you design an evaluation tool that will be useful to them? How can you engage them in the work of setting the highest possible standards for each stage or section of this unit? How can your rubric help to raise the standards?

_____

_____

_____

_____

Template for Designing Collaborative Classroom Projects

I. Project Planning Overview—for Teachers

Phases of Project Management
1. Initiating   2. Deciding Project Concept   3. Planning
4. Implementing   5. Evaluating

Phase 1: Initiating
- Set the overall project goal
- Clarify expectations: deliverables, due dates
- Select members of the project team

Phase 2: Deciding Project Concept
- Brainstorm alternative approaches to project
- Decide on criteria for evaluating alternatives
- Evaluate alternatives
- Choose a course of action

Phase 3: Planning
- List tasks that will lead to achieving project goals
- Sequence activities
- Assign tasks to team members
- Develop a schedule
- Develop a risk management plan

Phase 4: Implementing
- Hold team meetings
- Communicate with teacher or other "stakeholders"
- Deal with conflicts or problems
- Keep track of progress
- Make needed changes

Phase 5: Evaluating
- Recognizing positive results
- Acknowledging shortfalls
- Learning from the project experience

II. Guidelines for Assigning Group Projects — for teachers

Defining a project clearly is probably the most crucial step in a successful group project. Follow these guidelines to ensure that students understand what you expect of them and their project.

1. **Provide a brief overview of the project**

2. **State primary objectives. Good objectives are "SMART:"**
   - Specific
   - Measurable
   - Achievable
   - Realistic
   - Timebound

3. **Define required work output**
   - Be very clear about what you expect the group to produce
   - Include expectations about project quality, depth
   - Show examples of projects which met your quality expectations

4. **State expectations about process**
   - Are group members expected to contribute equitably?
   - Are groups expected to meet during non-school hours?
   - Are groups expected to check in with teacher at specified times?
   - Are groups self-selected or assigned?
   - Will groups use a pre-defined process for completing work or will they define their own process?

5. **State evaluation criteria**
   - How will you assess the project?
   - How will you assign grades to individual group members?
   - Will group members contribute to evaluation?

6. **Explain time frame**
   - When is the finished project due?
   - Any interim work products due before the final product?
   - For 6th through 9th grade students, it would be helpful to indicate how long the project is likely to take. (If you have no idea, how can you expect students to plan their time well?)

7. **Organize your assignment sheet to make information easy to grasp**

III. Project Assignment Template—
to be completed by the teacher

Project Name _____ Due _____

Overview of the Project _____

_____

_____

Project Objectives _____

_____

_____

Required Work Projects _____

_____

_____

Expectations about Project Quality_____

_____

_____

Expectations about Group Process_____

_____

_____

Evaluation Criteria _____

_____

_____

_____

Estimated time to complete project (person-hours)
(may break down by project segment or by group vs. individual time)

_____

_____

_____

IV. Deciding on Project Concept — to be completed by the students

Step 1

Brainstorm alternative approaches to the project you have been assigned

- Ask everyone in your group to give their ideas about what the finished project should be
- Encourage everyone to be creative and not to worry yet about whether the idea is practical
- At this stage, don't criticize anyone's ideas
- Write down everyone's ideas on a big chart, blackboard, or storyboard

Step 2

Decide on criteria for evaluating all the project ideas, for example,

- ✓ Some of the work can be done by individuals
- ✓ Can be completed by the due date
- ✓ Does not cost more than $10.00 [or whatever the limit might be; zero is an option]
- ✓ Uses special talents that group members have
- Write the criteria down where everyone can see them

Step 3

Evaluate alternative project ideas using the criteria

- This method will prevent people from being too pushy about their ideas:
  - ✓ Ask each person in the group to put a check mark by the two ideas which best meet the criteria
  - ✓ Count the number of check marks by each project idea
  - ✓ Usually it will be easy to see which project idea the group likes best
  - ✓ If there is a tie, do a second round of voting on the two "finalist" ideas

Step 4

Summarize your project concept

Write a project concept summary of 25 words or less that will explain to your teacher or classmates what you plan to produce:

_____

_____

_____

V. Project-Planning Checklist — for the students

Step 1

List tasks that will lead to achieving project goals _____

_____

Step 2

Determine how much time is required to complete each task _____

_____

Step 3

Sequence activities (put them in the order they must be done) _____

_____

Step 4

Assign tasks to team members_____

_____

Step 5

Develop a schedule _____

_____

Step 6

Identify necessary materials or other resources_____

_____

Step 7

Anticipate problems_____

_____

Step 8

Plan out-of-class meeting times _____

_____

VI. Project Task List and Schedule — to be completed by each group before beginning work

Project: _____ Due _____

Concept (describe briefly) _____

_____

_____

Group Members _____

Approved by _____ Date _____

Task	Time	Who is Responsible	Target Start Date	Target Finish Date

Materials/Resources	Source/Cost
_____
_____

VII. Anticipating Problems —
to be completed by each group before beginning work

Murphy's Law: *"Anything that can go wrong, will go wrong..."*

Potential problem	A. What will we do if that happens?	B. What will we do if A. doesn't work?

VIII. Group Calendar and Communication —
to be completed by the students in each group early in the process

Group Members

	Name	Hometown	Tel.	E-mail
1.				
2.				
3.				
4.				
5.				
6.				
7.				

Phone/Chat Dates & Times

1. _____
2. _____
3. _____
4. _____
5. _____
6. _____
7. _____

Get-together Times & Places

	When	Where	Who
1.			
2.			
3.			
4.			
5.			
6.			
7.			

Sample structure of a test or examination based on Bloom's Taxonomy

Sample structure of a test or examination based on Bloom's Taxonomy

Part I	Question Types	Evaluation Criteria
Knowledge/ comprehension	Short-answer fact questions; simple calculations; definitions/ simple translations; "ID"s	Basic accuracy; right-wrong
(Application—for developmentally more advanced students)	Short cause-effect relating to established facts or basic procedures; procedure choice (e.g., "preterit or imperfect?")	Accuracy, by "gross" degree ("That's pretty much it—full marks!")
PART II Application	Short essay, complex multi-step calculations, explanations, functional/procedural walk-throughs ("how would you...?")	Accuracy, clarity of process—fine distinctions okay
(Analysis—for more developmentally advanced students)	Parallel problems or calculations requiring application before analysis, more complex essays requiring student-developed thesis	Accuracy, clarity (and form, if in language-based class)
PART III Analysis	Word problems, essays, complex cause-effect explanations, cold translations target language → English	Accuracy, form, content, choices, clarity
Synthesis—as students become more advanced	Word problems, essays, complex or suppositional cause-effect essays, cold English → target language translations	Accuracy, form, content, choices, clarity
PART IV—maybe Evaluation	Call for self-reflection, critique (maybe in target language), suggestions for change/development	On clarity or form only

PART I. Identify/translate/define/solve each of the following (20 pts.)

PART II. Briefly explain/translate/solve (show your work!) each of the following (30 pts.)

PART III. Translate/write essay/draw complex diagram and explain function/solve and explain your solution (50 pts.)

The First Day of School Checklist for the Intentional Teacher

DO:

- ❑ Be ready for everything—minimize fumbling and back-filling. Be prepared for the arrival of students and have everything set up to complete only essential tasks in order not to waste time on them.

DON'T:

- ❑ Become bogged down discussing rules, summer vacations, personal stories and anecdotes, or even course goals. All these things can be done in passing (and in a more natural way) over the first weeks of school, AFTER you have established a classroom culture of intellectual productivity and respect.

Before the day begins

- ❑ Classroom set-up: desks, visual aids, materials
  - ❑ Your name on the board
  - ❑ The name of the course on the board
  - ❑ Your contact information
  - ❑ Course essential questions
  - ❑ Essential materials ready to be handed out—books, photocopies, tools, student contact and interest questionnaires
- ❑ The day's school schedule, clear and precise—and a timepiece
- ❑ Class lists, with seating charts, if age-appropriate
- ❑ A plan (Use "The Intentional Teacher's Daily Lesson Planner")
  - ❑ Doorway meet-and-greet, if desired
  - ❑ An opportunity to learn students' names, either by roll call or "introduce-around"—the teacher can challenge him- or herself to repeat all the names back, but do not spend too much time

After brief introductions, swift distribution of most necessary materials, and the assignment of homework, move to an intellectually stimulating discussion topic or activity

- ❑ A course essential question
- ❑ A brief text to be read and responded to (texts can be visual or cinematic, too)
- ❑ A rich, open-ended discussion topic

Be ready to call on as many students as possible, even those without raised hands. Use names if you can, or ask to be reminded—but focus on the thinking! The first day's activities communicate your priorities.

Index

Readers should also consult the relevant portion of the Resources *section for further specific references.*